Dialogues with Masters

Talking with Twentieth-Century Women

Dedication

Dedicated to the women in my life who profoundly impacted my spiritual journey.

Amlas and Daya of Wildquest for introducing me to the dolphins and facilitating the opening of my third eye with their meditations.

In loving memory of Suzanne for introducing me to the energy of Sedona, and to the wonderful world of channeling; not letting me stop until I was completely comfortable talking to the "Guys".

Most of all, to the sweetest person on planet Earth, my dearest friend Rosaire, for believing in me, pushing and cajoling me, and always telling it exactly as it is—with no sugar coating.

Toni Ann Winninger

Dialogues with Masters of the Spirit World: II

Talking with
Twentieth-Century
Women

Compiled by
Peter Watson Jenkins

Channeled by
Toni Ann Winninger

~ *Celestial Voices Inc.* ~

Talking with Twentieth-Century Women

Published by Celestial Voices, Inc.
13354 W. Heiden Circle, Lake Bluff, IL 60044

Cover design by Robert Buzek Designs Inc.,
Lake Zurich, Illinois

Library of Congress Control Number: 2008902059

ISBN: 978-0-9798917-3-1

FIRST EDITION   Second impression

Our Publications Policy
Celestial Voices, Inc. is a specialist publisher of works produced with the sanction of the group of Ascended Masters who have commissioned them. We do not accept any submissions from authors, and we will not enter into correspondence concerning their ideas, or return unsolicited manuscripts.

Contents

Acknowledgments

The authors wish to thank
Sonia Ann Ness for copy editing,
Robert Buzek for the cover design.

About this Book

It's exciting to find out about famous people we admire. Some fans collect pictures of their idols, go to movies telling their story, collect newspaper articles, autographs, and programs in a scrapbook, and even buy items of the clothing the famous people once wore. We visit websites put up by their fan clubs, or those whose authors want to honor their memory, just as we do. But when our idols die, their book of life closes.

Or does it?

What if it were possible to talk with famous people *after* their death? What if they could tell us more about themselves and their life? What if Amelia Earhart could actually give us details about the mysterious end of her pioneering flight around the world? What if Sharon Tate and Selena Quintanilla-Pérez could tell us what it felt like to be murdered, and Marilyn Monroe could reveal whether her death was accidental or deliberate? What if Mother Teresa could tell us if it felt overwhelming to be admired as a "saint"? Does Judy Garland enjoy life more now that she's living "over the rainbow"? Does Rachel Carson worry about global warming? Does Georgia O'Keeffe still visit the mountain in New Mexico that she loved to paint? With 21 famous women to interview we had tons of questions to ask!

Well, we really can talk with them, and we really can find out their answers. It's what this book and its companion book on *Twentieth Century Men* are all about.

1

In *Talking with Leaders of the Past*, we interviewed 15 leaders born in the nineteenth century, including: Pope John XXIII, Florence Nightingale, Oscar Wilde, Eleanor Roosevelt, Adolf Hitler, Mahatma Gandhi, Charles Darwin, and Albert Einstein. They answered questions we shot at them, talked about themselves, and discussed their life at "Home," which is the place in the universe where people's souls live after they have died—which people sometimes call "the Other Side."

A lot of what we learned from these souls blew our minds. It was all so different when they talked about God, Heaven and Hell, the purpose of our life on planet Earth, why human beings suffer so much, and lots more.

Our first book was organized in cooperation with a group of Master Spirits, who live at Home. Then the Masters encouraged us to produce two follow-up books of famous people of the twentieth century. The interviewer was Peter Watson Jenkins, MA. He's an author and former parish minister now working as a clinical hypnotherapist. Peter drew up a very long list of famous people, mostly American, and presented them to the Masters for review. For many different reasons a lot of these people were not available for interview, so they were deleted from the list. Souls are not idle at Home; they are involved in life reviews and have further spiritual training to undertake. Some act as guides advising the souls of people on planet Earth, or helping newly arrived spirits settle in after their time here. After being at Home for a while they are usually given the option to return to planet Earth. Even former princesses get busy—we had to drop Princess Grace and Princess Diana from the list, as well a lot of other notable people, but we know those who were chosen are outstanding subjects, both interesting and informative.

So how did these dialogues take place?

Contact with the spirit world was successfully made by a leading American channeler, Toni Ann Winninger, JD. The Masters first asked her to start channeling just a few years ago, when she was getting ready to retire as a prosecutor in the Cook County State's Attorney's Office in Chicago. Toni's training as a lawyer has given her a real gift of mental accuracy, and her regular practice of very deep meditation has resulted in her amazing ability to allow the thoughts of those souls whom she channels to flow *through* her mind with little or no interference from her. Toni spends much of her time as a psychic advising private clients. She enjoys working with the same large group of Enlightened Masters, which includes both spirits who have finished their task of coming down to planet Earth, and celestial beings (whom we call "Angels") who have never been down here in physical form.

Yes, we do know people are skeptical of channeling!

Psychics are really a mixed lot. Some of them, such as Echo Bodine, Sylvia Browne, Sonia Choquette, John Edward, Esther Hicks, Judith Orloff, and James Van Praagh, have fine reputations and deservedly have achieved great popularity. Many "street corner" psychics are also quite trustworthy, but, sadly, there are also many wannabees and frauds who cheat and manipulate innocent people. But that's unfortunately true for every profession—even in churches, temples, and mosques—isn't it?

As authors, we are more skeptical than you might expect, believing that we need to "test the spirits" as the Bible says, and also to test the claims of human psychics. We understand that some readers may prefer to treat this book as a work of fiction, but we sincerely believe that it is absolutely true and, with Toni's channeling, Peter really did converse with the souls whom we have named. We stake our reputations on the claim that what is printed in this book is an accurate record of our conversations. Those who have read the books of Dr. Brian Weiss, and of other pioneers in this field, will know how important it is to put your reputation on the line. We honor Dr. Weiss for his courage in publishing *Messages from the Masters*.

What if I don't know anything about these women?

It's easy! The questions that Peter poses fill in a lot of historic information, so we have not detailed every person's life story in this book as we did in volume one of the series. If interested, you can easily find out about each one for yourself by typing their name in an Internet search engine and harvesting the results.

We want to help readers discover how and why these famous people came to be who they used to be, what influences affected them, and if they were influenced at all by their past lives. As we talked together we asked them to tell us a little about themselves as they are now, to explain in what way they like to remember their most recent physical life, and also to comment on our life on planet Earth today from their spiritual perspective back Home.

Note

During each discussion Peter's questions and comments *are printed in italic type.* Replies by the souls involved are printed in roman type.

Special Terms Defined

Advisors. Souls who are given the task of advising incarnated souls.

Angel. A human term for a celestial being who, after being separated from Source, acts as a guide to those upon Earth, but may or may not at some later time choose to experience an Earthly body.

Archangel. A human term for a celestial being that is very advanced and experienced as a guide, whose soul has never incarnated.

Council. A group of guides who help us decide what lessons we wish to experience, and who help us make best use of the lessons we have learned.

Creator. See "Source."

Dimension. A waveband or stratum of vibrational energy. Planet Earth is at the third dimension. Home is at the fifth and higher dimensions.

God. See "Source."

God-Force. See "Source." Sometimes used as meaning "all souls."

Guides. Souls given the task of advising incarnated souls.

Heaven. See "Home."

Hell. A state of mind on Earth.

Home. Not a physical place, but an energetic dimension of unconditional love and of conscious connection with Source. It is where each soul works with its guides and council. Every soul who is not incarnated is consciously within the dimension of Home.

Incarnate. A soul who has gone down to planet Earth and is now in a physical body.

Shell. The living physical structure inhabited by a soul. No human or animal body can live without some connection to a soul.

Supreme Being. See "Source."

Souls. Individualized pieces of energy split off by and from Source, in order to have unique experiences outside the perfect. They are all particles of Source, so each and every soul is also Source. All souls are equal regardless of the human shell they have chosen to inhabit.

Source. The point of origin of all that is known by human beings, and all that exists. It is the energy of unconditional love, the highest vibrational energy anywhere, and is found in everything. The Source makes no judgments and does not reward or punish souls.

Transition. The soul's move from life in the body to life at Home. Physical death.

"The people we worked with were so rich in their culture and their work ethic but their needs were being put aside by those who had the means not to have to deal with mundane things."

Jane Addams

1860 – 1935

Laura Jane Addams, you were quite a sickly child with a severe curvature of your spine. Then, after your heart attack in 1928, when you were 68, until your death seven years later, you suffered terrible ill health. How do you look now on your experience of physical frailty?

Physical frailty, not being able to do what normal people did, was one of the lessons I wished to experience. The sense of having to sit back on the sidelines and watch as the world went by, so to speak, made me acutely aware of everything that was going on. I devoured literature, I devoured the newspapers of that time, and I keenly sought information about the outside world, from which I was semi-removed. I was also a keen observer—one of the things I saw was the way people interacted. I saw how the various types of people, because of their personalities, placed themselves in situations where they lacked the benefits others enjoyed because of a social classification which either they had given themselves, or someone else had given them. This made me long to find a way to level the experiences people had, giving them an opportunity to enjoy that which they had previously denied themselves or which other sections of society had denied them.

So your reforming zeal came directly from your being on the sidelines?

Quite certainly—it is what festered within me. When I was physically able to go out and do something about it, there was already within me a sense of urgency and the inkling of a plan of what could be done.

Did you fulfill the demands of that experience of ill health?

I know that I have learned what it is like to have such experiences in physical form, and I knew why we need to experience them when I came back Home again.

Do children with physical problems usually choose those problems prior to coming down here?

Yes. We plan our lives before we come down here in terms of the major things we wish to experience (though not exactly how we will experience them), but still they are major issues or lessons. My desire was to be in a position where I had problems with my body and was confined and restricted. This could have been accomplished (as in fact it was) with my spinal difficulties, or it could have come through having polio, or it could have resulted from an accident. I did not determine the exact way it was going to happen to me, just the fact I was going to have some physical restrictions.

Your father, a very positive force in your life, was an Illinois state senator, an officer in the Civil War, and a friend of Abraham Lincoln. Tell us about your relationship with him.

I adored him. For the large part, he was my eyes out there in the world. He indulged me with whatever type of information I wanted to have. He would give it to me even if it was thought to be unseemly for a young lady to be concerned with such things. He treated me as if there were nothing wrong with me, and would let me ride upon his knee in the carriage as he went to various places, and support me. He was my hero!

He taught you about the demands of work.

He taught me the value of time—you didn't twiddle it away and waste it by day-dreaming, as so many people do. You have a plan, a goal, and if you are day-dreaming it will be about ways to implement the plan that you want to see brought to fruition.

Your plan was to study medicine. At the Rockford Seminary for Young Ladies you were a good student and quite a leader. What happened to your desire to study medicine?

Not everybody was as indulgent as my father. There were several forays that I made into the field of medicine, when I went to hospitals and observed what was going on (Daddy had all kinds of connections and could get me into those places), but I was—even considering who I was and who my father was—treated with disdain, across the board, that I should wish to enter the male profession of medicine. I saw that, while I could accomplish things there, the medicine of the day was primarily reserved for the rich, for those who could pay for treatment. There were those who treated the indigent in the clinics but they were very few and far between. I wanted to help people at ground level and did not feel that medicine would allow me to do that.

After that disappointment you went to Europe, but on your return your father suddenly died. You became gravely ill and had surgery on your back. Was his death or frustration with your life in any way the cause of your illness?

All illnesses in the physical body are a result of what the whole body is going through. The whole body includes the mind, the spirit (which encompasses the emotions), and the way they impact the energy within the body. So, yes, I simply walled myself off in my grief for my father, and in so doing I stopped the flow and process of balance within the body. As a result I became gravely ill.

Was the surgery you received reasonably effective?
The surgery was something new, which had been recently developed. Its purpose was to go back to my initial physical problems and correct the malformation. It put me where I was in much less pain and had a greater degree of mobility.

Which lasted the rest of your life?
    Yes.

On your second tour of Europe, with your school friend Ellen Gates Starr, you discovered Toynbee House in the East End of London. It was the very first settlement house, where middle-class reformers went to live in a poor neighborhood, providing direct aid to the people around them. What did that experience mean to you?
    It showed me that some of my childhood dreams of equality for all were being put into action in a way that really helped everybody. It gave me ideas of what was missing back home. It gave me the desire to bring to people whom I had seen on the streets what was being offered to them in Europe, humanely and without that degradation which "helpers" make indigents feel, as if they were a plaything or just an indulgence of those with means.

Samuel Barnett, one of the Oxford University founders of Toynbee House, said they aimed "to learn as much as to teach; to receive as much to give." What gave you and Ellen the confidence to go and establish Hull House in Chicago, which was the first American settlement house?
    We knew that we could provide for the people, and as Samuel Barnett stated, that it would be just as much a learning experience for us as for them. The people we worked with were so rich in their culture and their work ethic but their needs were being put aside by those who had the means not to have to deal

with mundane things. The hope and the striving of these people...

Who were mostly European immigrants?

Mostly from Europe, but sometimes second- generation folk who had been in situations such as house fires where they had lost all of their money. There were many instances of women who were widowed with children, who because of the way they had been raised, and who had always been provided for by their husbands, did not know where to go. So we educated them as well as helping their families.

In 1889 the two of you bought a big but dilapidated mansion owned by Charles Hull, a rich Chicago businessman. You opened Hull House as a kindergarten, then added a day nursery, a care center for babies, and further education classes. How did you find the money and people for all that?

First we used our own money, but there were a lot of wealthy people in the Chicago area who had a conscience, and we were more than happy to let them assuage it by keeping our doors open. [smiles]

Three out of the four richest women in Chicago supported you?

That's correct. At first it was done very secretively, until they could sell their husbands and families on the concept of what we were accomplishing.

Then Hull House added an art gallery, a coffee house, a gym with a swimming pool, a boarding club for girls, arts and crafts, a library, and an employment bureau. Were you trying to bring middle class culture to the working class, or did the drive to have these facilities come from them?

It was a bit of both. We wanted to provide opportunities for people to experience things which might give them a passion to go beyond where they had thought they could go. To them certain things, like art, music, or simply swimming in the pool, were things only done then by the rich. We showed them the pleasure they could get out of their experience, how it could be an integral part of their lives, and how they could benefit from it.

A number of our first swimming students became life guards, which gave them an employment. Our employment agency dealt with things outside the realm of our teaching, a large portion of which was to introduce people to possibilities, say, within the field of art. We trained people to have an eye for things. Instead of walking blindly between home and work they began to see the city, the beauty that was in the world, and to know from that vision that they could enrich their life and, in some cases, be paid a salary.

During the depression of 1893 you fed hundreds of people every day at Hull House. Was it this experience of people's poverty that caused you to campaign for new labor laws?

A lot of things led to the campaigning. From the very beginning it was apparent in working with our people that they worked long, hard hours for very little pay. They were so desperate to bring home any money, however small, that they settled for ridiculous remuneration for the amount of work they did. It became very obvious to me that we would not have people in this position if those who had the money, instead of putting it in their own pocket, would pay a decent wage to those people whose work was actually putting the money in their pocket.

Two of the causes you championed were industrial safety and the protection of immigrants from exploitation. From your place now at Home, how do you view these issues in America today?

[laughs] Humans are humans! If they are in a position of power and think they can exploit people without having to pay them, they will. It is incumbent upon governing bodies or the general public to rise up and fight against exploitation of any kind. It is still for the strong and the rich to do as much as they can to help others, although their practice is to do as little as they can. There are many parts of the world where the problem

of sweat shops, child labor, and actual slave labor is still the norm.

You also campaigned for Women's Suffrage. Women got the vote, but does anyone's vote count for much against the powerful business interests in the government of America today?

From an overall perspective, if enough people get disgusted with enough things, and they put their energies together, they can have an influence. If the general public is nonchalant about the abuses brought down on them, nothing is ever going to be accomplished—and that is generally reflected by the fact they don't even care to vote, saying that they don't think their vote is going to count.

You campaigned for peace in the first world war, and in 1915 you founded the Women's International League for Peace and Freedom. Your opponents struck you off the list of the Daughters of the American Revolution as a result. How do you view the effectiveness of people's witnessing for peace in today's world?

There's a very complex energetic equation governing this situation. We must explain it in terms of how people's intentions affect the direction of the energy on the planet. Let's suppose there is a group which is constantly putting its energy into praying for peace and having vigils for peace. All the energy upon the earth is a dichotomy. So the more people pray for peace the more war you have to have to bring the scales into balance. So the very action of praying for peace can create war.

So, if nobody prayed for peace we'd have no war?

That's correct.

Then your efforts in the peace movement were useless because you only created more war?

Only created the energy for war. If instead of praying for peace—because praying for peace is saying there isn't peace, which is war—we had spent our energy in saying how grateful

13

we were for peace ... in order for us to be grateful for peace it would have to take from the energy for war.

But isn't this having gratitude for a peace which is yet to exist?

It will come into existence by siphoning off the energy for war. So, if instead of praying for peace (which means there isn't peace) we say we are grateful for peace, peace comes into existence.

So the peace movement campaigns for peace and tries to shout war down. Is that effective or non-effective?

It's non-effective because although they may not use the term "pray for peace," they are still working with the energy that there is not peace. And if there is not peace, there is the opposite, which is war.

You helped to found the NAACP and the ACLU as well as the Settlement House Movement in America. Some withdrew financial support from Hull House for your support of workers during the 1886 Haymarket riot. Do our spirit guides actively encourage our becoming involved in reforming enterprises such as these?

[laughs] There is a misunderstanding about our spirit guides. They assist us and help us see different things, but they don't interfere with our choices. They show us what there is but they don't campaign for anything. They leave it up to us to make our choices and then move forward in the direction we want to go. The mention you made of funds being withdrawn was because I was making people uncomfortable. When I was a lady who helped the rich assuage their guilt for being so nasty, making money off the poor, it was fine. But when I started to attack the various means by which they made their money, which would shift part of their funds out of their pockets into the pockets of the people of whom they were taking advantage, they decided that they did not need to support us any longer.

Did you ever have a previous life as a reformer?

Yes. I was very active during the French Revolution when

I was a young nobleman who was not part of the ruling set but I had the funds to get the masses of people together to help break the bonds they were under. Also I was back in the time of the Black Death. What I did there was to help people to understand that it was conveyed from person to person. The reform I did then was in the medical practices of disposing of the infected bodies.

People may have called you a socialist, an anarchist, and a communist, but toward the end of your life you received numerous awards, including that of being the first American woman to be awarded the Nobel Peace Prize. What do you remember as your finest achievement?

Bringing a sense of purposefulness to those who felt they were totally worthless, and were totally controlled by others. In particular, to be able to help children raised in an environment where they believed that they were just scum, and to then see them accept themselves and better themselves. To see them getting all the education they could possibly get, and then going out and exceeding the expectations of themselves, and their parents, and their grandparents. That was my greatest achievement.

Are you planning to return to planet Earth anytime soon?

I may possibly be back within the next twenty years, by your time standards.

Thank you, Jane Addams, for talking with us.

Commentary

Toni: Jane Addams had a very demure energy but it was as if there was a blow torch inside and if you turned it just the right way—look out! Then there was this dainty little porcelain figurine of the sick child. My feeling was that people had found her voice quite mesmerizing. She was like a preacher, someone whom everybody wanted to help because they felt they would be helping themselves. That was the way it was presented: help yourself, feel good about yourself. She made her appeal in that manner both to the poor people and to the rich.

Peter: Jane gave us a hard lesson in how the spirit world and Earth's energy works. It is already a well-established part of the reincarnation story that we all come down to Earth from Home with a clear life purpose and a set of life experiences that we agree to undertake, sometimes including physical weakness such as that which Jane suffered both as a child and toward the end of her life.

What is poorly understood is the issue of Earth's energetic balance, which she discussed. Her illustration of this essential balance had to do with war and peace. If we pray for peace, she said, we say in energetic terms that there is war (a lack of peace-energy). Statements like that strengthen rather than weaken war-energy. To diminish war-energy we must make a statement of our feelings or prayers of gratitude for whatever crumb of peace there may be in the world (a lack of war-energy), because by so doing we strengthen peace-energy.

This same energetic balance is involved in the issue of personal health. We can deduce some of this from Jane's breakdown after her father's sudden death. To pray, for example, for our cancer to be cured serves energetically to say that cancer exists in our body and, so, strengthens its energetic force. To express the conviction that our good health is restored, with gratitude for whatever healing has been accomplished (or is in the process of taking place), strengthens the energetic health of our body. This need to balance the opposing energies may baffle us at times, but is the way of the universe. So Jane, from Home, now sees her activity for peace as somewhat ineffectual, but her work to help poor people relish their new-found opportunities was done in exactly the right way.

One of the best historical examples of the energetic balance principle was put into practice by the study of auto-suggestion by the French pharmacist Emil Coué (1857-1926). His famous mantra, which people could repeat many times daily, was: "Every day in every way, I am getting better and better."

With such a powerful statement (always providing it is said without an inner contradiction of thought), he concluded anyone's positive energy could not possibly fail to strengthen. The problem lies in human dismay, doubt, and lack of awareness that the core of our humanity—our soul—is a powerful, eternal, energetic being. After seeing what was being done in the East End of London to help the poor, Jane Addams appears never to have doubted the possibilities. Hull House Chicago, with its national legacy, proves the power of her positive energy which has lasted until our own time.

Note:

You may wish to examine more of the Masters' teaching on healing and prayer contained in their powerful little booklet *Healing with the Universe, Meditation, and Prayer* (Celestial Voices, Inc. 2007).

"The highlight of my work with Pierre was being able to be with him every day."

Marie Curie

1867-1934

Marie Curie, you were born Maria Sklodowska in Warsaw. When you were 24 you emigrated from Russian-dominated Poland to France, learned to speak French, changed your name to Marie, became a French citizen, married a French physicist, and after your death the French people buried your ashes at the Pantheon in Paris as a national hero. What was the special appeal of France?

There were a number of things that appealed in France— a freedom present there which was not present in Poland. There was a sense that, providing women were understated in what they did, they would be given their head and could go forward into activities such as science (which was not allowed in my birth country). Also, there was a sense of romance—being near the water and having that free-flowing energy that was there. It was quite smothering in my homeland at that time— opportunities were given to me which I would never have had in Poland.

Your parents were well-educated teachers and you seem to have inherited a powerful memory and a furious addiction to schoolwork. Tell us about those early days.

Mama and Papa were all about letting your imagination direct where you wanted to go. They didn't push me into any

19

particular thing; they got me excited about what learning could do for me. I used to talk with Papa about his reading, writing, and experiments, which engendered in me a desire to explore and go deeper into some of the things I had read about. Across the energy of our family there was the desire to improve life, to make it better for ourselves and those around us. It was a quest to explain the unexplainable and in so doing make it so practical it could be used by all.

You suffered a real loss when first your sister and then your mother died while you were quite young.

It was very trying for me, but its effect was to force me inward and I became totally immersed in the books that were around me. It was probably the biggest driving force for me to dig into the depth of things in the way that I did. I took care of my loss and my depression by filling myself with exciting new ideas so that I wouldn't think about my mother and sister.

After graduating at the top of your high school class you were totally exhausted and went to the countryside to recover. Did overwork, followed by physical exhaustion and depression, become a pattern in your life?

I didn't know when to stop! When I was on the trail of something, just like a bloodhound, my nose was down on that line until I got where I was heading. I didn't think about sleeping. I didn't think about nourishment. I didn't think about balance. All I thought about was the target I was going toward, and what I was trying to accomplish. When I would complete whatever it was that I was chasing, then it was as if you had pulled the plug out of me and I was thoroughly drained. That was when I went to the country.

You were not permitted to go to university but you attended the illegal "Flying University" instead, and then left Warsaw after being involved in student protests. Tell us about that experience.

The student protests were for women and for those of lesser financial backgrounds. University was only for men who were rich or who had connections. I protested that women should be allowed in, and that those of high intellect should also get the opportunity, because training such people always led to the betterment of society in general if they were given the chance. I was not looked upon as bringing myself into compliance with what was desired by the government and the ruling parties.

Then you and your elder sister Bronya came to an arrangement. You worked as a governess for several years to pay for her studies in Paris, then she in turn supported yours. Your goal was to take a teacher's diploma and then to return to Poland. How well did those plans work out?

In Paris we found new ideas, that life as we had been introduced to it in Poland was not the only life that existed. We discovered that with hard work you could accomplish whatever you wanted. We also sensed that, were we to go back home, all of the gains we achieved would be for naught because we would not be able to put our newfound education into practice. To be a teacher was a very noble thing, something I thought early on that I would like to do, because it was semi-accepted as a woman's role. But when I got into my education I became excited by the possibilities of not being restricted just to learning sufficient to instruct others, but being able to fly beyond what was currently accepted and written in the books.

At age 24 you moved to France and lived in an attic on a shoestring. You started at the Collège Sévigné, then studied physics and mathematics at the Sorbonne, later becoming the first woman to teach there. What gave you the impetus to go into science?

It was something that had the biggest question marks for me, as if I had to find the answer to things. Physics was a ride! It defined who we were, and could also be used to explain all of the advances that I saw being made in the world around me at that time. I wanted to be a piece of it—to be one of those who contributed to those changes.

So in 1893 you were top of your class for your physics degree, and then you excelled in your master's degree in mathematics at the Sorbonne. Was this confirmation of your life purpose?

It was confirmation that I could accomplish what I had set my mind to do, though it came with a price. That was when I first began to be a workaholic, as they say now. I did very little but spend time with my books and my ideas.

With your present perspective, would you say it was your life purpose to be a physicist and chemist?

It was my life purpose to go beyond the trends of the times, beyond my station in life of being born a woman in a semi-oppressive country, and to be able to recognize that I did not need to remain within it—that I could do whatever I wanted providing I had the time and faith in myself to accomplish it. My life purpose, as you call it, was to discover the potential within me and to develop my self-confidence, then to go beyond that and to implement it all.

Had you lived lives before which contributed to your skill as a scientist?

I had a number of different lives prior to this one. Some of them had to do with what is known by us as "spiritual studies." I was also a very skilled pick-pocket when once I was a gypsy. That gave me a sense of yearning to mix in and become a part of something instead of being a vagabond. I also did early mathematics, which I studied with Copernicus. At that time I got my desire to discover how things worked and were interrelated.

Did you know Galileo Galilei?

Yes, but unfortunately I was then one of the hierarchy who debunked what he did. Yet even in debunking something you get to know more about it, because you know what it is that does not work, or does not exist. So that was another way in which my desire to look into things was stimulated.

22

In 1895 you met and married Pierre Curie, who was also a physicist. Two years later your first daughter, Irène Curie was born. She went on to win the Nobel Prize for Chemistry in 1935. Had you known either Pierre or Irène in past lives?

Pierre, yes, we were soul mates. We had been in many lives together. It was for him to be there and for me to be with him so we might collaborate in bringing new information to the world that would change the way things were seen (I refer to our experiments with x-rays and radiation). We needed each other to stimulate and to direct a pattern that would set the standards down for everyone else in the future.

But you did not know the soul of Irène?

We had been together but never as intertwined as Pierre and I. Irène came to us because she wanted to be born into a family that was all scientific. That was what she wanted to experience, and she wanted to have the encouragement and the work ethic which she knew coming to us would instill in her as she grew up.

How much do genetics, as opposed to the environment into which we are born, play a part in determining our direction as human beings?

Genetics have something to do with it. There is a "soup" contributing to who each person is in their physical form. The ingredients of that soup are the physical genes which give predispositions for some things to be easier than others. There is our learning done in past lives, held in the Akashic records. There is the environment the soul chooses to enter, which may either stimulate or supplement the genetic mix which predispositions our physicality. Over all, there is the soul who is the major ingredient to give the basic flavor of how that entire life is to be lived; and there is the amount of awareness and recognition that the physical body allows the soul to have within that lifetime.

Then you and Pierre guessed that pitchblende contained traces of a previously unknown substance that was far more radioactive than uranium. You spent years refining tons of pitchblende to concentrate the elements. Finally you isolated radium chloride and two new chemical elements: polonium, and the strongly radioactive substance radium. Was this immense work the highlight of your partnership with Pierre?

The highlight of my work with Pierre was being able to be with him every day. The academic highlight of our career? Yes. We were both intensely workaholic—it was as if we were like one body with four arms as we did our work. The fact that we were able to share what we were doing was the highlight.

Why did you and Pierre decide not to patent the radium isolation process?

It was too cumbersome, and we were aware that there had to be an easier way to do it. Were we to patent the process it would tell people that this was the way they should do it, and it would not allow them to experiment and go further. We also had moved on to other things by that time.

So it wasn't an act of supreme generosity on your part?

No, we hadn't considered that at all. We thought afterward, during our physical life, that it was a mistake as we could have received additional financial help from a patent, but that wasn't what we had gone into the experimentation to do.

Did you realize at the time the immense danger of handling radioactive substances?

No. We were not certain what the effect would be. We were in virgin territory, so to speak, of how the human form might deal with such things. This was not a time when people were aware of the interconnection of toxic substances and the frail human body.

Later in your life you criticized physicians and cosmetic manufacturers who used radioactive material without precautions. How do you view the dangers to consumers of radio waves today, such as in mobile phones?

When I became aware of the dangers of repeated exposure from the physical ailments I observed, it struck at my heart that, since I had this knowledge, I must convey it to those who did not have the experience (just as we didn't when we first began). When I saw the potential problems and saw the casual way in which various companies and groups of people subjected themselves to this potential danger, I regarded it as my duty to make them aware of my knowledge. When they would not listen to me [laughs] I became a little forceful at times, and maybe not subtle with them. It was the way I did it, and maybe it was saving lives, which is what all good scientists do.

As for the potential dangers to which the current population are subjecting themselves, these vary with the amount of use, the overall vibrations within which people allow themselves to exist, and the vibration of the body itself. So to be able to say that exposure to a cell phone tower will do this amount of damage to a person, or the damage of holding a cell phone to your skull will impact your brain in such and such a way, is not as formulaic as people would like you to believe. It varies with each individual. Is there potential danger? Yes, there is potential danger to everyone from these microwaves. The extent of the danger depends on the individual human body, exposure level, duration, and any one of a number of factors, but it is like any potential toxin—user beware!

In 1903 you were awarded the Nobel Prize in Physics together with Pierre and your mentor Henri Becquerel for your "joint researches on the radiation phenomena." Do you feel that human science has made good use of your discoveries?

[laughs] They did for a period of time but they have moved beyond our accomplishments. The importance of radiation and x-rays in their use for diagnostic purposes opened things up from archaic methods to what you might call space-age ideas. But the whole field has continued to progress. The thing now is magnetic resonance, which can be used on the body

with minimal impact. Whereas the potential in radiation is still damaging in use for diagnostic purposes, magnetic resonance is not. But, in the opposite direction, based on our initial experiments with radioactive substances and the deleterious effects radiation can have on the body, things have now been turned around for treatment protocols where it is necessary to kill cells, such as cancer cells. So things have come full circle, beyond what we had established. It has been replaced as a diagnostic tool in favor of a treatment.

A year after your first Nobel prize, your second daughter, Ève Denise Curie was born. Then, two years later, Pierre was run over by a horse-drawn dray in Paris and died instantly. Do you know now why he died so young?

He died as an agreement with me so I might go beyond even where I had been.

Was that a prior agreement made between your two souls?

Between our two souls. I had become as a part of him, not as myself. We played this little game that some of the time he was the author and the leader, so far as the general public were concerned, and sometimes I was the star.

In your past lives?

In past lives and even in our life together as the Curies. One would be recognized as the lead researcher, so to speak, in one particular area, then the other would be recognized as the leader. In point of fact I was blessed by having the majority of the ideas, but I shared them with Pierre. Our spiritual agreement was that I was going to be put into a situation where I had to recognize my own potential. Also I would be re-visited by the feeling of being abandoned as I had felt when my mother and sister left. So it was another lesson for me to experience while in the throes of all of my research and while I was trying to raise the girls.

Four years after losing your twin soul Pierre, your name appeared in the press in a scandal. It was alleged you had had an affair with a married physicist, Paul Langevin. Historians have suggested that the press were especially hard on you as a Polish immigrant. What is your opinion?

First, Pierre and I were not "twin souls," who are those souls who complete each other. We were soul mates, those who are very close but not the other half (the Siamese-twin half). The affair was not all that the press made it out to be. It was a very close working relationship that grew in respect and then, in times of joy, was released for both of us. There were those who believed my awards at that time were things that I stole from Paul. They thought that I was using his name to further my nefarious affairs, he being a native of France. So it was partially because of where I had come from, and I was not French.

In 1911 you won a second Nobel Prize, this time in Chemistry, but one month later you went to hospital with depression and kidney trouble. Was this the first sign of the effects of radioactivity on your body?

The depression was because I was in a break between being totally immersed in something and, having completed it, was stepping back. During those periods when I stepped back I became immersed in thoughts of all that I had done throughout my life, and what had been done to me and with me, such as gaffs and illnesses. It was one of those periods. The kidney trouble was the effect of toxic radiation. The result was a hardening of tubes entering the kidney.

You lived until 1934 when you died at the age of 67 from aplastic anemia, a form of leukemia. You were almost blind, physically exhausted, your fingers burnt and scarred by radium. Were your discoveries worth the price of your suffering and the subsequent suffering of other people from radiation?

The sickness I endured was part of who I was. It was part of my experimentation, part of what needed to be gone through for us to recognize the potential of the dangerous substance with which we were dealing. It became a map for other people of what *not* to do. Some of those who were harmed by it had carried our experiments further to find out what else could be done with radioactivity. Those who were the subjects of treatment with radiation (done by others) understood that it was something new. For them it was the person who managed their experimental treatment who was to blame, not our initial work. What I was able to provide for humanity has saved thousands if not tens of thousands of lives, and has impacted millions as a diagnostic tool. Was my life worth that? Very definitely it was worth everything that I endured. To be able to impact beneficially one, ten, or one hundred people was quite enough reason for everything I undertook.

Marie, you were raised in the Roman Catholic Church but later, like many scientists, you became an agnostic or atheist. What can you say to scientists about your understanding now of the Creator and of life in the universe?

My withdrawal from the Catholic Church was because it had no true understanding of the power of the inter-connectedness of nature and the universe. I could not live by what I knew was not correct because of what I was doing with my science. At one time the Church had believed that the Earth was flat, then that the sun revolved around the Earth. As a scientist I knew such ideas were disproven—even I disproved some of their beliefs! I went through a period when I was an atheist and did not believe there was anything but matter. To me, rays of energy given off by radium, though unseen, were still material because of their impact on things. I thought that everything could be explained with the realm of what we could measure, and that if we couldn't measure it, then it didn't exist.

Toward the end when I stepped back from my pure scientific research and took a look at everything else in the universe, I softened into believing that some power existed outside of us and became what is considered "agnostic." Then I believed there was some power beyond us but I didn't know how it interacted with us. Now I know that all energy is

28

connected and that there is a point of origin, a supreme Source which is part of anything and everything. As a particular belief pattern this does not mesh with anything you have on the planet at this time.

But it is a reality?

The word "reality" is difficult to use between my sense of being and your sense of being, because a reality for a soul is the illusion you create in the moment. As my illusion at one time was Roman Catholic, and then my illusion became first atheistic and later agnostic, my illusion now is what some call spirituality—that spirit is in everything and is interconnected.

You wrote, "You cannot hope to build a better world without improving individuals. Each of us must work for [personal] improvement and, at the same time, share a general responsibility for all humanity." What improvements do we humans most need to make?

I was speaking only of physical improvements then because I did not believe in anything beyond the physical. That was my reality at the time. In order for people to expand and grow they must become aware of the interconnection between their physical and their non-physical self, their soul. They must realize that they experience the physical in order to experience lessons by which the soul grows. The perspective I now have is of the non-physical witnessing the physical. My statements then portrayed precisely what our physical side needed to do. The non-physical needs to become aware of itself.

Thank you, Marie Curie, for talking with us.

Thank you for having me.

Commentary

Toni: During the interview I had the sense of Marie Curie's having several personas. One was enmeshed in scientific experimentation, obsessed by everything to do with it, and very concerned by its impact on other people (and by the impact other people had upon her). Then there was an extremely physical person. The third person gave out a nervous energy, fringed with anxiety that she wouldn't be understood and would not be able to accomplish all she needed to do. Then, finally, there was another quite different person, whom I felt as a distinct shift in her energy took place toward the end. She was totally peaceful, looking at all of the steps which she needed to accomplish while in physical form in order for her to be in the place she is in right now, a place of total balance and tranquility.

Peter: We have experienced a number of variations in the way subjects carry on the dialogue with us. Marie had adopted France and its language, and she often puzzled us with her use of formal repetition and by the apparent French construction of her sentences. To make what she said a little more plain for modern English readers, these characteristics have been smoothed somewhat in our editing, which has met with her subsequent approval.

It is somewhat amazing to observe the nonchalance with which painful human experiences are viewed from the vantage point of our spiritual Home. It is difficult not to suggest that Mme. Curie's stoical attitude to the agonizing end of her physical life is a spiritual rationalization: "Was my life worth that? Very definitely it was worth everything that I endured." Her bravery took place only in the context of her physicality. Spiritually speaking, the suffering that Marie endured was all part of a plan worked out before she came down here, just as she had a contract with Pierre's soul that he (whom she loved so intensely) would abandon her by dying suddenly in a street accident.

If all this seems foreign to you, keep on reading. We have found that attitudes adopted by souls are constant and loving. It is we who must be open to allowing a shift in our thinking so we may accept the very different view they have of human life, its hardships and difficulties. Marie starts us off by showing us a new angle on life to which few people have ever been so exposed. The manner in which souls at Home (living within the energy of unconditional love) reason about life is hugely different from the way we human beings (living within the polarized energy of planet Earth) look at things. Perhaps we should recall the scripture: "For now we look through a mirror dimly, but then face to face." (I Cor. 13:9 - RSV)

"I felt that my physical restraints were unjust—even though I know now they were things I chose to experience."

Helen Keller

1880-1968

Helen Keller, thank you for being with us. The doctors never identified the childhood illness that resulted in your deafness and blindness. Was it scarlet fever or meningitis?

It was scarlet fever that attacked the nerves.

You wrote, "When one door of happiness closes, another opens; but often we look so long at the closed door that we do not see the one which has been opened for us." Will you tell us what you had in mind?

Well, the first door that we access as an incarnate soul is that of being able to live in the world with all our physical senses—being able to see, being able to hear, being able to interact with things, knowing the near, and knowing the far. When that door closes we have to interpret everything from inside ourselves, to find the strength that we have within us, and not be dependent upon what we can grab hold of, or lean on. During the time after it was discovered that I did not have my normal senses, my parents indulged me in every way, shape, and form. I became quite a brat because I was allowed to. Everything I wanted, I could have. I did not have to learn any of the normal proprieties or anything else. Because I couldn't hear disapproval from anyone, there was no realization of my going beyond the norms of society. Since anything I tried was in essence rewarded, I thought my behavior was normal. It wasn't until dear Anne Sullivan arrived that I discovered there were rules that applied to me as well.

You were under two years old when you fell ill. Much is made of your childhood anger (you just called yourself "a brat"), but by age seven you had actually invented more than sixty different signs to communicate with your family. Had you already begun on your own to open the door to your future?

I guess you could say that. I had an insatiable need to be able to interact with people, and communication is the only way to do that. Not having had, at that point, formal training in any organized or recognized means of communication, I found ways to make myself known and to be understood by other people. If you look upon it as substitution for what I later learned, sign language and Braille, then yes, I was on the way to a form of communication that opened a door of interaction with other than the recognized five senses.

In what ways did your mind and body compensate for your loss of hearing and sight?

Well, my body got used to being bruised [laughs] until everything was put so that I knew where it was. I became very aware of feeling and touch. I could find things with my hands and feet; I could find things by brushing against them with my body; I became very aware of things around me. It got to the point where I could sense some things energetically. If I was getting too close to a wall (and was open to it) I could feel the vibration sent off by that wall, not unlike sonar. So I was becoming more aware of everything around me.

Did you have any connection in previous lives with your teacher and companion of 49 years, Anne Sullivan?

Quite certainly. We had been together several times

before. None of the lives was as violent as at the beginning of the life of Helen and Anne. We had been two men who were inventors and collaborators in the development of the printing press, which is a little ironic as in Helen's lifetime I could not read what we had produced then for others. We had also been sisters in a prior lifetime at a vineyard on the French-Italian border where we both had very happy lives, raised families, and lived in the same village.

Tell us a little of what you do at Home. Do souls work together in groups?

Sometimes they do, but your description of a group is somewhat misleading as it means distinctly separate individuals coming together. Energetically we can bond together and be perceived as one, although we have input of the background of each of the individual parts coming to form the one. So we do work in groups as needed. The only time when we don't work in groups is when it is necessary for us to assume some type of physical appearance to put at ease the new arrivals from earth, who have not yet realized the pleasure of being in energetic form.

Is your being together in a group for training courses or for recreation? What do you actually get up to?

[laughs] You are looking at our existence in terms of what is familiar to you in human form such as physical recreation, learning, and family experiences. Everything here is an exchange of unconditional love, and through unconditional love allowing others to feel the experiences which have been unique to us while we were in a particular form on earth—so it is a sharing in that regard. There are specific moments when souls transition (come Home) but are not ready to rejoin the whole or are in a state of denial as to their authentic being. They may need to retain their individual characteristics before they can become part of the collective again. In that case we work one-on-one with them in small groups. It happens particularly with children and with people who are totally unaware of their spiritual

aspect while in physical form. When they come over it may take them a period of acclimation (sometimes, by your standards, over years) to become comfortable with who they are. It is during that period that we work one-on-one as guides, or in small groups, to help them become comfortable with being back Home.

You mentioned the word Work; what about the word Play?
Everything we do is "play." (We are trying to get a lexicon by which my impressions may be conveyed to you and your leaders.) In fact, for the pure soul, everything is work and play, enjoyment, excitement, and enlightenment.

You appear to have chosen to have a life with an enormous challenge. Are souls sometimes overwhelmed by the experiences they request?
They can be overwhelmed in the physical sense. A soul itself cannot be overwhelmed in its purest form. The physical sense of being out of control or overwhelmed is the biggest part of the lesson. This ascertains whether the soul can tap into itself and gather all the strength within itself, to learn lessons and to make progress through those difficulties or disabilities it has chosen to experience.

Although your family, paid companions, and friends were constantly beside you, was your inner life lonely and baffling?
It was initially, when I went from being able to hear the soothing words of my parents into a place of total silence. The only noise (as it were) of which I was aware was of the internal workings of my own body. It seemed as if I was cut off, yet could still feel the presence of people around me. It was very confusing though I acclimated to it very easily because everything I did was accepted, or appeared to be accepted. It was a transitional change in my human body. I did not even know then if it was physically accepted that we have things withdrawn from us. At one point I thought that, perhaps, my loss was just for a temporary period and then it would be over, as the cessation of

sound while sleeping.

As time went on and my senses did not return I tried to accommodate my own feelings by little games that I would play and things I would do. I can't say I was lonely because I was aware of other people around me. I did not have easy communication with others which was very frustrating to me, but that is why I developed my sign language to let them know when I was hungry or thirsty, when I wanted things. It was, granted, a one-way communication because I never knew what they wanted at that point.

Can you now compare that experience with communication you now make at Home, because you don't use eyes or ears at Home, do you?

No. The type of communication we have here is, as some of your movies show, a type of extra-sensory perception, or clairvoyance, or thought projection. We all know everything if we tune into it at this level. We don't need words; we don't need touch; we just need the intention to tune in. Then we know exactly what it is that the other spirit is attempting to communicate with us. We direct an intentional thought toward someone to get our point across.

Just as you are to us now!

Yes.

How did you get along with Alexander Graham Bell? Do you have contact with him now at Home or has he reincarnated? No, Alexander is still around; he hasn't reincarnated. When we were in physical form we used to play games, trying to stump each other, finding different ways to get points across. Alexander loved games and puzzles as did I. Now we just laugh about the various positions we put ourselves in, the things that were successful and those we considered failures.

At Radcliffe College, when you were only 24, you became the first deaf-blind person to graduate from an American college, and you did so with distinction. Did Anne pay for your immense labor with the severe eyestrain she suffered?

Anne's eyes never were strong. That was the situation that found her getting her own education in Braille. She had such an insatiable desire not only to provide service to me but also to get as much information as she could. She could not feel herself worthy of the status of a college graduate, but she earned the degree just as much as I did. The ideas that came through for the test papers were mine, but without her I would not have been able to graduate. Her support was tremendous.

Then John Macy came into your life as your editor, and he married Anne. You later wrote about your views as a suffragist, pacifist, birth control advocate, and socialist, in your book Out of the Dark, *which he edited. Later in 1924 you helped to found the ACLU. Was he the catalyst for your social agenda?*

I don't know that he was the catalyst, but he was the grease under my wheels. I had a sense of what injustice was, partially because I felt that my physical restraints were unjust— even though I now know they were things I chose to experience. He allowed me a forum to express my inner anger, energy, and turmoil surrounding what I considered to be injustices. He easily facilitated ways to overcome the hurdles in front of me.

You wrote twelve books, lectured, and even toured with a vaudeville act. You made a movie, Deliverance, *that was unsuccessful. Finally you started fund raising for non-profit organizations to combat blindness. Did you ever feel that, although it was easy to be on display, it was hard to have a normal life?*

[laughs] I'm not sure exactly what "normal" is! Normal is what every person experiences; it is normal for them. When someone presented a proposal to me of something I might do, if it was beyond that which I had experienced before and it seemed interesting, I would try it, almost as if to put another notch on my belt, that here was another thing I had accomplished. I went into some things that I now look back on as

kind of ridiculous, like the vaudeville act. The movie was another thing. When I examined the proposal, I knew it wasn't going anywhere, but how many deaf-blind people are ever seen in movies? It was something I had to do.

You had a run-in with the editor of the Brooklyn Eagle *newspaper over your socialism. He said that your disabilities put you out of touch with reality. Did you have to put up with much prejudice like his?*

To a lot of people anyone with whom they could not easily communicate (by which I mean "dictate to") was someone who was out of touch with reality. In fact the point was that they were the ones out of touch with the reality of the abilities each one of us possesses in physical form, regardless of the shape or condition of the vessel within which our souls are contained.

The *Brooklyn Eagle* editor was annoyed with me because I was able to accomplish so many things in what he considered to be a fragile, injured, persona. He would have been much more comfortable had I not spoken out, and just been placed on a shelf to vegetate. The very fact I succeeded in most everything I tried infuriated him because I did not fit his definition of "disabled." He picked on aspects of my work he didn't care for and chose whatever way he could to discredit me. His main way of discrediting anybody was to say she was "out of touch."

Did you have such treatment from other people or was he unique?

He was unique in the vehemence and strength of his attack, which was facilitated by his publication. There were a lot of others who thought the same, but because they were not walking in my shoes they did not know what my experience was and were prejudging what I was doing, and attacked what they perceived as a person who was less than they. There were also those who were jealous because I appeared able to collect a greater audience than theirs.

Did this also have to do with your socialism?

That was like the "three strikes and you're out" rule in

baseball. Whenever I championed a particularly caustic cause for some groups, people would find some other way to attack me rather than on the principles, because they could not argue with my viewpoint in most cases, but they could argue with me as a person.

If you were living here today, would you still be a socialist?
Socialism changes with the times. I would still stand up for the rights of all people, that all should be treated equally. If that is the current definition of socialism then, yes, I would be a socialist.

From your vantage point at Home, what do you view as your greatest achievement?
My greatest achievement was showing that physical form does not have to be restrictive. By that I mean that some of the most treasured people incarnate at any one time are not cut from the same mold as the majority of the population but get their inner strength in overcoming the dysfunctional mold they are put in.

Helen, in 1960 your book Light in my Darkness *advocated the teachings of the eighteenth-century Swedish scientist, philosopher, and mystic Emanuel Swedenborg. What drew you to his work and how do you view his teaching now?* Swedenborg was a visionary.
He tried to blend a sense of the self with what the existing society recognized as being concrete—showing that the energy within us, combined with the material world outside of us, allows us to create whatever we need to manifest in order to have a more fulfilling physical life. I believe now that some of the things he said at that time were a little restrictive in that there was a pattern that had to be utilized in order to manifest what you need to experience. At Home we know that you can manifest your own illusion of life (your physical perception of your surroundings), what you get out of life, what you interact with in life, and that you don't have to follow any particular formula in

order to accomplish that. You simply need to go inside and connect with the soul within!

Thank you, Helen Keller, for talking with us.

Commentary

Toni: Helen's powerful soul energy made me feel that I was being lectured. She seemed to blend different lives here on Earth with many concepts, and there was a feeling of total certainty in the energy coming through which said, "this is the way it is." I sensed she would not allow anything to get in the way of communicating her feelings to anyone. I felt her frustration that others, without the extensive strengthening brought about by her disabilities, would never be able to understand totally what inner strength can create within the human experience and how rewarding that battle can be.

Peter: What Helen Keller said was quite remarkable. She went inside the mind of the infant Helen and told us about her inner feelings. We sensed the little child's optimism, wondering when the absolute silence would come to an end, accepting the attention given her, exploring her own senses, making small advances, and finally reveling in the gift of the tough-minded "Wonder Worker," Anne Sullivan. I found myself reading this part of the transcript as though I were myself disabled, sensing the enormous strength her words impart. So the uncompromising energy of which Toni writes is part of her larger vision, a vision that we must all undertake the challenges that we chose for ourselves, and that, whatever happens to our mortal shell, it is up to our soul to tackle our situation head on and triumph.

It seemed as if Helen's fury toward the obtuse Editor of the *Brooklyn Eagle* is still simmering. This was one of the few truly angry moments we encountered in our dialogues. Of course, Adolf Hitler (in volume one of the Dialogues series) was very much worse!

"I put energy into my painting, I put my being into my painting,
so that whatever people perceived was
my energy as well as what they saw visually."

Georgia O'Keeffe
1887-1986

Georgia O'Keeffe, your early days were spent on your parents' dairy farm in Sun Prairie, Wisconsin. Flowers, rocks, shells, bones, and landscapes became very important in your colorful painting. Was your childhood experience of nature your basic inspiration?

Life as a whole was my inspiration. I felt the energy of everything and wanted to convey that to other people because, as I talked to my friends of the vibrancy and the energy coming out of a rock or plant or bulb, everybody thought I was crazy. So I thought, "Let me show them what I see." So that's what I did with my art.

You once said that you didn't know where you got the idea of being an artist. Do you know now?

Well, I had been an artist in past lives. I had been a scribe and a recorder. It was a combination of all of those things that I did in my life as Georgia O'Keeffe because I was a recorder of energy as I felt it, and of life as I saw it—and the medium I used was art.

As a child were you aware of your past lives?

No, I had no recollection of anything. Later on, as I

traveled, there were some feelings where I knew (even before I had arrived) that I had visited places. It was a kind of comfort—not a disquieting feeling—but I did not dwell on it.

At home in Wisconsin you studied with the watercolorist Sara Mann. Tell us about that experience.

She was able to help me remember the mixing and the vibrancy of color, to feel the energy and the magnificence given off by some of the colors, and to use the play of colors in order to modulate and modify what was being presented. She was a wonderful teacher when it came to conveying what the eye saw onto the paper.

You just worked in watercolors at that time?

Yes.

Were you still using watercolors when you went from the Midwest to Williamsburg, Virginia, where your art tutor was Elizabeth Willis? What was her gift to you?

I was primarily still in watercolors, but when I was working with her I began to experiment with oils. Her main thing was depth and perception, taking and building layer upon layer to capture the feeling of whatever nature was presenting to us. With her I experimented in almost monochromatic paintings to get from the depth and from the layering the sense of what was there. I had studied color before, and now I was studying formation and conveying the sense of being able to pick something up and hold it.

In your paintings, you often transformed natural subjects into powerful abstract images. Was this approach to art spontaneous, or did you learn it from William Merritt Chase in New York?

I was an admirer of William but it came from myself—I didn't mimic anyone in my paintings. I simply took the energy and what it was trying to say to me. If you look at some of my abstracts, the geometries were what people today call *feng shui*.

They set the energy of the painting, which was what I was putting on canvas and paper.

While you were in New York at the Art Students League, you visited Gallery 291 to see an exhibition of Rodin's watercolors put on by Alfred Stieglitz the photographer. Did you meet your future husband then?

Yes, it was not the first planning of the rest of my life but a chance meeting.

How did you feel about him then?

When I first met him I thought he was a bit egotistical and puffy, but at that time I was finding my own personality and what I thought about my own work. Anyone who could present something that was so well received by people was to me "hands off" and above me.

In 1912, at the University of Virginia Summer School, you were introduced to the ideas of Arthur Wesley Dow. How did his ideas shape your painting?

They got me to think from more than one angle. Instead of being uni-directed with blinders on, it was taking a perception of the entire canvas, and not only the canvas itself—one could be perceived as being just off the canvas and directing the viewer into a scene, into an energy, into a movement, while just representing a simple subject.

Alfred Stieglitz exhibited ten of your drawings in April 1916. Your first solo show opened at Gallery 291 a year later. You fell in love and started modeling for him. Then his wife Emmeline found out, they divorced, and later you married him. Was it a good marriage?

It was a very insightful one, both artistically and romantically. I found out how fickle some things can be and that things are not always the way you envision them to be as reality sneaks in and colors everything.

You said about it that you "put up with what seemed to me a good deal of contradictory nonsense because of what seemed clear and bright and wonderful." What was the contradictory nonsense?

That was me—taking my expectations of how things were, based on romance novels that I had read, and then bringing them into the day-by-day real life experience of being married to somebody.

Was he faithful to you?

Not totally.

Alfred took 300 photographs of you, and in 1921 the Anderson Galleries displayed 45 of them, some showing you in the nude. How were they received at that time?

[laughs] That was a period of time when the human form could be talked about, could be hinted about, but could not be exhibited *au naturel*. They were not received very well, except by the art community.

How did you feel then as a photographer's nude model?

I was so much in love with my expectations that posing for the photographs was a matter of just being there and sharing with him. I had no idea what the photographs were going to be used for. To me it was just a way of being part of a relationship.

Did you go into the Anderson Galleries and look at yourself?

Only when they were closed.

From your perspective now, how do you view the enormous rise of nude photography and pornography today, especially on the Internet?

Nude photography, for the sake of honoring the body and the beauty of the human form, is of the highest calling. Pornography, with a prurient interest, is sick. It has nothing to do with art at all. A nude photograph, if it is viewed as a piece of art, does not evoke a human sexual response and is not intended to do so. It is intended to be a thing of beauty, a replication of perfection.

So there's no place for someone who looks at a piece of art, which is truly a celebration of the female form, and has erotic ideas about it?

No. Nor is there anything wrong even with a piece of art showing a human coupling, if it is viewed as a piece of art and not as a "turn on" for a person who is incapable of having a relationship with someone of the opposite sex.

Many painters have denigrated photography, but you seem to have drawn inspiration from the work of your husband, Paul Strand, Ansel Adams, and others. Were your large-scale pictures of natural forms, close up in great detail as seen through a magnifying glass, meant to appear photographic? I experimented with photo-realism because that seemed to be what people wanted at the time. For me it was also a means by which I might transform myself into the thing that I was painting, and live within that area. My pictures were like a movie in my mind, with a vibration rising out of them that enabled someone viewing them to feel the earth, the rocks, the air, and the sky.

Your art took New York by storm, and in 1928 your calla lily paintings sold for the largest sum ever paid to a living American artist. How did you feel about success?

At first I was a little embarrassed by it because, again, it was a type of photo-realism that I was giving to people. I put energy into my painting, I put my being into my painting, so that whatever people perceived was my energy as well as what they saw visually. It was the "energetic bounce" that drew people to my pictures.

Did you have an understanding of that at the time?

I knew the effect that my pictures had on people, but to be able to say it was an energetic bounce, I didn't perceive that then. I just knew how great my pictures felt and what they could accomplish.

There was a darkness in your life. Early on while working in Chicago you fell ill and returned home. In 1933 you were hospitalized for psychoneurosis, a stress affliction. In the 1970s your eyesight started to fail; you suffered from macular degeneration and had to stop painting for good. What did illness teach you?

It taught me to be more connected with energy, the same thing I began to realize was in my paintings. The period in 1933, which I called "burn out," was when life caught up with me because I was trying to do too much too fast. I was trying to be everything I thought people wanted me to be, instead of just being myself, instead of going inside and finding comfort within me. I tried to be the debutante; I tried to be the belle of the ball; I attempted to present people with what I felt *they* needed and wanted. This took everything away from who I really was as a person, sapping the energy right out of me—the energy I drew in my paintings. I so allowed the energy that I put into my paintings to be siphoned off that I was no longer able to draw on that energy and put it down on the canvas.

And macular degeneration?

The macular degeneration was, at first, a cooling down period for me. It was a time for retrospection, when I went back and re-lived within my mind the paintings of my life. But it was still a time when I could convey things with energy; I still taught people who came to me. I was able to teach them the feel of color, and depth, and energy. This was easy for me because I was not distracted by wanting to jump in and change this little piece or that little piece within the pictures they were creating.

In the summer of 1929 you went with Rebecca Strand, Paul's wife, to New Mexico, and over the next twenty years you spent part of each year there. Tell us about that part of your life spent between New York and New Mexico.

I was never truly alive in New York in the sense that I was in New Mexico. There I was able to feel the earth, feel the life. New York was a place where I lived among other humans; New

Mexico was where my soul thrived, where feelings inside me were ignited by the air, by the sand, by the wind, by everything that breathed.

Then you discovered Ghost Ranch, a 21,000-acre retreat center in a desert area of dramatic cliffs and hills which inspired some of your most famous landscapes. After your husband had died you bought and restored an abandoned adobe hacienda in Abiquiu. Was that a true homecoming for you?

It was like returning to the womb. Everything about it felt as if I were at home. There were no distractions, no silly society life, no trying to match what other people had done, or please other people. It was the period in my life when I became myself.

Your world travels in the 1950s resulted in a series of cloudscapes. Tell us about them.

It was during this period when I had the majority of my *déjà vu* feelings. If you take a look at those cloudscapes, they have reflections of what I was experiencing from the past. Within them are intricacies of the time that I spent in those locations in other lifetimes.

Tell us about your other lifetimes.

Some of them were quite ordinary—a milkmaid when I raised a brood of chickens and kids. I was a gypsy wandering throughout eastern Europe.

A male or female gypsy?

Female. I danced for coins at different points (and helped myself to coins in different places). I went back to times in the British Isles when the Celts were there, when I was very connected to the Earth and the energies of the Earth. There is some very subtle symbolism in my paintings which came through. The lives I became aware of as I traveled were mostly female, but as a soul I have been male a number of times, on different continents, and even different planets.

In 1973, a potter called Juan Hamilton came to the door. You once said, "He came at just the moment I needed him." He helped around the house and became your friend. Had you asked the Universe for help?

Indirectly, I had. I was in a period of despair when nothing seemed to be working right and I simply said, "What next?" Then there was a knock at the door!

What did Juan's friendship mean to you?

He was a person who saw me as another soul, not as somebody he could use, learn from, or even steal from. It was soul-to-soul sharing, both the spiritual and physical experience.

He taught you pottery?

He taught me a feel of what the Earth is, what solidity is. So much of my mind was fluid and had no stabilizing foundation to it. In the pottery I could feel the energy of the Earth and sense the connection that existed between the physical human being and the incomparable living Mother Earth

Juan's final act was to scatter your ashes on your favorite mountain, the Pedernal. You had painted it many times from your Ghost Ranch house and said, "It's my private mountain. It belongs to me. God told me if I painted it enough, I could have it." Were you with Juan when he did the scattering?

Of course! My soul is still upon the ranch—quite frequently. When I wish to re-experience the magnificence of that time and place, I return there and stroll amongst the cactus and sand. A soul has the ability to recall in intimate detail the experiences of each lifetime, but also the ability to return and relive the desired moments.

Once you said, "When I think of death, I only regret that I will not be able to see this beautiful country anymore—unless the Indians are right and my spirit will walk here after I'm gone." Well, are the Indians right?

Without a doubt! But I didn't quite believe it then. I didn't remember it until I had crossed over and was able to see everything from every location. I could be in whatever part of the planet I wanted to visit and experience the beauty and the energy that I knew. Yes, I can walk upon the planet and I can feel it, not physically but energetically.

So when are you coming back?
    I don't have any plans right now, but we shall see.

Thank you, Georgia O'Keeffe, for talking with us.
    You're most welcome.

Commentary

Toni: It felt as if I were waltzing. There was rhythm and energy to Georgia—I felt alive and able to feel her artistry in everything. Hers was a very light energy but she possessed depth of emotion as well. It was an interesting soul to deal with. At the end, when she spoke of returning, there was a wistfulness for being able to return to the physical at the moment of our conversation. I sense that when she left us she returned to her beloved mountain again.

Peter: My conversation with Georgia O'Keeffe shows how very different souls are in their approach to life, both human and spiritual. She displayed a naiveté with a passionate artistic purity. Her concentration from early days had been on the abstraction and replication of energy—of both color and form—so that she might share her beautiful experiences with anyone who saw her work. She appeared to have been unfazed by the public furor over the pictures of her nude body in the Anderson Gallery in 1921, unimpressed by the battle over the photographic style of some of her pictures, and even embarrassed by the stunning reception (and prices) her work fetched once New York had woken up to her presence. Indeed, she seemed to have given of herself somewhat uncritically to all those people who demanded more, from her adoring patrons to her egotistical and wayward husband. Then (it seemed not a

51

moment too soon) came the trip to New Mexico with its stunning vistas and colors, and she could be herself, at last, in the little hacienda she bought and renovated.

We have been told by the Masters that the spirit world has an intimate connection with our own. The detail with which ascended souls comment on what is happening on planet Earth is astonishing. It seems they can view just about everything going on here, although they refrain from invading the privacy of our thoughts, and everything is viewed with unconditional love. So now, just as the native American Indians foretold, Georgia delights in re-visiting the scenes which she once depicted so vibrantly in paint and watercolor, though she will have to return to human form before she can ever pick up her palette knife or brushes again.

Those who are unfamiliar with the activities of spirit guides are sometimes quite put out at the thought of people on the other side being able to read our thoughts and view our daily activities. The Masters have assured us that our privacy does matter to them, and that, after many lifetimes lived over countless generations, the desire to engage in voyeurism has gone. As their Home truly is a place of unconditional love, we can expect them to take note of our sensitivities.

"I could lose myself completely within

that energy in the air."

Amelia Earhart
1897-1937

Amelia Mary Earhart, you were the first woman to fly the Atlantic alone twice, to fly an autogiro and to fly across the U.S. in one, to fly non-stop in a regular plane across the United States, to fly from Hawaii to the U.S. mainland, and almost the first woman aviator to fly round the planet. Which is more important to you, your daring achievements or the fact that you were a woman doing them?

It all depends upon your perspective. Mine was that I didn't do things just to be first, nor to prove that a woman could do them. I was proving to myself that I could do them. It was the adventure, the excitement. I would get on a project and find out ways to do it with ease, cut down on time, and make it something that all people might realize they could do if they put their mind to it, whether they be female or male.

There was much said about the fact that I was female, and that presented a lot of barricades and difficulties for me. When I first got into aviation it was considered a lark by the "boys' club" that here was this woman who *thought* she was able to perform as well as they. When I outshone a lot of their derring-do they grudgingly began somewhat to accept me and the fact that I was a fellow aviator. It wasn't a matter for me to try to prove that women could do it; it was just trying to prove to myself that I could.

53

When you became famous you said, "Girls, especially those whose tastes aren't routine, often don't get a fair break. It has come down through the generations, an inheritance of age-old customs...that women are bred to timidity." How true is this in the world today?

It depends on where the woman is located. If it is in an area where by custom and family tradition they still have that timidity and deference to the male, then it continues as it did in my day. But in all of Western society and throughout Europe, and even now into such areas as Japan, women are beginning to put aside any restraints, and the veils they are supposed to hide under, and are following their hearts as I did.

You wrote, "Women must try to do things as men have tried. When they fail, their failure must be but a challenge to others." I don't know if you are planning to return to earth any time soon, but, if you did come back as a woman, what issue or task would you choose to tackle today?

Medical research. In my experiences as a trend-setter in the field of aviation and in politics and in world involvement, I got the excitement of being able to go beyond the written barriers which were supposed to define what a woman is. In medical experimentation and research at this time the majority of trendsetters are male, just as they were in my field of aviation. So I am dealing with a plan at this point to come back as a medical researcher, to link cancer with all of its causes.

To prove that women can do it?

Well, I didn't go into aviation to prove women could do it; I went there because I wanted to do it. That would be the same thing—I would do it because I wanted to. The choice of coming in as a female rather than as a male would be more accepted in the medical community. It's the excitement that I would add to the mix.

You were briefly engaged to Samuel Chapman, but eventually married George Putnam, your publisher and publicist. You seem to have been ambivalent about marital commitment, and concerned lest you would be tied down by marriage bonds. Did this attitude relate to your feminism?

Not if you are using the term "feminism" as the rebellion which is the normal role of the feminist. I followed my heart in all things while in human form. I followed my heart, my soul, my yearnings, my passions. If it did not match with what other people wanted me to do then I stepped aside.

You wrote to your husband, "I shall not hold you to any medieval code of faithfulness to me." Apparently you were looking for an open marriage. Was that feminism or a desire to play the field?

Neither. It wasn't feminist because I did not care what the rest of society did. I didn't want to be the little woman tied with apron strings to half a dozen progeny, and not be able to go out and step into my plane. My idea of an open marriage was that I could follow the pursuits of my passion rather than be confined to household tasks. The open skies were the definition for me of an open marriage, and I did not feel that George should be tied to the house when I was out flying around the world.

You were a tomboy when young. Were your previous lives lived more as men or as women?

They were about 50:50 men and women. I was everything from a very rich, spoiled princess to a shoe-shine boy on the streets. I shined shoes, carried coal, did anything I could to get money because I was a waif. So I had had the experiences of both. In this lifetime I came in with a female body with the idea of being a rebel, a trend-setter, breaking the rules, stretching them, seeing how far they could be pushed.

That was your life purpose?

My life purpose was really to be able to identify myself and follow my passions, without living under the pressures put upon me from outside. To learn to identify myself from within, from the soul, rather than from without—the belief systems of society.

We understand that, where you are now, souls do not have a gender. Doesn't that make life at Home rather bland?

Oh, not at all! It takes away all of the issues that might come from being in an area of unconditional love and then having problems of jealousies or ambivalences develop. Here we can simply be the energy force that we truly are.

Isn't there excitement in having male and female relationships?

When you are in physical form, yes. When you are in energetic form it doesn't matter—you are always within the excitement and you contain the energies of both sexes.

When you are looking back on your own life, do you feel the energy of that life?

I can envision the excitement in completing the tasks into which I put myself so wholeheartedly. Being up in the clouds was as close to the feeling of being at Home in energetic form as you can possibly have on Earth in physical form. I could lose myself completely within that energy in the air. I can still remember the little sub-plots in my life, and laugh at the idiocy of some of them. I only hope that what I was able to accomplish, by sticking to who I was, helped others realize that they have the same potential.

In addition to your flying career, you worked in a Canadian military hospital, then became a social worker, wrote books and magazine articles, gave lectures, promoted products from Kinner aircraft to pajamas, and even promoted cigarettes—though you didn't smoke. Then you became a careers counselor for Purdue University women graduates. What aspect of your working life gave you most satisfaction?

The overall feeling of being able to help people. With the exception of the advertising, where actually the only help came to myself in monetary form, every position I had was oriented toward helping others—to find out who they were, or to overcome their barriers, or to help them through the difficulties they were experiencing. That was the big mission of my life.

As a future medical researcher do you now regret once having promoted cigarettes?

[laughs] No, I needed the money at the time! Were it not for people today smoking, some medical researchers wouldn't have anything to do!

When you were 23, you attended a stunt-flying exhibition where you had your first 10-minute flight. Later, you wrote, "The lure of flying is the lure of beauty." Was it beauty or the thrill of danger that motivated you most to take up flying?

The beauty of it, the freedom of it, the fact that you were one with the plane. I envisioned myself out there as a bird, and the plane was my bone structure, my wings. I was able to soar and not be restricted by anything. I didn't sense any danger at all—it was the excitement, the exhilaration.

Did you do gliding?

There was no type of aircraft then known to man of which I did not avail myself.

You got your flying lessons at Kinner Field with Anita Snook; then you bought "Canary," your yellow Kinner Airster biplane. In about two years you had achieved a women's world-record altitude of 14,000 feet. What do those early experiences feel like now?

Now they are just like a recording in my journal, my akashic [celestial] record, because this was only one of many lives that I have had. If I put myself totally back into my persona as Amelia, that was the beginning of my dream, my passion. It was what told me I was on the right track, that I could get away from the restrictions being imposed upon me by society, and that I was the one who determined my destiny. I could do it in a manner where I felt free, where I felt a part of nature and all-that-is, just as now, as a soul, I feel a part of all-that-is.

You said that your ambition was to "produce practical results for the future of commercial flying, and for the women who may want to fly tomorrow's planes." Weren't all the record-breaking feats which followed much more truly your personal quest for fame?

I don't like the phrase "quest for fame." I didn't do things in order to be recognized for them by way of a return. I did them in order to show that each one of those milestones could be surmounted. Of course, fame was the necessary return at that time. But it wasn't fame that I sought; it was the accomplishment of doing something that was believed either impossible to do or, at least, impossible for a woman to do. I wanted to prove that impossibility was only a self-imposed restriction. If we set upon a course and were conscientious in getting the right materials—the right plane, the right fuel—we could accomplish what we set out to do. But if we just took an ordinary plane with a simple mixture of fuel, we could not reach the heights or the speeds, because we were allowing what general aviation said was the norm to dictate who we were. I chose to step out of that and to experiment, to prove I could do what was real. Not for the return of fame but to prove to myself (in my human form) that I could accomplish whatever I set out to do.

The Boston Globe described you as "one of the best women pilots in the United States." Some have doubted whether that was really true. How do you evaluate your own skill now?

I was as competent as I could be. The reason everybody touted me as the best was because I was known. I did a lot of things that other women did not do, and was fortunate enough to have the backing to be able to do it. So, with my name prominently in the press, I was dubbed "The Wonder Woman." There were other women aviators who were just as competent, but they did things which did not get into the news as much as mine did. There were those who flew mail and things like that, which sometimes was just as dangerous at the time, and they were just as good. I was extremely good on the equipment I had, but then I surrounded myself with the best people, so it was easy to be the "best."

In 1927 Amy Guest paid for you to fly across the Atlantic as a passenger. You actually did some piloting on the flight. The plane was forced to land in Wales, but later you all received a ticker-tape reception in New York and visited President Calvin Coolidge at the White House. Tell us about your feelings on the flight and as the woman of the hour.

My feelings on the flight were fantastic—I was getting a sense of the variance of weather over a large body of water, which I had not experienced before to that degree. It was the beauty of everything which was beyond description. It was a very "spiritual" experience, you might say. The designation of me as "Woman of the Hour" was rather embarrassing because I was, after all, just a passenger, although I did a lot of stick time [took the controls]. People wanted heroes. In particular, people of my age wanted female heroes, because they needed to know that women could do something beyond being home, taking care of the family. So it was very easy for them to adopt me as a hero.

Did you enjoy visiting the White House?

It was interesting meeting Coolidge. He was one whom I had admired from afar for his free thinking and his decisions.

Then, among other achievements, came your courageous and successful solo flight across the Atlantic. You wrote about courage that it is "the price that Life exacts for granting peace." How do you look at the human virtue of courage from your place now at Home?

Courage, on a spiritual level, relates to the courage to find out who you are and what you can do. It's not the physical type of courage that is known when we are in the body. Physical courage is trying that next step, going beyond the norm, experimenting, "pushing the envelope" (as they say) of what is accepted. Courage at any time has to do with your intention. If you have the intention to do it so that you become the lady of the hour, it's the wrong way to do it because you are doing it for the ideals of society. If you have the courage of your conviction to prove that *you* can do something, and your intention is not to get a reward but just to prove it can be done, and to accomplish it, that is true courage. It does not make any difference if you go inside yourself to get that information or you fly across the water to get it.

Your Atlantic crossing was a copy of Charles Lindbergh's successful solo flight to Paris in 1927. People even gave you the nickname "Lady Lindy." Do you have any contact with Charles Lindbergh, "Lucky Lindy," in your present life?

We sit around sometimes talking about early aviation, knowing now, as we do, how far people are able to go into the air and into space. We laugh at how archaic some of the things that we did—and had to do—seem at the present time.

What's your view of space travel?

I wish I could have experienced it in the flesh. I would have loved to be in that first ship that orbited the moon, because the moon was always something that hung out there enticingly when I was in the air.

So is there life on the moon?

In some dimensions, yes.

What do you mean?

All time exists at the same time for us. There has been life on the moon before, and there will be life on the moon in your time-line future. So depending on when you pop onto the surface of the moon, there's either life or non-life.

Physical life with which we could have contact?

Yes, if you are in the right dimension. And because there was prior life there before it became dormant.

Finally there came your attempt to fly around the world. We know a lot about the first part of the flight, but mystery surrounds the final act which started when the Lockheed L-10E Electra, with you and your skilled navigator Fred Noonan on board, left the city of

Lae in Papua, New Guinea, on July 2ⁿᵈ, 1937. You were to fly across the Pacific to the tiny Howland Island, 2,556 miles away. The plane was last seen over the Nukumanu Islands after flying 800 miles. Historical records of voice contact with the U.S. Coast Guard cutter Itasca and other operators do not give a clear picture of what took place after that. Please account for what happened to you and Fred after you had passed the Nukumanu Islands.

First off, our mission—if you want to call it that—involved a secret agreement with the U.S. government that we would provide them with an excuse to be able to go in and blanket that whole part of the Pacific, mapping and finding out the strength of different nations within that area.

What part of the U.S. government was that?

It started with the President himself and the War Department. There was a belief that in the not-too-distant future there would be war waged in that part of the world. There was very little known about a lot of the islands and nations in the area. It was thought to be impossible for the government to go in there and map other nations' property. So it was determined that if we were able to land in a place that was not thought to be near where we were heading, we could be picked up off that location, which was an island to the north of our route. Meanwhile, the Navy, Coast Guard, and other services would be able to blanket the whole area, gathering intelligence information.

I'm interested you should say "north of our route" because there are quite a lot of islands to the south of Howland Island but nothing much to the north. Were you intending to go on a lot farther?

Yes, that is why we stocked up with so much additional fuel. Unfortunately we did not have enough for the headwinds we encountered, and the weather was not as good to the north as it had been on our projected path. But we couldn't not take off when we did, since the weather conditions around Howland Island were good. We couldn't say, "We can't go because of the

61

weather," because then people would know we weren't going where we said we were going. The plan was that we were to go north to a very small uninhabited island, and land near the island because it was too small to land on, and then be surreptitiously rescued by the military while they were surveying the area.

Is that why the US Government spent the huge sum of $4,000,000 (in 1937dollars) looking for you?
Otherwise they could not have invested that much time and trouble. What happened was a miscalculation in our search for the small island from which we were to be rescued. We ran into some air currents which prevented us, and we ran out of fuel before reaching that particular island. When Fred and I determined that we weren't going to reach our destination because of the fuel shortage, we decided we could not make radio contact because people would be able to guess what we were doing since we were "so far off course." First, Fred was just too good a navigator to have made a mistake like that, and second, if we went near to populated islands at all they would suspect or know what we had been about. So it was decided between the two of us that we would just ditch at sea. We never reached the island. We went down at sea some distance from it. And because we had sworn to maintain radio silence, we floated around for a while, but then we ceased to exist in human form.

When you ditched were you north or south of Howland Island?
We were north of it. The particulars of exactly where we went down were irrelevant to us. Finality in physical form is finality. We gave up, knowing what we had been recruited for and what we had promised to do—and that was it.

So it wasn't that you couldn't find the other island?
We ran out of fuel. It wasn't that we couldn't find it. The weather conditions changed and there was more turbulence, which prevented us from making the speed we needed. It was going to be a very, very close call as it was. We had more fuel on

board than was reported, so that when they were looking for us, they could say there was no way we could have gotten as far as we attempted to get. Still, even with the additional fuel we had on board it was at the very edge of the range of the plane.

Can you check with Fred on your last position?
He has reincarnated. He didn't stick around here very long.

What's he doing now?
He's actually in electronics.

Was any part of the aircraft or any part of your bodies recovered?
No. The water was very deep where we went down.

What was it like to drown?
It was just cutting loose and floating downward—instead of upward! That was the last sensation.

You don't seem to be too troubled by the memory.
When you go from a physical form, where you might have pain or some other affliction, into unconditional love, there's nothing to be troubled about. We had prepared our physical selves psychologically for such an eventuality, and had dedicated our lives to being able to help the government get the information that they needed. Looking back on it, I see that it did allow them to map some of the area that hadn't been extensively mapped before, so that when the war began in the Pacific they did have much more reconnaissance than they had had previously, before this little expedition.

So the search for you was more of a mapping exercise?
It was a mapping quest. They mapped the depth around different areas so they would know what could be used as deep sea harbors, where they could run various sized ships through, which islands had concentrations of people on them, and which

islands already had a build-up of such nationalities as the Japanese.

That all seems to me very courageous of you and Fred Noonan. Does it match your own criteria for courage?

[laughs] In physical form, yes. Actually, it was just another adventure.

But what about Fred? He had a future of his own.

He did, but he was very aware of the danger of what we were doing. He was a truly patriotic person. He believed in the government very strongly, and in what they could do to help protect the country.

How do you feel now about that venture?

Taking into account where I was then in my mind, my belief, and my ambitions, I would do the same thing again.

With or without the government's involvement?

I think it would be inevitable that I would have become involved again with the government because that was all part of my journey of helping in every way I could to make life better for people. The feeling at that time was there would be war, and if there was a way to give the government an edge to save lives, I would give my life again for that.

Roger! Amelia Earhart, thank you for talking with us—over.

Over and out.

Commentary

Toni: I felt Amelia's powerful personality but she resonated with a lovely gentleness as well. She seemed to say, "I am comfortable with my decisions, even if they were wrong. It was easy to make them because I was being true to myself, and that's why we go into physical form." There was a calmness, a peace, even a lightness about her, as if everything were conducted in the air, floating on a cloud. There wasn't any static cling—it was very free flowing. The ending brought out a dynamic mixture of nonchalance and purposefulness. This feeling was so strong it was like being in her physical presence, yet at the same time I felt she conveyed a lot of understated energy.

Peter: There have been decades of speculation concerning what happened to Amelia Earhart and Fred Noonan. Two theories predominate: The first is that President Roosevelt personally authorized a spy mission to discover what the Japanese were up to in the North Pacific, and that Amelia and Fred provided an excuse for the ensuing far-flung "search." The second theory is that the aviators were captured by the Japanese. Amelia's statement confirms the first theory but denies the second.

The plane was battling headwinds aiming toward a secret location, but failed to make landfall when fuel supplies ran out. We were unable to identify where the target island might be as our request for details of the secret location was simply met by silence from the Other Side, and Amelia indicated that Fred, having reincarnated, is not available to help. We do not rate this detail central to our purpose of contacting the eternal soul of this amazing woman aviator, and letting her tell her pioneering story as she chose.

The issue about life on the moon was also discussed with us, in the first volume of *Dialogues*, by Albert Einstein, who also claimed there was life on the moon. Briefly, the points these souls make are:

First, as Einstein discovered, time is only a reality to us human beings in the way we experience life on planet Earth. The universe outside Earth's dimension does not use the concept of time—everything happens in the Now. So the simple phrase "life on the moon" involves its chronological past, present, and future manifestations, all observed together.

Second, just as the vibrations of a dog whistle sound clearly in a dog's ears but human beings cannot hear it in the *dimension* of their hearing, so all life vibrates in many physical dimensions within the universe. Life may exist somewhere (such as on the moon), yet neither our human senses nor our electronic instruments can observe it.

As Amelia's soul was communicating to us from the dimension of her spiritual Home, she was observing life on Earth's moon within the higher vibrational frequency where the whole truth may be observed. She was telling us the truth as she observed it from her vantage point in the universe.

"My people, the African Americans, instinctively felt the historical message of slavery, freedom, hope, and redemption in my music."

Marian Anderson
1897-1993

Marian Anderson, at the age of six you were called the "Baby Contralto" in the junior church choir. When you were only ten you sang in a duet at the Baptist church. Did you imagine at that time how music was going to shape your future?

Even at that time, music was my life. I couldn't have a single waking thought without music being a part of it. I would feel the rhythm of the music as I walked down the street. I would feel the rhythm of the music as I ate food. I would feel the rhythm of the music in the wind, and in everything. I breathed music.

You had to teach yourself the piano because your parents could not afford lessons. Your hardworking father was proud of your singing, but when you were still young he died in a work-related accident and your family was plunged into poverty. What did that experience mean to you?

At first we were all crushed by his leaving and the struggle that ensued. The experience told me that if we want something in life there is always a way to get it, if you put your mind to it, and also that family is very important. The strength and support you can get within the family take you from a place of total deprivation into a place of peace and beauty.

That's the story of your own people.

Yes, it is. I didn't look at it with a global or racial viewpoint when I was young, but as I step back from it now I can see that I was but a little microbe in the huge growth of what was going on at that time.

As a child, were you very aware of segregation?

Not in the beginning. It wasn't until I started moving around that I noticed it. I was fairly well protected within the community as a child.

In the African American area of Philadelphia?

Yes. I rarely ventured out of familiar territory when I was young.

At the South Philadelphia High School you did get some musical education. How much did you benefit from that public school's teaching?

It gave me a way to communicate with other people in musical terms. Up until then the music came from without and from within me, but it was difficult to talk to another person and say "this is what I get out of it." Once I had learned about the music on the page and how to work with it, I was able to communicate with other people and to give them a sense of what I was feeling.

Did you try your hand at composition?

Well, it's rather interesting because it's almost as if the compositions were already written within me. I don't know if you could say that I did anything more than copy down what was a part of my existence.

What do you feel about musical education in American schools today?

There are some schools that have beautiful programs, some that allow the soul to speak through music. They treat music as just another language to be mastered. Other programs have marching bands for the football team and things of that sort, which are not wrong because they still give the sense that music can unite and be a common thread, even if it's just having the band march to instill a unity within the people. There are some programs in the school orchestras where people can let their hearts sing. True, they can let their hearts sing with the trumpet and trombone, but more so when you play the string and let it reverberate. There are some schools that do a fantastic job, but of late, when they start talking finances, music programs seem to be the first thing to be cut, and what they are doing is cutting the heart out of some of the students who are there.

You were refused admission to a music school because you were African American. People raised money for voice teachers, and in your last year at high school your tutor was Giuseppe Boghetti. What did he do for you?

He gave me a sense of who I was. He gave me confidence and introduced me to the depths that the vocal chords can reach, and the way that the soul can change the very timbre of what is being expressed. The man had an incredible heart and an incredible soul. He spoke volumes with a simple note and you could know exactly how he was feeling by that note.

You had a broad range. You could reach the D below middle C, couldn't you?

Yes I could and that gave me versatility. It's almost as if I had a foreign language on top of my own with the breadth I could bring to my singing.

Do you see a voice like that as a gift you had already asked for, before you came down to planet Earth?

It's a combination of things. While we are in spirit form we decide what lessons we wish to take and what our spiritual purpose, our pathway, will be. I had decided that, first, I would be in a situation where I had to learn my worth and to claw myself out of oppression. Then, with my physical tools, I would be able to lift people out of the emotionally binding places from whence I had learned to release myself. A number of my prior lives had been musical, so I already had a feeling within my soul of the vibration of music. That's why from an early age the vibration of music was my entire life.

Any musicians we might know about today?

None were famous—because I was always working on a lot of other issues. I was a peasant performer. I spent several lifetimes in monasteries where I discovered an innate quality of vibrating the whole body with chant. I was an instrumentalist so I could feel the vibration from the instrument outside as well as the vibration that was created within by my singing.

You began to earn a little money singing in churches, at the National Baptist Convention, and on tours of black colleges and churches in the South. You were well known for your singing of Spirituals. Was this the time when you developed your interest in this musical genre?

At the time I was black and my exposure was with blacks, so the way of reaching them was to talk their language. In using recognized symbols for them I was able to help them more than if I had tried to bring something else into their parlors, saying, "Take hold of this, instead of what you are used to." The rhythm of the South was still the rhythm of the slave chain; it was the rhythm of the constant movement of work and of the feet on the soil. If you take that and put it into any type of music, it speaks to the heart of the African American. It speaks to the oppression but also to the possibility and the joy that can be had if they get out of the restrictions they think are being placed upon them, and relate to their current problems. I could feel all that in the music and I conveyed it in my music. I could see the effect that such music produced in my brethren, so I honed it to such an extent that it became magical for them because it released the shackles and allowed them to come into their own.

People used to write to you with their spiritual ideas and concerns. Were you a religious person?

It depends upon your definition of religion. I believe that the faith of the people was what kept them going in all of their adversity. A lot of them needed the churches to give them a foundation, since the families were not all that strong during that time. In that regard I believed very firmly in what the various churches and religions were doing for the people. But I also had a sense of who I was as a spirit, and that overrode any of the restrictions placed on people either by religion or by society. So, if faith in myself and a sense of who I was (what you now call Spirituality) is what you are referring to, then I was very religious.

Were you in contact with your spirit guides?

I was in contact with a lot of energies from the other side, but they all came as music. I now know that they were my spirit guides, people whom I knew before, and people I had helped. They came to help me celebrate my life, and I experienced them as music.

You worked tremendously hard at your career, but were kept out of many venues by segregation. In 1924, you gave a recital at the New York Town Hall which was badly attended, and the critics were unhappy with your voice. Is it true that you then contemplated abandoning your career?

I did contemplate abandoning going outside what was accepted for me, in other words the churches and gatherings of my people. I imagined, from what happened in that concert, that I wasn't going to be able to communicate with those who did not feel the rhythm of the Earth and of the shackle. So, for a time, I withdrew somewhat from promoting anything beyond where I was graciously received.

71

Were you sensitive to criticism during your career?

To a degree. Whenever I received what would be considered a negative review I figured that I had failed to get the message across, and if my message was not conveyed I felt there had been no reason to give it. My people, the African Americans, instinctively felt the historical message of slavery, freedom, hope, and redemption in my music. Those who had not experienced such hardships saw it only as some warbling coming from a revivalist church.

The next year you entered a voice competition, beat 300 rivals, and won a chance to sing with the New York Philharmonic Orchestra. Your subsequent triumphal concert led to a contract with Arthur Judson, a leading impresario. Then you started looking to sing in Europe. Why was that?

Even though I had won the competition, and even though I had the contracts, I did not feel a graciousness in working with people in the United States. I continued to feel indulged—an outcast.

The white people?

The white people. There was still that edge of how did I dare come to their venues? How did I dare to think I could be as good as people they considered wonderful? I had heard from other black entertainers how graciously they had been accepted in Europe, and I wanted to take my message, my song, my rhythm, my vibration to a place where I could be appreciated and affect those who came to hear me with open hearts and souls and no agendas.

In 1927 you sailed to London, where Roger Quilter introduced you to composers and performers in Britain. Am I right that the first tour wasn't very successful?

It wasn't very successful primarily because I couldn't believe they were truly sincere in their appreciation of my music. It was as if I had set up a roadblock for myself, sabotaging my feelings, taking the impression of my difficulties in the

United States and placing them over those gracious people, thinking that they all must have had agendas. So it did not turn out as successfully as it could, but it was my fault, not theirs.

Back in New York you gave a recital at Carnegie Hall and received very favorable reviews. Then you went again to Europe, successfully performing at the Wigmore Hall London and at 142 concerts in Scandinavia. You even sang before the Kings of Denmark and Sweden. Tell us what success meant to you.

I can feel it now as I go back over it—as if the heavens had opened and had allowed me to be the sunshine, allowed me to warm and influence the hearts and souls of the people with whom I came in contact. It was a beautiful thing, a place where people opened themselves to receive my message. They didn't have any preconceived ideas, or hold to any restrictions. They were all like sunbathers on the beach and I the sun warming them.

One of the people who fell under your spell was Jean Sibelius, who wrote his song "Solitude" for you. What was your meeting with him like?

That was like meeting a soul mate, someone who understood the vibration of music—which is the vibration of life. He knew that it can be shared with others, that it can affect others, that it can change the course of continents if people will receive it. It can defuse rage, misunderstandings, petty differences and let all see and feel the unity of a single vibration; discord will not be tolerated.

You went to Europe to study as well as to perform. What did Europe teach you as an artist?

It broadened my understanding of orchestration and of musical possibilities. Up to that time my musical education had been quite simplistic, centering around just belting out a song that would be felt! It didn't include all of the intricacies of some of the music that had run through my head. It wasn't of the spiritual genre.

Such as German lieder?

Yes. Europe exposed me to all the various aspects of music that were understood and employed around the world, and gave me possibilities to use them.

Did you start singing oratorio then?

I experimented with it.

But it wasn't really your genre?

No. It didn't vibrate well with me. I could do it but I couldn't feel it as much.

In 1935 there was a magical moment at the Salzburg Festival. The great conductor Arturo Toscanini heard you sing and said, "A voice like hers is heard only once in a hundred years." Do you recall the occasion?

Yes, it took my breath away to hear that accolade after everything I had been through. I wept when I thought of all the people who could have been in the same position had they persevered and had they availed themselves of the opportunities that I had. "*Once in a hundred years?*" No! Once in a million people, but there are billions on the planet.

That same year you took on a new manager, the impresario Sol Hurok. As an artist you depended on the skills of your music teachers, accompanists, and managers. Were any of them in your soul group at Home?

Not in that particular bunch. It was almost good that they weren't because it would have been a distraction from whatever they were helping me to develop in this lifetime. A soul mate comes along in a lifetime to have a particular impact in your life, either positive or negative. If you have reached a point where you are in service to assist others, it is better not to still be working on your own lessons at the same time. My entourage was enabling me to interact with more and more people and to bring them to a feeling of themselves.

Then in 1939 discrimination came to a head. The manager of the Constitution Hall in Washington, DC, refused to book your concert with an integrated audience. The hall was owned by the Daughters of the American Revolution. First Lady Eleanor Roosevelt, a member of DAR, resigned in protest, and was followed by thousands more. How did you feel when the row became so public?

I had mixed emotions. I felt like a child venturing out of the home town to experience racism for the very first time. I wept for my country's being so backward, after the graciousness that had been extended to me throughout Europe. Here was a nation that put itself above all others, and yet it had created an elitist mentality for but a few of its people. I wept at the ignorance of what was there and I was gratified that such a great lady as Eleanor would stand up and say, "This is not right."

In fact Mrs. Roosevelt helped you further. She supported the NAACP that arranged for you to sing on that Easter Sunday from the steps of the Lincoln Memorial in Washington in a free recital. It was attended by 75,000 and millions of radio listeners tuned in. Tell us about that experience.

It was a healing, a sense that the nation was in recovery, and that the bigoted people who had placed themselves as the guardians of the country were not as powerful as they thought they were and not universally accepted. They were but little people with little minds, who were going to be put in their place in the years to come. There was the possibility of an equality for people of color, of nationality, of any distinction imposed by those with bigoted little minds. When I projected musical vibration from that lofty location, with all of its accumulated history, I felt that I carried the hope of a nation. As that music went out, it traveled across the country and told people that they do not have to be oppressed. There is hope. There is a new age coming. And so I felt a pride and a sense of gratitude that I could be a part of such a great transformation.

You wrote, "I could see that my significance as an individual was small in this affair. I had become, whether I liked it or not, a symbol, representing my people." Later you broke the color barrier again by becoming the first African American to perform as a member of the New York Metropolitan Opera. Was combating racism one of your pre-assigned life lessons?

My life lessons included dealing with racism, prejudice, difficulties, self-imposed restrictions, and restrictions imposed from outside. I was to go inside myself and define who I was as a soul—not who I was in the eyes of other people but only in my own eyes. And also as a soul, I was to acknowledge who I was and not to let myself be suppressed by the majority of people.

How do you view racial relations among Americans today?

[laughs] There is so much going on right now. In some parts of the country there are pockets of racism as strong as any I experienced, and there are whole areas of the country that are totally color blind and see nothing because they see the soul. As there is such a large number of people on the planet, there will always be prejudice and racism, whether for the color of your skin, your ancestry, or the religion you follow. It is one of the primary lessons allotted to souls who enter into the earth plane to experience and to work with. But it is as it should be, one huge melting pot of people experiencing life.

From then on you remained highly successful but found time for a private life, and you married Orpheus Fisher. You settled on a farm in the Connecticut countryside with him. Was he your childhood sweetheart?

Yes, he was my dream partner. In the very beginning, whenever I thought I could not accomplish something, we would do a "let's imagine." Let's imagine the possibilities. Let's imagine we had different skills from those we have. Where can we go? What can we do, or what do we want to do? He always stayed in the background because, as he said, I was the shining star and he but the platform for it. In a lot of ways he was my mentor. He was my hope. He was my love.

Did you keep in contact all your life before you married?
    Periodically, we came in and out of each other's
lives all along.

Did you mind not having children?
    I had millions of children! I did not have any physical
children, but then I did not have the time.

*Your success led you to sing at the inaugurations of Eisenhower
and Kennedy. You sang when Dr. King gave his famous speech. You
became quite an icon of the American Establishment. Was that
constrictive?*
    It wasn't constrictive for me because I did not allow the
ideology of those events at which I performed to dictate where I
was. I participated because they had a venue that would allow
me to showcase my talents and to convey my heart to people,
always with the hope that they could do exactly what I had done.

*You once wrote about segregation, "If I were inclined to be
combative, I suppose I might insist on making an issue of these
things. But that is not my nature, and I always bear in mind that
my mission is to leave behind me the kind of impression that will
make it easier for those who follow." looking back, do you feel that
you achieved your objective?*
    Don't you?

Thank you, Marian Anderson, for talking with us.

Commentary

Toni: What a sweetheart! There was such gentleness in her, but
an incredible depth of energy and, definitely, no combativeness
whatsoever. She gave a sense of "I've got this mission, and I'm
going to find a way to fulfill my dream, and in doing so I will
share it with whoever is ready to receive it." She is a very old
soul with strong energy, very firm in her intentions. It was a
pleasure meeting her.

Peter: Toni is sensitive to energy of all kinds, of course. I'm only a little intuitive, but when Marian Anderson's soul entered the room I was stunned by the overwhelming feeling of love and peace that she brought with her.

Marian's great contribution through her music was to deepen African Americans' sense of pride in their own heritage, and to awaken all other Americans, of every color and race, to the beauty and incredible power of black music. Indissolubly linked with their music is the dignity, personality, and suffering history of the black people themselves. So when Marian sang from the steps of the Lincoln Memorial on Easter Sunday 1939, she did not just sing old Negro spirituals; she blew a celestial trumpet for an end to racial segregation, for healing, and for a deepening of understanding between the many peoples of America. It was a sound that reverberated throughout the nation.

Reading her answers to my questions provides us with a quite precise blueprint of her development as a national artistic and spiritual leader. We see her face up to each of her challenges step by step, then succeed and move on to the next. This is truly a clear object lesson in how the soul works progressively through the physical body it inhabits, and the human ego with which it wrestles. I sense it is also an example of how the universal God-force gives its support to the individual soul's endeavor. If only we were all as sensitive to these possibilities in our own life, as she clearly was in hers, the world would be a better place.

The Masters of the Spirit World have made it very plain to us that the purpose of each soul in coming down to live in a physical body on planet Earth is always the same—to take advantage of the experiences it has received as life lessons and to use the knowledge gained in its quest for personal growth toward full maturity.

These lessons may appear to be overwhelming, as Helen Keller and Wilma Rudolph describe in this book. Some are subtle and persistent, as Marian found in dealing with the negative receptions she received from the ranks of predominantly white American concert goers.

She was up to the task. Her personal maturity as a soul showed through the choices she made and enabled her to sound a note for equality and freedom not only for her own people but also those who had been freed from the shackles of institutional racism by her engaging and peaceful presence. Her answer to my final question was not smug but quite truthful—she really did achieve her objectives in life—and we honor her for that.

"I did the best that I was capable of doing.
I always gave my physical all to whatever was going on."

Golda Meir
1898-1978

Golda Meir, let's go back to a high point in your career. The date is May 14, 1948. You are one of the 24 people who signed the Declaration of the Establishment of the State of Israel. Tell us about that experience.

I was very humbled by the experience. It was the fulfillment of a dream, not only for me but for all of the immigrants who had hope of having a homeland, of being able to have a place that represented our way of life, our beliefs, that gave us a stability—a place to call "home." We had been dispersed to so many places throughout the planet with never a central location where we could say "this is our home."

You were one of just two women there?

Yes, but at least they acknowledged that women had a place. There have been a number of advantages to that throughout the progression of the country.

You likened the experience to the signing of the Declaration of Independence in America.

It was, and it established a nation that was responsible for itself, could make its own laws, could inscribe an identity, could be recognized as an independent state capable of controlling itself and moving forward and making a name for itself within the world community.

Did you have contact at that time with Yitzhak Rabin?
    Yes.

Do you get together now?
    Not often. Sometimes we sit down with some of the others and talk about what we considered insurmountable difficulties of that time, which were really things that we put in our own way by the manner we looked at them. It's interesting. Now we laugh about how seriously we took ourselves at that time.

Laughter seems a common thing at Home.
    Very much so. Who better to laugh at your self than you!

Have you any contact with the signers of the Declaration of Independence—Washington, Jefferson, Adams, and the rest?
    We could feel them applauding us both then and now. We sometimes hold a round table discussion with Jefferson and other people who have formed nations. We discuss the difficulties that were unique to us because of the varied elements of resistance, and geographical difficulties— everything that made our experiences so diverse.

When a soul has been involved in a major enterprise like yours, does it come down again or is it employed permanently in other activities?
    It's simply a matter of choice. There are so many things going on at this time on your planet. For me, I am choosing to be a spectator now. Were I down on the Earth again I would have a very small idea of what is going on, just what would be within my field of observation. Up here I can observe everything that's going on.

What's your feeling about the immediate future for the Earth?

Planet Earth is going through a transformation. It's also fulfilling some of the biblical predictions for the planet. Those of you on the planet right now chose to be around for the fireworks. Me? I chose to be in the grandstand.

To which are you referring?

The revelations of the end times. Brother fighting brother. Were I to come back from whence I left [the same geographical area], I would be going into utter turmoil. But I had my experience of turmoil in that part of the world, so now I choose to see how others handle it. It's interesting for me to notice how various peoples use their religion as an excuse for what they are doing—that they are maintaining what they call "the purity" of their religion against the heathens and infidels who believe in a different way. In fact, were they to go into the *spirit* of their religion they would be able to see that the basis of all religions is love, and it is not going off and wiping out the opposition so that they can say theirs is the one true religion. People use religion to mask their greed in taking over and controlling their particular sphere of influence.

What kind of government is running things at Home where you are now?

We have no government. We don't need one because a government implies that there is right and there is wrong. Such a duality only exists where you live.

What about good order—knowing what to do next?

It's difficult to explain because, energetically, we are all connected. Most of the time up here, unless we choose, we don't have individual bodies, but an amorphous energy that is anywhere and everywhere we choose to focus. So, being that kind of energy, if my amorphous energy passes over your amorphous energy there is a merging (at least during the period when I am passing over). During that period I know your thoughts and you know my thoughts. So, with everybody knowing what everybody else is thinking, there can be no plotting or planning or, say, ambushing or whatever. We therefore waste none of our energy on such trivial pursuits.

Is there still some kind of individuality?

There's still individuality because the source of each energy bundle, the soul, has had many differing experiences. It is as if you read a book on how to perform surgery. Everybody can read the book and have the *knowledge* of how that surgery is performed, but the one person who goes and practices that surgery has the *wisdom* of that knowledge. So we all share in everyone's knowledge, but individual souls have the wisdom of having actually gone and experienced the knowledge we all have.

Is that wisdom the main reason why souls come down to earth?

You're right. We cannot experience physicality here. With our intention we can create what would appear "physical" to the eye, but we cannot experience the depth of the things in the way a human body can. You have to be within the density of the Earth plane, and in that density experience all the emotions that are present on the planet within a particular lesson. Our emotion here is unconditional love; we have no hate, we have no doubt, we have no fear.

Many people opposed you, Golda, in your lifetime. Why do people take on hatred?

They take on hatred as a lesson, in order to know the intensity of love. When we are in soul form and are in unconditional love, the concept of hatred (if we have not already experienced it) is beyond our comprehension. So we have to go to the planet to experience it, and to be on both sides of it. In my life as Golda Meir I did not choose to practice hatred, but I was well aware of hatred directed toward me. It felt like a coldness— the opposite of love and warmth—biting, cold, abrasive energy that struck out and tried to grasp my being and suck it in.

You were called the "Iron Lady" of Israeli politics long before the epithet was given to Margaret Thatcher. Was it your experience of Russian oppression as a little girl, or the influence of your strong father and of Sheyna, your radical elder sister, that put metal into your soul?

It was a combination of all. I had very good role models and I chose to come down into a strong family so that I would have a pattern for self-development. Growing up in Russia as I did, I felt the disdain and hatred directed toward my people, and others as well—anything that did not agree with the current ruling ideology. Of course, my sister, whom I dearly loved, was just the perfect little rebel [laughs] from a very early age. Anything she didn't like she would protest, even within the family. It became quite a joke. Then, when her whole purpose for being here played itself out as the protester, the revolutionary, it was like being part of an on-going schoolroom to watch her. Father had such strength within him; he refused to be bowed by the pressures exerted against him.

You took on responsibility early. After emigrating to Milwaukee, Wisconsin, and while you were quite young, you had to look after the family's grocery store whenever your mother was away. At school you founded the American Young Sisters Society to raise money to pay for poor classmates' textbooks. Then you rebelled, fell out with your parents, and ran away to join Sheyna and her husband in Colorado. What was all that about?

That was priming, prep work! It was getting me ready for knowing within that whatever I did would have repercussions that reached not only the area around me but around anyone else who was alive with me. It also told me that, if I wanted to follow a pathway and hold firm to my beliefs, I had to be responsible for the way other people reacted to that. That was my leaving home into the arms of Sheyna.

They say you left home in order to avoid being put up for marriage.

That too. After a while, though, father was tolerant; he felt that he did not want two radicals in the family. One way to calm me down was to have me "wed and bed."

So you ran away to Denver and then fell in love with a sign painter, Morris Meyerson, who was a little older than you?
Yes.

A poet, interested in music, and not a radical. So you jumped from the frying pan into the fire?
No. I jumped from the frying pan with high walls that contained me, onto a griddle that I could skate upon. It was my choice where I went, and what became of me. It was a decision to experience things that some people would consider of a frivolous nature, the arts—something I had viewed from afar but had not delved into much. So it was a great experience of freedom for me.

You kept in touch with Morris when you returned to Wisconsin to get on with the rest of your life, but eventually you married him. Tell us about your relationship.
We were soul mates. We had had prior lives together. He was very calming to my rebellious nature, but also a directive force for me. Calming in that when I got on my soap box, much as I had seen my sister do, he would remind me that there had to be a purpose for what we did. That is was not to do something in order to be known, it was to do something with a purpose. He would always ask me, "What do you seek to accomplish, Golda?"

In 1917, after Britain declared support for a Jewish homeland, you married Morris on condition you would both emigrate to Palestine, which you did in 1921. You bore a son, Menachem, and a daughter, Sarah. Did you enjoy motherhood?
Yes, I did. It was totally different, and I had sworn that my children would have a freedom of expression and a freedom for growth that had not been afforded to our people—that they could do it in the open, expressing who they were and being

proud of who they were. They could openly proclaim our great religious heritage.

Why did you and Morris separate in 1945 if you were soul mates— did you not see eye-to-eye?

I chose to put the country above my family, and he was asking the questions, "Why do you seek to do this? For what purpose?" He thought that I was giving up my family for the limelight and not for the country. He did not understand that I was driven internally to accomplish what had been started. When first I heard that we were to have a country it was my pledge at that time that everything would be done by and for the people. It would not be some protectorate that is guided, directed, and mandated by someone from the outside. There had to be an internal agreement among the people. Morris did not see that as anything other than (as you would say today) "an ego trip," but my vision, my journey, my passion had nothing to do with ego. It had to do with providing a base, a country, for posterity.

The Zionism that you talked about was socialist. Did it have the political intention to control of the means of production, distribution, and exchange?

It had to in the beginning because we were taking in so many diverse people, so there had to be a basis of organization and control, which could morph over the years into something that was palatable to all.

You once said, "Above all, this country is our own. Arab sovereignty in Jerusalem just cannot be." From your perspective at Home now, was it fair to the Palestinian Arab population, to create the State of Israel and to form new boundaries by openly annexing captured lands?

[laughs] It totally depends upon your perspective (even from my perspective at Home), because everything that was accomplished was done for various parties to add to the experiences that they already had. So it played out exactly as it

needed to play out. All souls are identical at Home. They just have different costumes that they wear as they play different roles. The costumes and the roles exist down on Earth only; we're all the same inside. When in a particular lifetime, in order to gain experience, you have to find the means of writing the pattern that goes with that particular role. In order to form the homeland on Earth that I had envisioned, there had to be boundaries for that homeland. For it to be, as I had envisioned, for the Zionists, for the Jews, Israelis (whatever you want to call us), it had to be contained, it had to be unfettered by outside influences, because we were taking a stew of people and forming a beautiful compote. If we had ingredients that did not wish to be part of our compote, they would sour our creation.

Is it a good policy today to throw a wall around the State of Israel?
No. A wall says, "I am intolerant." A wall says, "I will not participate in anything other than my game." It's like a little boy taking his ball and going home in the middle of an organized match.

Isn't it a logical consequence of Zionism that, if you are going to establish a state, you are doing it openly and knowingly in the face of opposition?
Very true, but that was when it was being established. It is well established in this day and age. It has an identity. Once an identity is established and a cohesive ideation is in place, or is in a place such that the people can change some of the parameters if they choose through regular parliamentary procedure, there is no need to remain in a boxing ring. You simply proclaim who you are on your turf and invite your neighbors to recognize your sovereignty. In order to grow there must be interchange and a degree of tolerance.

When you and Morris got to Palestine you joined the Kibbutz Merhavia. You represented it at Histadrut (the General Federation of Labour) and, later, got a job with Histadrut's Council of Women Workers and so began your rise as a Jewish leader. What qualities made you successful?

There were a number of qualities. I think the best way to explain it was that, having spent so much time in America, where nothing is impossible, I had a way of looking and thinking about things that was different from that of those people who had come from oppressive situations. While others would say, "I would like to do that but nobody has done it before, so I'm not going to try because it's worthless or hopeless," I would say, "This is what we want to do; let's find out how to do it."

Despite the British crack-down on Zionism in 1946, arresting many leaders, you were never arrested. You took charge and negotiated with the British. Tell us about that time.

During the struggles a number of the men believed the only way to get independence and to exert a degree of autonomy for ourselves was physically—with power, with guns. I believed we could talk it out in a rational way. So I was not perceived as a threat because I did not advocate open warfare. Also I had very good English (although American and British English are really two different languages), and I was very flexible and accommodating of differences.

The day after the Declaration of the Establishment of the State of Israel was signed, Israel was attacked by Arab nations, but you went to the United States. Why?

Various things were happening over there. I had the idea that there was wealth in America which could begin to be tapped as a resource to help strengthen what we had in Israel. I knew there would be many, many years of conflict with our neighbors. That was going to entail the necessity for financing. With my ability, having lived in the United States for so many years, and also with being recognized as a woman leader, which was an oddity in both locales, I would be heard—at least as an oddity! Once I got my foot in the door, I believed my persuasiveness would allow me to set up a base of operations to funnel the funds that were needed back into Israel.

Did you have success with the United States government as well?

I had an idea that the government would like to have a foothold in that part of the world. I wasn't as successful as I would have liked, and believe that was because of my sex.

Then you were assigned to be Israel's first ambassador to the Soviet Union. What was it like to return to the country from which your family had fled?

When I first got there, it was one of the only times when I felt apprehension because there was still quite a bit of oppression going on. I feared (particularly as a woman) that if I disappeared it would not be questioned too much. I went with the idea that I was going to present our cause to the people there, and also to find a way to open the door of passage from the Soviet Union to Israel.

Were you successful?

It took a long time, and some of the initial diplomatic discussions were clandestine. Their officials believed that they could not openly advocate that educated people should leave The Motherland and emigrate to any other country—but eventually the discussion was successful.

You became a member of the Knesset, Israel's Parliament. You were Minister of Labor and after that Foreign Minister. Then you were diagnosed with lymphoma. Was cancer a lesson you had agreed to experience before incarnating?

It wasn't specifically determined that it was going to be cancer, but it was decided that there would be something that would stand as a huge roadblock, something of a physical nature. It was also partially because, at that time, I was overwhelmed by what I saw as roadblocks within the Knesset and with several procedures that we were attempting to get carried through. There were factions starting to form that were interfering with a smooth transition of things. I took all that to heart, so part of the lymphoma was a blockage of energy within myself, created by myself, because I was not fully aware of the energetic nature of my self. I had become so totally physical that

I was unable to reverse it. That was the lesson I needed to learn, that if I could project my spiritual knowledge into the physical aspect of myself and remember who I truly was, I could reverse the deleterious effect that such a disease would have upon my body.

You are said to have hidden the disease and resigned your office on the ground of "exhaustion." Did you finally recover from the lymphoma?

I reversed a large portion of it when I spent time examining who I was as a person, who I was as a soul, and where I was going. Then I became conscious of myself versus the public persona, the mover and shaker.

Then in 1969 your party chose you as Prime Minister and you had to deal with the War of Attrition with Egypt. Was it you who created the Israeli military strategy of "asymmetrical response"?

Not me personally. The plan was proposed by several knowledgeable military men, and we played it almost as a board game to see how it would work.

This is the strategy still followed against Hamas in Gaza and Hezbollah in Lebanon?

To one degree or another, yes.

Does it work?

It works when there are not too many variables.

As Prime Minister, in the short space of two years you had to deal with the Munich massacre at the 1972 Summer Olympic Games, and then the Yom Kippur War. Your government was blamed for having been caught napping by its enemies, and much of the blame was directed at you. Looking at your leadership now, how do you assess the situation?

From the personal energetic standpoint, I did the best that I was capable of doing. I always gave my physical all to whatever was going on. From an historic standpoint, I reached a place where my sphere of influence was so large that it was impossible for me to micromanage simultaneously everything that was happening in all the spheres of influence.

I delegated to a lot of people responsibilities that I had myself assumed at one time early on. Those who looked from the outside said I was falling down on the job. This was for the reason that, in previous years, I had been responsible for the things where we were hit the hardest. They did not see all the other things, the behind-the-scenes negotiations with other major countries, the building up of the private sector, the building up of the scientific community within the country, that was going on at the time when I was hands on.

How I am judged is only for those who are now in human form in judgment to say. How I am evaluated back here is that I accomplished what I set out to experience.

Golda, 60 years after its founding, Israel today is still not free from trouble. What policy would you now follow to realize your dreams for a Jewish homeland at peace?

For a nation to have been developed to be totally at peace, we would have had to have created a homeland in a location where the history of so many diverse peoples did not coalesce at one place. In other words we would have had to eschew our connection with what we felt we absolutely needed—going back to our roots. Then we would be transplanted to a place which was not in contention. It would not have been accepted by those who felt that the only place to build a city and a country to bring us together in our religion was in the place of our Holy of Holies. Through the centuries, the vortex of energy in Israel—in Jerusalem and various other locations—drew to it Islam and many of the Christian sects. So to go to the place where all of these religious groups' histories were interlinked, said automatically that there would be a fight to control the intersecting territories.

Is Israel in danger of annihilation?

There are a lot of things that are going to be happening, and the variables involved with them make it too hard to be able to tell exactly the energies going this way or that way. One day the answer would be "yes," the next day the answer would be "maybe," and the third day the answer would be "no."

What can we do about it?

We can only encourage people to go into their hearts, to connect with their souls, to find that spark within them which is unconditional love, and know that is all that any of us are. If that can be acknowledged, we can all co-exist—with a multitude of languages, a multitude of customs, a multitude of religious parameters—on the head of a pin, in peace.

Thank you, Golda Meir, for talking with us.

Commentary

Toni: An extremely powerful woman with a dynamism about her—but it was understated. I felt that she wanted to be the game player, the one behind the pieces letting them all move in synergy. When she talked about the game board, I saw several games with pieces being moved about strategically. It was a constant intellectual experience for her to try to get everything to fit, to plan ahead—anticipating the next step, and making sure everything was prepared. It was a complex energetic experience because she was clearly re-living some of the things she had gone through as she was speaking about them, and I could feel her pulled in a dozen different directions at once, trying to create something that was for the good of all.

Peter: Loyalty to a cause and a people does not end at our physical death. There was no questioning the devotion Golda Meir still has for Israel, even though, like Ronald Reagan at Berlin, she would "Tear down this wall!" because: "A wall says I am intolerant." Proud of her nation, she looks back to the day she signed her name as a Founder of the State of Israel as a high point in her life.

Golda has a new angle on the present and potential future of Israel, as well as her past role. She seemed proud of her accomplishments but recognized her personal difficulties. She had been too engaged in politics to save her marriage. Then, perhaps because she was a woman, she had failed to impress the US government as she tried to get funding in the immediate post-independence period. Despite popular acclaim among Polish Jews (which we did not mention), she had a tenuous time as the Israeli ambassador to the Soviet Union. Then came the big one. Pre-occupied, she had failed to give adequate oversight of her government's operation under her premiership during the Yom Kippur war.

Having the perspective that being at Home affords, makes her glad to be watching "in the grandstand" as her successors wrestle in the mud of the human playing field with the harsh lessons that each of them had requested before incarnating. In coming days life at the Ground Zero of the three faiths will be especially tough. Israel will not know peace, because that was the hand that had been dealt the nation from the beginning. "Earth is going through a transformation. It's also fulfilling some of the biblical predictions for the planet." Judging from comments that the Masters and several leading individuals have made to us recently, there is more than just conflict in the Middle East about which the spirit world has a real concern.

Before incarnating, every soul now here on Earth, has been made aware—at least in outline—of what will happen to the planet in the next few years, and those who have decided to rest on their laurels will have plenty of human drama to watch. Every life on Earth is thoroughly planned in advance. We make contracts with our soul mates; Golda mentioned one she had made with the soul of her husband, Morris. But when we arrive, the decisions we make of our own free will then become the experiences and lessons of our self-imposed predestination.

"Souls are here to learn the lessons they choose,

and those may have sexual aspects to them
that are not what society thinks is normal."

Margaret Mead
1901-1978

*Margaret, on one occasion you said, "Fathers are biological
necessities, but social accidents." I get the impression that, in fact,
you chose both your parents with great care.*

We all do. We all decide exactly what the lessons are, and
what energy we need to surround ourselves with in order to set
up those lessons we wish to learn.

What did each of your parents give you?

Well, outside of the background DNA that they gave me,
my mother gave me a sense of tolerance and an ability to
examine all of the energies surrounding a situation—not to take
things at initial face value, but to know there is something deep
beneath the surface that motivates and sets up the patterns that
develop. From my father I inherited fire; I inherited the desire to
take an issue and go forward with it and to overcome patterning
that people might say exists. He instilled in me the possibility of
going beyond whatever others had done.

Did you have past lives that also contributed to your forcefulness?

Yes, I was a researcher in a number of lives, where I
researched everything from the scientific, to the social, to the
patterns of what the enemy was going to do on the battlefield. I

95

was in all types of examinations of the human psyche as well as of the animal kingdom.

Was it a work ethic or was it more a passion to express yourself that drove you to write all those books and articles and travel all over the world?

It was a combination of both, because without the drive and the passion, the work ethic wouldn't have gotten me anywhere. A work ethic without an engine behind it wouldn't have made me succeed as I did. A desire also to inform and to educate was part of that passion, which resulted in the plethora of information I delved into and regurgitated for the public.

At Barnard College you met Ruth Benedict, who became your lifelong friend. Was it she who persuaded you to become an anthropologist?

I don't know that it was "persuaded"—she was my sounding board, she was my friend. It wasn't very seemly at that time for a woman to be an anthropologist. It was still primarily the purview of the male, because it was simply unheard for a woman to go out into primitive areas, to deal with people who might harm her or not be truthful with her—all, of course, belief systems from the society I was part of, not from the societies I wished to examine.

Another important person at Barnard College was the anthropologist Franz Boas, and when you went on to study at Columbia University he became your mentor. Tell us about his influence.

Franz had a way of igniting within you a fire that burned so deeply you couldn't imagine existing without it. He took all of the other lives that I had lived, all of those things that were in the shadows, and seemed to be able to go by an instinct of what was deep inside me and pick them out and put them together into a pattern that showed me what I could do in this particular lifetime. Then he equipped me with the car and the railroad tracks upon which to run it and gave me a push!

You're almost suggesting he was psychic.

The man was able to feel within a person what connected that person to a passion. It was as if he could see the ingredients for a cake lying around the various parts of the individual, and seeing the ingredients that were there, he knew exactly what the finished product would be. He knew from the interests I had, from the things that excited me, and from the questions I asked, that I would be a perfect—as he called it—"field operative."

From 1926 for the next 50 years you served the American Museum of Natural History in New York. You wrote, "Anthropology demands the open-mindedness with which one must look and listen, record in astonishment and wonder that which one would not have been able to guess." Did the Museum fulfill that test of open-mindedness then?

Initially, no, they didn't. There was a lot of hesitation. There was the desire to be in the forefront of saying they had employed a female anthropologist. There was the desire to say they were completely open-minded, but they still had to be pushed. Once I brought back to them examples of exciting, never-before-seen customs and ways of life which stirred the imagination, that they had never thought could exist, then they became the platform to propel me forward. I accomplished this with my descriptions and my recounting of what I had experienced in the field.

You were very learned, of course, so that appealed to them.

Had I not been learned, I wouldn't have gotten in the front door.

How do you view the Museum's, and also anthropology's, contribution to our cultural understanding today?

For those who even know what anthropology is, it is like a large arrow that shows the way to live this life, if you wish to interact totally with it and utilize all of the possibilities that are out there. Taking and studying the motivation behind a culture that is diametrically opposed to your own, being able to feel the reason that these individuals (just like you and me) take a different path, allows you to become totally open to whatever exists in the world, to be able to have an interplay with it, to understand it, to accept it, and—if carried beyond that—to be able to help others to understand why your neighbor does not have to be the same as you. It also puts people, if they enter the feeling of it, into a place where they recognize the soul as the basis within all humans that makes us all the same.

Anthropology has got into souls these days?
  [laughs] The energy behind it, what it can do if you are open to what is there . . . no, anthropologists as a whole still have not accepted spirituality.

Before you joined the Museum you did fieldwork in Polynesia, which resulted in your first book, Coming of Age in Samoa, *published in 1928. Looking back, are you satisfied with the research you did there?*
  I am, for the period in my life in which it occurred. It was a coming of age for me, as well, so the title of the book referred as much to my opening into my profession as it did to what I was recording. It was a total awakening. You can study things in school, but even when you have a teacher such as I had, who gave me the basics, until you go and experience and are totally immersed in a different type of culture, you don't have a good feeling for where something like anthropology can go and what your part is within it, and that you are primarily an observer. You cannot interact with what is going on, because then you change it. If you put your ideas, your beliefs, into your recording, you are then only taking and presenting from one point of view. If you allow yourself to go into a culture, accept it totally without question, feel the motivation behind its mores, then you are truly presenting to other people the beauty of the differences.

The National Catholic Register suggested that your findings were projections of your desire to eliminate restrictions on your own sexuality. The Intercollegiate Studies Institute declared Coming of

Age in Samoa *as Number One of its "50 Worst Books of the Twentieth Century." Considering these responses as an anthropologist, how do you evaluate the battle over human sexuality in the last century?*

Well, my first comment is that the fact that it caused such a stir is indicative of the fact that I did a good job. The strong reaction from the Catholic Church was in response to the fact that they wished everybody to abide by their ideas, their belief systems. They could not imagine a place where people did not fear sex, did not fear someone seeing the naked body.

To them, and to a lot of other people, because of the prudish tenor of things at the time the book was published, seeing any naked part of a body immediately created a sexual response in their minds. To a people where nudity was normal and just the way they grew up, there was no sexual response simply because of the presence of a naked body. There had to be much more put into it. There had to be the initiation of a flirtation. There had to be energy exchanged between the parties, which could occur in America or in England or anywhere else in the world, even if the person is fully clothed, with the same energies.

Because the cloth made the difference to people of closed minds, both book reviewers and theologians, they would not feel, would not even try to accept that this could exist somewhere else on the planet. Everybody had to have the same ideas, the same principles, the same mores that they were raised with, or it was horrible, it was taboo, it was the worst thing possibly imagined—hence, it was the worst book.

Rather unfairly, it being after your physical death, the Australian anthropologist Derek Freeman denounced your analysis of Samoan culture as being "sexually liberated." So now it's your turn! What's your response?

I respond to Derek that by the time he examined the culture it had totally been indoctrinated by those from the outside, as opposed to when I dealt with them so many years— decades—before him ....

About fifty years ...

It was as if he were looking at a contaminated culture, while I had looked at a pure culture. So his findings in his lifetime were true, my findings in my lifetime were true—we were both right—and yet the findings seem diametrically opposed.

You were married three times and are reported to have enjoyed a relationship with Ruth Benedict. In your commentary on teenage sexuality in Samoa and New Guinea you rejected promiscuity but suggested that attitudes toward sex in Western society might be more relaxed. Can you say now what are desirable norms for human sexuality?

I think that has to be determined by each individual person. It has to be determined by the pathway that that soul is walking upon in the physical life now being experienced. We cannot say for other souls what is right or wrong or *normal* for that matter, in a third dimensional way, for them. Souls are here to learn the lessons they choose, and those may have sexual aspects to them that are not what society thinks is normal.

So there's no norm for society as a whole?

No, because if you are experiencing the lesson of frigidity, or you are experiencing the lesson of promiscuity, both of them are perfectly normal for that lifetime. If you are experiencing a mastership of your body, where (even while being bathed in sexually explicit things) you wish to be celibate to increase the energy within you so that you can use that to, say, preach, that is normal as well. Whatever is the path of the individual soul is normal for that soul.

I'm sure you've answered me correctly, because you keep using the word "normal," but what about societal needs? How about trial marriages (which you advocated), and student sexual romps at Spring Break (which you did not)?

Well, there were a number of things that played into my do's and don'ts, and it had a little bit to do, sometimes, with where my head was at the time. A human individual is an animal with needs. One of those needs is sexual expression. Society, in my day (it has changed slightly in the present age), believed that those animal needs should be fulfilled only within the bounds of a marriage, but someone with the need for a sexual outlet (and, of course, masturbation was taboo) also needed to have a partner.

If it was because of the need and not because of procreation, nor because the two souls were energetically connected such that they wished to live their lives together, society's mandates then would restrict them from fulfilling the need that they had within their bodies. It would condemn them to partnering up to see if they were even compatible with each other.

I still do not advocate free love, open sex, but I do believe that it is something that is an animal need, and when it becomes so overpowering, it needs to be satisfied in order for the person to be able to give time to anything other than an obsession with it. Having it in a freer form prevents sexual predators from existing, because they can get by agreement, if society allows it, what they would need to take if they couldn't get it by agreement.

What was the most socially successful tribal attitude toward homosexuality that you discovered in your research?

Just to accept people for who they were and for what their needs were, that you couldn't make them something that they were not. That homosexual tendencies did not mean people were "sick," nor that the dictates of the remainder of society were able to switch them to normally accepted sexual preferences. Let people be who they are.

Did you find tribes that did that?

Yes. There were those that didn't have somebody coming in and telling them what they should think; they just accepted various sexual desires to be normal.

How much is the issue of sexual freedom linked to the support given to adolescents by their village or extended family, as opposed to their experience in the nuclear family?

That is totally individualized. It depends upon the amount of influence allowed from the various sources. For those who are very close to their nuclear family, the nuclear family is the controlling factor. If they get very little support from their nuclear family, then their peers are very important.

But often within the extended family there appear to be very strict rules of behavior that do not necessarily exist in the smaller units.

That is done primarily to keep peace and to keep petty rivalries from existing. It is very much like our laws, when it comes to who can force oneself upon another individual. It more has to do with aggressive behavior than consenting behavior.

Has the dominance of media-disseminated attitudes toward sexuality changed the norms of the world society for the better or worse?

That completely depends upon your perspective. I have to give my perspective based upon what I see. Those who want an excuse for what they're doing can find it somewhere in the media. If they want to fit into society, they might have difficulty. So it depends on the psyche of the individual. For a lot of people it has definitely loosened up their impression of things and their view of things, because instead of getting input from one little place—their nuclear family, their church, their close associates—they now can say, "Well, that may be your idea, but the rest of the world permits this."

Isn't there a degree of chaos in society in this respect, with people getting hurt?

There is what you would call chaos, because chaos indicates that there aren't strict patterns. Are people getting hurt? On a soul level, no, because they can't be hurt on a soul level—they chose to be on the planet at this time, knowing what the energies were going to be like. Does it play with their minds sometimes in the physical, so that that is an added lesson they have to learn? Most definitely.

In your study of relationships in New Guinea, you compared the different gender roles in three tribal cultures, concluding that human nature is "malleable" and that masculine and feminine characteristics do not reflect basic biological differences but cultural conditioning. Were you correct?

All physical beings do what needs to be done to be accepted. If they are born into a family where the matriarch is the primary source of all decisions, the females will be very strong in that family. If they are born into a family where everybody bows down to the father in that family, the males will be strong and the females weak. So it depends upon what you chose.

And it can change?

It can change if a woman who is born into a patriarchal family marries a weak man—weak in that he has come from a matriarchal family—and he therefore allows her to have more power within the family, to assume the responsibilities that would normally be handled by the titular head of the family. She can totally turn around and assume those responsibilities, if she so chooses.

You wrote, "If we are to achieve a richer culture—rich in contrasting values—we must recognize the whole gamut of human potentialities, and so weave a less arbitrary social fabric, one in which each diverse human gift will find a fitting place." Looking at the world now, what is our greatest success and greatest need in this respect?

I'll handle the greatest need first. The greatest need is for people to go back and recognize their individuality. So many parts of the world in your time have gone back to the patterning where someone—some group—tells them not only what to do, but even what to *think* about what they do, taking away all degree of individuality, taking away any curiosity (even about something that may be beyond), and in some cultures that is adhered to with death hanging over people's heads if they vary.

Would it be fair for you to name any of those cultures?

I think it would be unfair to point fingers at the Middle East.

And the success?

The success is what has happened in the countries that have become melting pots, such as the United States and some different places in Europe that have opened up, where people can do anything that they put the effort into doing. Governments allow the culture from an immigrant's homeland to be assimilated into their culture if it enriches what exists. Freedom is often the catchphrase of these countries. The greatest success that individuals can have is to recognize the power within themselves. Those who do are aware that they create their own reality, manifesting the peculiar illusion that they call their life. Those whom society might call Spiritualists are living through their hearts and souls, feeling for themselves, and not just complying with the expected. As long as you recognize that a possibility exists, and you are willing to take the responsibility of following your own path, even if it is divergent from that of society, you are able to grow and make a change.

You're not only known for sexuality; you're also known for your interest in the environment, and you once said, "We won't have a society if we destroy the environment." It's more than global warming isn't it?

It's much more than global warming; it's the reasons for global warming. It is the pollution of the mind and the spirit as well as the pollution of Mother Earth—when we allow the energy of a group of people to change what we think. To most, a very benign example would be that everybody has "the right" to have a motor vehicle. That motor vehicle will use fossil fuels that pollute, but it is our "right" to be able to go anywhere we want at any time we want to—and the result is the greenhouse effect.

We can say that in order to provide ease for people, we will make Styrofoam products for them to carry home their hamburgers and French fries, or their fish and chips, something that is consumed in a moment, while the container will exist in its same condition for hundreds of years, and also the very manufacture of it produces chemical byproducts that pollute streams and the Earth. But we're "helping" the people, because we're keeping their food warm for five extra minutes.

On another occasion you wrote, "A small group of thoughtful people could change the world. Indeed, it's the only thing that ever has." What are the most vital, urgent changes we need to make?

We need to get people to understand consumption of natural resources, and that there are alternatives. We need to have them understand that when it comes to cattle, we don't need the beefiest of the beef, shored up by antibiotics and growth hormones that then enter into our body and weaken it and put it on a path of decay. We need people to know that they can get just as much energy out of a windmill or a solar panel as they can out of a coal-smoke-belching power plant. We need to let them hear the environmentalists who live off the Earth. The "small group" that can initiate the change might be one manufacturing plant that changes to green energy and through that stops pollution within the industry and makes a handy profit as well because green energy is cheaper.

It's hard to do much with the huge population that exists on Earth at the moment.

If we start with small groups—since money rules the planet—if they see that they don't spend as much on medical supplies because they aren't sickened as easily, that they don't spend as much money on fuel or electricity, that they don't spend as much money on food, then the movement will spread out. But then the major companies don't want that to be known, because we would be cutting the strings, the profits. Medical supply companies would try to find a way to legislate against changes that make them unneeded.

Where do we look for that group of thoughtful people: science, religion, the young?
They're spread across the surface of the planet. There are those who have chosen no longer to be sickened by the environment, nor to contribute to the pollution. They are the ones who have created "green villages," as they call them. They are the ones who have gone into what is known as permaculture. They are the ones who have gotten groups together to non-violently protest big industries that pollute. I would not, however, include the environmental groups that have become quite violent in some of their protests, although a good portion of environmentalists are still on the right track.

Margaret, your leadership was broad and thoughtful, ranging from the issues we have touched on to the women's movement, to nuclear bombs, ecology, and education. If you were to leave Home now and reincarnate, what issue would you most like to tackle?
I don't know that I could choose one, because as I watch what takes place on the Earth, I get moved by the direction that some groups are going in, and then I have another interest grab me, and another, and another. It would be very difficult for me to choose just one. The environment would be the biggest for me, and cutting down the pollution of the planet, and easing the pressure put upon the various plates of Mother Earth that doesn't allow her to stretch, and when she does stretch, results in devastation and loss of life.

Is this devastation a certainty?
As the world exists now, yes.

How soon?
There are pressures building now. If there is not a major change in the greenhouse effect, with the melting of the poles there are going to be a lot of places under water that are now

106

above water. There are going to be whole island groups that no longer exist for habitation. There will be a change in the growing patterns on the planet. There will also be shifting of the plates as the temperatures change in the oceans, which will create earthquakes and tsunamis. And this is an ongoing, progressive increase over the next few years.

From which there is no retreat?

The energy needed to prevent this occurrence is right there on the planet. That is the energy of the creative power inside of all the mass of people that inhabit the planet. If they were to organize with their intention of changing their over-consumptive ways, this could be slowed and, in some cases, even prevented.

As an anthropologist, do you see that as likely?

Way too many variables exist at this time to make any type of prediction regarding that.

Finally, do you know when you will return?

I'm having much too much fun being able to observe, not just one place, but dozens of places at the same time from my current position, so I don't have any plans at the present time to return and get only a single viewpoint.

Thank you, Margaret Mead, for talking with us.

It has been my pleasure.

Commentary

Toni: Margaret had a highly polished energy. It was almost as if she knew what the questions were going to be and had decided exactly how she was going to respond. It felt more like a play being enacted than a spontaneous interview, but her sincerity ran very deep. Her connection to the planet was palpable (like a live thing that she was watching intently), which she presented dispassionately just like one of her field observations. It was a very individual perspective.

Peter: I had expected comment on issues of human sexuality, but Margaret's concern for Mother Earth proved to be stronger. It was as if sexuality were a discussion from the past but global warming and the list of disasters—that was for real!

Margaret's take on human sexuality centered on physical need. There is no case to be made for a single social norm of behavior. Each of us is responsible for dealing with the lessons we chose before incarnating. How do we deal with frigidity? sexual compulsion? masturbation? social restrictions? homosexuality? parental edicts? media liberalism? In reality, the norms are within ourselves, whatever the world may say.

Of course there are social pressures, social "standards," but Margaret's answer is rooted in the life of the individual soul, because each soul answers for the way lessons are tackled, difficulties overcome, experiences are processed, and a passing grade achieved. This "leave it to the individual" does not ignore religious teaching or legal rules—but they are just part of the total experience of which the individual soul must be aware.

When it came to environmental issues, I felt a new direction. The anthropologist became the campaigner. One of her answers began: "If we start with small groups..." She was personally caught up in the drama. There was an urgency for us to examine our pollution profile: our addiction to cars, plastic cups, needless manufacture, and other excesses. She was urgent about the need for sustainability and for a new transforming spirituality based on an awareness of the needs of planet Earth.

"It was as if I could transport myself into the environments I wrote about, so it was a living, breathing thing to me."

Rachel Carson
1907-1964

Rachel Louise Carson, you were born on a farm near Springdale, an Allegheny Valley town in Pennsylvania, where animals roamed, the birds still sang in field and forest, and where your mother taught you to look deep into rivers and ponds to see the life that was in them. Was this childhood experience the source of your commitment to nature?

That's correct. I was raised with an appreciation for every living thing upon the planet. I was given insight into the interconnectedness between what the two-footed human did and how it affected not only the animals but Mother Earth herself. I was raised with a reverence to let me see the higher purpose in everything that is on this planet earth, and to know that nothing exists in its own little vacuum.

You were shy, but loved writing poetry as well as prose, and were first published at the age of ten. Then came that insight in college when you, an English major, declared, "I want to make animals, in the woods or waters where they live, as alive to others as they are to me." What caused you to put your writing skill at the service of the environment?

In talking to my fellow students, I found that their world was all concrete and stucco and brick. They were totally unaware of what lay beyond the houses that they existed in. I wanted to be able to give everyone a feel of what insignificance

109

man has when seen in the context of all the other living, breathing things upon the planet. I knew that from my expertise in the use of language, I would be able to find a way to turn on and tune in (as they say) those around me to take notice of and to be able to communicate with and to feel a part of the whole of nature.

Much later, when your sister died, you adopted her five-year-old son. Did you ever wish for a husband and family life?

There was some longing within me for it, but I knew that I was more driven to be a communicator than to be a "hausfrau," or a mother. Not that mothers are not very powerful in this world, and not that mothers do not have a very special place, but with the abilities I had in that lifetime, I wished to be able to affect not just a familial unit but an entire generation, an entire planet.

So you switched your studies from English to zoology, went to John Hopkins University for your Master's degree, and then studied at the Marine Biological Laboratories. Were sea creatures your first passion?

Sea creatures were a terrific passion for me. At that time, I knew little about them and their environment. I had always just viewed them through the surface of the water. I hadn't been able to go down and examine their neighborhood, so to speak, their way of existence. I was given this terrific opportunity, with the laboratories there, to step into a world that was almost alien to me. For some people it would be like being able to go to an amusement park and have all of their fantasies created in front of them, and they'd be part of them.

Did your past lives help you to become a marine biologist?

Well, except for the life I now know of when I lived as a dolphin, I wasn't conscious of any past lives that had to do with it. I was a fisherman, but I would say that was probably the antithesis of what I was doing as Rachel.

What was your experience as a dolphin like?

It was a very peaceful existence, an existence of community and of a shared consciousness, of being able to feel, almost in the way I do now as a soul, that I am interconnected with everything that is.

Dolphins have an acute awareness of life, don't they?

They really do. They are the librarians and the historians of this planet.

Can you say more about that?

Dolphins did not evolve on this planet. Dolphins came from a galaxy named Ashfar that is a water planet. They and the whales came down here around the time of what you know as Atlantis, a time of transition for humankind. They were the ones who provided the information on how to commingle the species upon the planet. They knew what would be needed, and what would help to facilitate the growth of your current species upon the planet. They also were the historians in that they kept the records of what was going on, and even as the planet evolved through all of your different ages, there were dolphins present on the planet.

It is not a mistake that in places such as Sedona, Arizona, they have found dolphin skeletal remains. Dolphins were throughout the planet whenever there was an opportunity to be there. They also tried to keep the consciousness of the planet alive, and to keep the spiritual connection with soul alive. When man became very, as you would say, "third-dimensional," only concerned with the ego, only concerned with physical desires and wants, the dolphins kept the purity of spirituality alive. Those who communicated with them in their environment felt that spirituality. They felt their connection to the Creator, to the interconnection, the web of all that exists.

[Toni: She just showed me dynamic energy going from place to place, and a web that appears to connect

111

everybody, as if individual beings were like little dots or little spiders upon this huge web.]

So you had what Charles Darwin, in his discussion with us, called a "human interchangeable soul."
Yes.

How common is that?
It's not that common. If you want Earth percentages, I would say no more than one to two percent of all souls have interchanged and spent time within another animal species' body.

Do whales and dolphins have a higher percentage of human interchangeable souls than other animals?
They do. They also have a higher percentage of brain mass than puny humans.

So how do you view the present trade in whale flesh?
It saddens me, but not all of the whales that are on the planet have souls that have been human. Some of them are just there to provide a food source, as a supply within the ecosystem, and those that do have a flicker of a soul (that has been in other existences), put themselves up for sacrifice because that is something that they wish to experience.

Your writing skills were developing fast. Marine zoology was your main topic. You wrote an essay, "Undersea," for the Atlantic Monthly, and radio scripts for the US Bureau of Fisheries, which resulted in your getting a job there as a junior aquatic biologist. Tell us about that experience.
I would say that the slowness of bureaucracies was the first thing it taught me. As with all things, whenever we wanted to try something new or innovative, it took a long time to sell it up the chain of command, so to speak. But at the same time, whenever somebody at the top of the command chain had an interest in something, it was amazing how fast funds could be

provided and materials gathered. So it gave me a very good look at what was possible when you had the power behind you, and when you didn't have the power behind you, how very slowly things could grind away.

Then in 1941 you published your first book, Under the Sea Wind. *The Bureau promoted you until in 1949 you became editor-in-chief of the Fish and Wildlife Service. This was your favorite book, wasn't it?*

It was my favorite book because some parts seemed to be almost autobiographical. It was as if I could transport myself into the environments that I wrote about, so it was a living, breathing thing to me. It was not simply black ink upon white paper.

What is your assessment now of the work done by the US Fish and Wildlife Service today?

Well, some of it is a little astray of its purpose, as proposed at the inauguration of the Service. Now it is more like trying to have fishing ponds for people who want to fish, and things like that—not the preservation of the species, necessary as it has always been. There is a small percentage of those within the Bureau who are interested in that, but they seek more to please the people who fund the Bureau than to protect the environment and provide a means for the common person to experience the complexity and beauty of nature.

In 1951 your second book, The Sea Around Us, *was published. You became famous all over the world and received many awards for your work. You retired and built a cottage on the Sheepscot River near the coast of Maine. Four years later came your book* The Edge of the Sea. *What was it like for a shy, country girl to become a world celebrity?*

Scary! It put me into a spotlight that never seemed to turn off. I was recognized everywhere I went. Essentially I had no private life, except around home where the local people accepted me (once they got over the fact that I wasn't born there). I tried to maintain my life as it had always been, but of course it had changed. By then I was a voice that was listened to, and I had the ability to impact trends that I saw were damaging to the environment because, very seriously, nobody wanted to get on the wrong side of the woman with the words.

At that point did you see yourself as a marine biologist?

I was always a naturalist, concerned about all of the environment, concerned about all of the creatures and the interconnection of all species upon the planet. My recognized expertise at that time was marine biology. I was recognized as an expert in that because of my work experience and my books, and how well they were received. They became almost textbooks within some institutions because I was able so to intermingle my energy with what I wrote about that they were first-person reports from both the fish world and the human world.

Tell us about the state of the waters and marine life on planet Earth now.

There are a lot of transitions going on right now that are the result of many things. There are pollution issues where whole bodies of water have been irreparably destroyed due to the run-off of chemicals, toxins from industry and various other sources. There are the changes occurring because of the climatic cycles caused by the shifting of planet Earth. There are also bright spots in that some nations and some people are trying to reverse the man-made disasters. I would give the whole planet an ecological grade of D-minus at this time.

Or, rather, you'd give it to human beings, because the planet herself is a living spirit, isn't she?

Oh, I didn't mean Mother Earth! Mother Earth is doing everything that she can, and her response is that when things get to the point of needing to be reclaimed, needing to be done over again, then she helps with an earthquake, a tsunami, a volcano, a nice storm.

Was there a spiritual plan that prepared you for the huge publicity and criticism that Silent Spring *engendered?*

Not that I was conscious of while in human form. I was just being myself, and that is a spiritual path in itself, accepting who you are in the physical covering that you have down on planet Earth, and still bringing out the essence of who you are, regardless of the reaction that causes. So in that respect you could say there was a spiritual plan.

You'd been monitoring governmental abuse of chemicals and pesticides since 1945, but you did little speaking or writing about it. Were you put off by the Reader's Digest's *rejection of your article attacking official insecticide experiments?*

There were a number of things happening at that time. I knew that an exposé of what was going on needed to reach the eyes and ears of a vast number of people. I determined from the reaction to my article that it had to be done on a grander scale than in a small magazine. At that time I was also very cognizant of the fact that anybody criticizing the government or Big Brother in a publication had an uphill battle. All publications of the time were monitored by the government and the publishers for the effect they might have upon the people after the war. A magazine's reputation was directed by these higher-ups; compliance with the desires of the censors was necessary for the self-preservation of the magazine. It was then very much my awareness that, in order to create this explosive revelation, if you will, so that it got across all lines (socio-economic, ideological beliefs, etc.), it had to be done in such a way that one person (myself at that time), was the full point of focus. It was then I decided that I could get away with it because of my reputation as an author.

Later you wrote, "The more I learned about the use of pesticides, the more appalled I became." What was it that drove you to begin writing your most famous book?

The fact that the government had such total disregard for the effect of wholesale use of poisons on the planet; that for a very small benefit, they were willing to unleash those effects upon masses of people. They were willing to allow something that would irreparably change the soil and the water for decades, merely to increase production (and that not even to a monumental degree, but to a small degree). There was a total disregard of the whole picture. I could see that if this continued to the extent it would, the planet would become barren because of the deleterious effects of those chemicals.

You said, "What I discovered was that everything which meant most to me as a naturalist was being threatened, and that nothing I could do would be more important." What do you recall as the main issue at that time?

The main issue of the time was: Do a few people who want to realize monetary gain have the power to affect everyone else on the planet, and the planet itself?

What gave you the idea to call your book Silent Spring*?*

There were a lot of different things that the title meant. I know everybody refers to it as that "spring" which is the budding period, but in my mind it was a little joke. I was referring to a mechanical-type spring, a coil of information, inside a sort of jack-in-the-box that sat there very silently, very innocently, until somebody came to open up the cover and then, unexpectedly, got it in their face. They thought that it would be very innocuous, but then they got the punch.

I don't think anyone has ever guessed that! Chemical industry corporations threatened you with lawsuits and, supported by the Agriculture Department, suggested you were hysterical and unqualified to write the book. Looking back now, what do you make of their opposition?

They demonstrated their fear that with the truth exposed, their livelihood was in jeopardy. The chemical moguls saw only that the more they sold, the more they took home. The

116

government saw only the support that they got from the lobbyists who helped create the budgets for their continued existence.

Can you forgive them?

Oh, absolutely! Everybody was just doing what they came to planet Earth to experience.

Half-way through writing Silent Spring, *you were diagnosed with cancer and died at 56. Why did you get cancer?*

It was part of my plan to go out with a bang, so to speak—the bang being that I would put myself out there as the sacrificial lamb, the person to be blamed for exposing this stuff, but without any way to totally discredit me and what I had said because I wouldn't be around. I had not pre-planned the exact cause of my demise. The physical cause was that I had done many, many tests with the various chemicals and had exposure to the chemicals, which had an effect upon my body.

Is there a link, then, between human illness and environmental contaminants? I'm thinking of Cancer, MS, Alzheimer's, Parkinson's—and, if so, which pollution?

Certainly. The link is that for the frail human body to remain in a living, viable condition, it must be in balance. The body is an electro-chemical device. When a contaminant is introduced into the body that interferes with the production of the various chemicals needed for the electrical process within the body, the body does one of two things: either it breaks down because of the contamination, or it creates blockages to attempt to prevent the contaminant from having an effect. Such blockages cause normal function to be impossible. That said, you have also to take into consideration each individual soul's pathway.

Do they choose to experience this disease or this disturbance within themselves for some learning experience?

It is possible for two bodies to be exposed to exactly the

same environment and for one, who has lessons not dealing with sickness and disability, to be unaffected by the same substances that cause illness in the second body, which wishes to go through various disabilities, various struggles with trying to overcome the effects of the contaminants.

Do children's mercury-based vaccinations cause autism?

They do in a very small percentage of cases. The cause of autism is the relationship of that particular soul with the body that it is in. In some cases of autism the soul has not totally integrated with the body, and there is a misfit of the energies within the body so that the centers for what we would consider normal speech and normal behavior do not line up. In a lot of cases the soul is more connected still to its spiritual side, to the Other Side, than it is to the physical body.

Some of these cases are the result of the parents' making a contract to deal with a situation like this so that they in turn can learn more about themselves (whether their lessons be those of compassion, of overcoming hardship, or of trying to find the cause for and the way to work through difficulties). Sometimes the physical reaction of the body is caused by the introduction of a substance from the outside, such as a vaccination, but that is because the individual contract calls for a calamity or a grave condition to come into what began as a normal existence, so that the parents and relatives deal with both situations—first a perfect situation and then one totally askew.

What harmful ingredients should we avoid in our food, and does that include genetically modified plants?

Let me speak first to the genetically modified (GM) plants. In most cases they are not as harmful as the alarmists would have you believe. While the genetic modifications are occurring because of outside stimulus, which is now available, it is not too much different from the experiments of Mendel and people like him, who mixed plants with cuttings and clippings. They altered the genes, as well, but they did it in what would be considered a natural way because they did not have the knowledge of what electricity and microwaves and things can do in this day, but it's the same thing—it's genetic modification.

In most cases GM is pushing evolution a little bit further. Some of these modifications would take place a hundred generations down the course of the life of that particular substance, were they allowed to do so naturally. The only negative reaction with GM for some human beings is if they have a sensitivity or an allergy to the new species as opposed to the old species, and that can occur even with something that is recognized, such as the common goober—the peanut. That triggers a sensitivity, an allergic reaction, in some people, and it is very similar to the reactions that some say they are having to the genetically modified plants. It's that some bodies are comfortable only with things they are used to, and when something new is introduced they don't tolerate it as well.

What about other harmful ingredients in food?

Chemicals added for the sole purpose of adding color or enhancing flavor—sweeteners, monosodium glutamate, various other things intended to appeal to the eye and the tongue—can be very harmful to bodies that are resonating at a very pure level—in other words, to very sensitive individuals. Again, this is a matter of whether it is something they want to experience, or whether they wish to maintain a state of purity that is changed by the addition of things that are not natural.

Your book Silent Spring *is credited with kick-starting the current environmental movement. In 1962 you wrote, "Now I can believe that I have at least helped a little." How do you view its success from your position now at Home?*

Well, it was a contract that I had wanted to fulfill to be able to awaken, in an environmental way, a larger portion of the population. I don't view that in an egotistical way, as some people might, because we have no egos here. I view it only as something I wished to experience and as my contribution to a process of allowing the thought patterns and the behaviors of people to come into line with Mother Nature if they so choose.

In the face of global warming and other natural calamities, what do we here on planet Earth need to do most urgently?

We need—or rather, you need—to be cognizant of continued pollution, that pollution intensifies the shifts in temperature. You need also to be aware of the fact that if the intention of the massive number of souls currently on the planet is to reverse and to balance the planet, it can aid Mother Nature in reversing some of her current problems—an energetic healing, so to speak.

Thank you, Rachel Carson, for talking with us and, as you put it, for "trying to save the beauty of the living world."

I hope that the work I began there will continue to be a stimulus for change.

Commentary

Toni: Rachel was a fantastic, loving soul. There was no sense of her trying to be more than she was, or trying to change the thoughts that people had about her. She just didn't care. There was a really authentic feeling about her. When she spoke of the planet, and marine life, I had a vision of being in the water communing with the fishes, swimming around as a part of it. It was almost like being projected into a village, but the whole village was of marine life, which gave me a sense of comfort and relaxation and enjoyment.

Peter: The inner compulsion that made Rachel Carson a true prophet was revealed. Her childhood experiences of nature, her decision at college to employ her skill in future as a writer to enlarge people's vision of planet Earth, her progress in achieving her goals and handling her fame—all were made crystal clear by her insightful answers.

There were some real surprises. In common with Charles Darwin (interviewed in the first volume of this series), she spoke of the tiny percentage of souls who incarnate in animal bodies. She also gave a flavor of how the universe can move animal species between galaxies, and of the role played by dolphins as record keepers of life on our planet. But if such remarks might be thought to smack of New Age fantasy, they must be read in the context of a passionate, very down-to-Earth account of the horrors of pollution, and the havoc wrought by chemicals on Earth's environment and on human life.

Rachel had a laundry list of pollutants' deleterious effects. What environmental campaigners may find a little muted was what she said about the effect on humans of the genetic modification of crops. I was sure there was much more to be said by her, both on pollution and GM, but this was not meant to be another edition of *Silent Spring*, only a brief dialogue with a remarkable and courageous pioneer.

One issue contained a new challenge. It was for us to re-examine our current attitude toward autism, which is of such growing concern in society. Autism turns out to be, in large measure, due to the relationship of the soul with the body it inhabits. In some cases a soul has not fully integrated with its young body, and in others a soul is more connected to the Other Side than it is to its physical body. The whole of her remarks is worth an in-depth study by those spiritual healers who are competent to deal with the issue. This renowned scientist raises a problem which, I fear, most scientists are less than likely to consider relevant. Yet, once again, Rachel Carson has taken a lead by challenging our desire to do the right thing.

"I was caught up in a tornado, and I didn't know how long it would last, so I just played it for all it was worth

and let it take me wherever it was going to go."

Carmen Miranda
1909-1955

Maria do Carmo Miranda da Cunha, you were nicknamed "Carmen" by your father, who loved Bizet's opera Carmen. *Did you share his passion for opera or just his musical nature?*

Primarily his musical nature. It was difficult to get up and dance around to opera, and I liked whatever moved the body. I liked to be able to fly upon the notes and have the freedom of conveying to others with my movement what I felt inside.

Was your mother a dancer, as well?

My mother was primarily involved with running the household and found some music to be a little frivolous.

Where did you get your talent from? Was it from a past life or some ancestor?

A combination, including the present life. There was a lot of music on my father's side, from the village I grew up in, and the children I played with. In my background there was a flamenco influence from my past life as a dancer in Spain. As a traveling gypsy I had also done a lot of free-form dance to the lute and other instruments. Music ran through my veins from all directions.

They say that you hid your desire to be in show business from your parents for years. Why?

My mother thought it was totally frivolous, and my father didn't approve of anything other than the classical, the highbrow. He felt that such things as show business and street dancing gave a poor impression of our national culture, that they were demeaning, and that we should be looked upon as sophisticated, rather than as moving to the beat of our hearts.

Was your father more Portuguese than Brazilian?

Yes, and while they rumba a little bit, their butts don't move when they do—just take a look at their posture when they dance.

Some people say that your parents' attitude was because of their Catholicism. Is that fair?

It's not totally fair. It was more because of their perceived culture. They wished to be considered highbrow and more important. Of course at that time the priests did not go along with anything that was considered too free, as well. It was considered sinful to shake one's booty.

When you were a small child your family emigrated from Portugal to Rio de Janeiro, Brazil. You never went back, and later you said, "Look at me and tell me if I don't have Brazil in every curve of my body." Why then did you keep your Portuguese passport?

Just in case at some time I did decide to go back. I never totally threw out the possibility that I would go back— somewhat in honor of my father, because I thought very highly of him. I thought it would cut him to the heart if I eschewed that last little connection that he had with his homeland.

In fact, your elder sister, when she had tuberculosis, went back to Portugal and stayed there, didn't she?

Yes.

Did you keep in touch with her?

To some degree, until my life became so divergent from everything that was our home that there didn't seem to be that much of a connection with us. There was a very deep fondness between us, though.

But were you really Brazilian? After you'd gone to the U.S., you returned and had to defend yourself with the song, "They Said That I Came Back Americanized."
Things were going on in the country at that time—there was a strong degree of nationalism. I became a doll within the United States, a doll that depicted Brazil to the American people. The Brazilians took offense at that, because it was on such a small scale, considering the entire depth of the culture. They said that it trivialized what a true Brazilian was—I did not have the heart of the country, I did not have the religion of the country, I did not have the seriousness of the country, and therefore I was just a carpetbagger who had come in from another place, adopted the name, and then used it as an excuse.

There must have been racism in their judgment—a black issue, because the samba you pioneered was music from the black slums, and the costumes you wore, which had exposed midriffs, headgear, bangles, and gaudy colors, were modeled on the Baiana, the poor black fruit sellers of Bahia, Brazil's northeastern province. What attracted you most to them?
The spirit that depicted those beautiful people. They did not allow life, as they were living it, to take away their energy, or to take away their sense of who they were, or to take away their spirit of being able to express themselves and get away from the troubles of the day. They were free in their expression of who they were. They didn't consider themselves to be restricted by somebody telling them exactly how they should feel or how they should comport themselves when they were enjoying life. They exemplified a sense of freedom little found elsewhere, containing a core of purity in the sheer joy of living and loving.

So was that one of the reasons why you were criticized for not being Brazilian enough—because you had taken on their music and their style?

Those who criticized me were what you would consider the highbrows, those who had the identity of being above the common folk, who were proud of the fact that they did not have to scratch for an existence, and proud of the fact that they could spend their money to go to the opera or to the theater, and they did not have to get their entertainment from the street corner or the local bazaar. They were jealous when they recognized the sheer joy of what I portrayed to the world, and they were embarrassed that they could not join in that joyful activity because they had no idea how to do it.

You eventually became a very successful businesswoman. Did you learn how to be one when you were selling ties and then making hats for La Femme Chic *boutique?*

That was the beginning of my entrepreneurial experience. Up until then money did not have an import for me. My parents provided what I needed as I grew up, and until I began working, so I did not equate the amount of work that you put into something and the return that you get from it, and what that return could bring you. My experiences in the United States also gave me a lot of understanding of the importance of money, and how fast it could go through your fingers. Then I decided that I would be a little more cautious and watchful of where the monies that came to me were used and what they were used for.

Then in 1928 came your lucky break. A local radio employee, Josué de Barros, introduced you to a Brunswick record company director. Singing Josué's lyrics you recorded "Samba Não vá Simbora," your first song. Tell us about that experience.

It was like a fairy tale. They mentioned that I could actually get paid for what I loved doing to a degree that I had never envisioned possible before. Then there was the hint that this would make me known, so it would open the door for me to be able to pursue, with even a higher percentage of my time, that

126

art of the enjoyment of life that I had had time to do only when I wasn't trying to pay bills. It was an awakening to me that I could also bring to others the joy that I felt through my music.

Then you signed up with another record company, RCA Victor, and the Brazilian composer Joubert de Carvalho heard you sing "Triste Jandaia." Wasn't there a surprise meeting with him?

It was a surprise meeting, because I thought that all the interest in me was coming from a distance, and that there wasn't any compatriot understanding of what I was doing—because I was breaking the mold of what most Brazilians were doing at the time. They weren't bringing the streets to the studio but were presenting to the world the accepted and recognized appearance of the country. So in that meeting I found that I had ignited a flame of interest through a large portion of the people who had never even been exposed to the type of music that I was giving them.

Looking now from your perspective at Home, do you feel that your soul organized that meeting with Joubert de Carvalho?

Absolutely. Everything was done with the idea that I was going to be the instrument to loosen the strings of restraint that held so many people so tightly. I would allow them to feel the way that the energy within them resonated with music, the vibrational language of the universe.

All music, or just some music, the vibrational language of the universe?

All music is the vibrational language of the universe, with many different dialects.

Even heavy rock?

Even heavy rock talks to some souls.

In the next two years you signed a bigger contract with the record company, appeared in a theatrical show, Vai dar o que Falar, *then starred in your first movie,* O Carnaval Cantado no Rio. *Did you feel a success, or was it rather like a dream?*

It was a whirlwind. I felt that I was caught up in a tornado, and I didn't know how long it would last, so I just played it for all that it was worth and let it take me wherever it was going to go.

What did success mean to you?

It had very different meanings for me. The first thing, on a deep, personal level, was that what I had always felt about the music and about letting others feel it, letting others be exposed to it, was my true calling. Initially my mission was something that had to be forsaken because my parents disapproved of it. It reaffirmed for me the importance of letting the soul speak— letting your soul help you decide how to play the lessons and missions for which you had come down to the physical world. My mission was to let people *feel*, in whatever way was possible. As I began this venture, it was like being in an impossibly fantastic place where I could shine the light onto different groups and, for the first time, help them to see and feel themselves.

In 1935 you appeared in the movie Estudantes *as an actress as well as a singer. Was that the realization of another dream?*

My entire life I had played parts. I had played the part of the dutiful daughter; I had played the part of the adoring sister; I had played the part of the milliner; I had played the part of the granddaughter, the niece—I had played all of these parts. I did not go through life unconscious of the effect I was having on other people. I would present myself to people as I felt they wanted me to, so during all my life I had played parts. I wanted to go into a situation where someone else would direct the part that I played, and would just let me have the fun of playing the part without having to constantly revise it as I went along. I found that very freeing and enjoyable.

You were now receiving million-dollar contracts to sing on the radio; you performed at the Copacabana Casino, and you appear to have been furiously busy for years. Was this when you began to take drugs?

Yes, I found that I needed something to stabilize the energy. Everything was so frantic that I didn't have a sense of where I was in a physical form, so I turned to chemicals to help me go through the various things that were asked of me.

In 1939, you made your sixth movie, Banana da Terra, *and wore your baiana costume to sing "O que é que a baiana tem?" The Norwegian Olympic ice skater Sonja Henie and Lee Shunert, a theatrical producer, invited you to perform in the Broadway show* Streets of Paris. *How did you feel about the chance to play in America?*

As you would say, I found it a hoot. I had fought to be accepted in my home country, and now I was being courted by other nationalities just for being who I was, and I found that exhilarating.

Were you embarrassed there by your strong accent and difficulty with spoken English?

I didn't realize how music would not take care of everything for me. Because music was my choice of communication, when it came to having to deal with people outside of the theatrical realm, I realized that I did not have the preparation I should have had prior to going to the United States.

You made lots of money in America. In 1945 you were the highest-paid woman in the United States. Your movie Down Argentine Way *was a hit in the US, but it was sharply criticized in Brazil and banned in Argentina. Did you understand the sense of betrayal Hispanic people felt—or had your life become simply doing what the studio commanded, and making more money?*

I can't say that money was the driving force. I can say that pleasing people was very important to me. It was going back to my early roots when I played the part that people wanted me to. That was something I never totally got away from. I was somewhat of a rebel from the beginning in going where my energies took me, where the music took me, such as when I went to the slums because that was where my heart really beat and I really felt it.

So I didn't have what they evaluated as a "national identity" as *they* wanted the national identity. I can understand where they thought I betrayed them, but I was only being myself. I was not and did not claim to be a representative of the country. I was a representative of myself and of the music and the movement of the country, so I can appreciate their disdain for what I was doing.

In 1940 your sister Aurora was married and you spent a few months with your family in Brazil. You and Aurora had sung together. Tell us about that relationship.

I guess you could say I indoctrinated her into the flow of the music, and she wanted to be a part of that. Together, it was as if an echo of myself performed with me, and it was very uplifting for me—and I'm sure for her, as well.

You were fairly close at that time with her?

I was fairly close—as close as the distances geographically between us allowed.

When we have been close to someone in a physical lifetime, do we remain close after going Home, as Aurora has recently?

Not necessarily. It depends if that person is part of your close soul group, those souls that we reincarnate with over and over again. In the case of Aurora, we had been together in two prior lives, but we are not from the same soul group. We do not continually go back and forth. In that case you are aware of the energy of that soul, and when you are near them you exchange pleasantries, but you do not spend a lot of time together because you're not planning for the next journey to Earth together.

Tell us about how the soul groups work.

The soul groups are composed of individual souls who break off from the Source in the same proximity of time.

Time? I thought there was no time at Home.

Well, I have to explain it in time terms or you won't understand it. There is no time at Home; there is progression, where things began as the Source split off and branched out as the branches of a tree. Those individual twigs, as you would say, along the same branch are all part of a soul group because of their proximity of awareness.

Is that group a large number of souls?

It can be up to 144, but generally you have a close association with a couple of dozen of them.

Were you aware, when you were on Earth, of having a close association with any of the people who were in your circle?

Within my consciousness, no. There was a feeling of affinity toward certain souls, who I now know were, in fact, soul mates of mine. Interactive soul mates are those who are most important to us during each physical lifetime, those with whom we make contracts for the lessons we wish to experience. They provide for us circumstances that on Earth may be considered negative, and they provide positive influences for us as well.

You worked tremendously hard during the war, making films and singing. During the shooting of Copacabana, *in which you sang the hit song "Tico-tico no fubá," you met and later married David Sebastian. He was abusive in the marriage, wasn't he?*

Yes, he was. He sort of took some of the energy of my explosive music and turned it around on me.

Why are men so often abusive in relationships like that?

Well, it's not that males as a whole have a tendency to be abusive; it's the lessons that we both wish to experience. In his case, as a soul, he had wished to experience feeling insignificant, feeling betrayed, feeling that he was being put upon, and his response was to overreact and try to dominate and take care of everything on his terms. For my part, I had wished to experience someone trying to control me. At first, while learning that lesson, I was very complacent, even docile, within the relationship. I allowed him to be abusive as it was part of my program to do whatever I thought people wanted. My lesson was to realize that I wasn't honoring myself and being true to myself by allowing him to physically take advantage of me and be abusive, and following that realization, to take action to honor myself by getting out of the cycle of abuse.

Is he a part of your soul group, and did you have a contract with him to do that to you?

Yes he is. I had a contract with him to be a wake-up call, turning me from being outer directed in getting my cues of who I should be, to being inner directed to express who I truly was.

So when someone is in an abusive relationship—whichever way round it is, male to female or female to male—they should recognize it as a lesson to be learned. Does that mean they can get out of the relationship if they want to?

It is their freedom of choice to learn the lesson in that particular lifetime—to recognize that they don't have to put up with what's going on, to know that they don't have to be controlled by another and that they have the right to remove themselves from that situation. If they do not learn the lesson in that particular lifetime, then they'll come back and do it again to some higher degree of intensity.

Do you feel that some women love too much?

It depends upon your definition of love. If you mean infatuation or romantic love and that feel-good, human feeling, my answer would be "yes." What I would more truly say is that most women look for love outside of themselves instead of connecting with the unconditional love of their soul inside of themselves.

132

You suffered from depression and received electric shock treatment in rehab. You had become an alcoholic, smoked, and regularly used barbiturates and amphetamines. Now you were having trouble with your heart. Had Hollywood robbed you of both your health and your personality?

I don't know that Hollywood was the mover and shaker, the initiator. I chose to do what I did. Granted, the stimulus was the pressure of Hollywood, but it was my choice to respond in the way I did, numbing myself with different chemicals that prevented me from feeling the situation that I was in. The abuse did cause my body to deteriorate, which put me into a situation where my health failed drastically.

The abuse you are talking about: was it David's abuse or taking the substances?

Chemical abuse, I'm referring to, not abuse by David. That did not have much of a physical effect on me, but it did have an emotional and mental effect upon me. The result was that I was put back into the situation where I had to try again to be truthful to myself, and for a long time I ran away from the truth with more drugs and more chemicals.

Looking at shock treatment as it is given to a large number of people, is it, in fact, an effective treatment?

It depends—effective from whose point of view? Does it make people change their behavior? Yes, because it destroys the memory centers that put them into the pattern that they are aware of. Does it make them more compliant with the desires of society and their family? Yes, because they become very docile, having so much of the stimulation within them removed.

Does it help their soul?

No, it does not help their soul, because what it does is remove the possibility of continuing the lessons that they were engaged in that were perceived by others as destructive behavior. They are in a situation where they are unable to complete that lesson and will therefore have to experience it in another way or at another time.

In 1955, while shooting "The Jimmy Durante Show", you collapsed, dying later that night at the age of 46. The autopsy said the cause of death was preeclampsia, a heart condition linked with pregnancy. Had your soul decided to die then?

My soul recognized that I had experienced all of the lessons that I had come down there for, that I was in a pattern where certain things were prevented from being completed because of what I had done to my body and what had been done to my body, so that there was no reason to remain in physical form.

Were you physically aware of being pregnant?

No, I was not.

Had you ever been pregnant before?

Yes.

And did you have abortions?

Yes.

Tell us about your feeling about abortions.

The feeling I had at the time of the decision to have the abortion was that it was totally inconvenient for me to bring another being into the world who would compel my attention away from the career that I was embarked upon at the time. I had totally eschewed the religion of my upbringing, so I did not let that influence my decision. It was done completely on a convenience basis.

From my position now, I know that these were decisions I made so that I would have the energy of the memory to haunt me to come back into my thoughts in subsequent periods of time in that lifetime. I know now that the conglomeration of cells within me never contained souls, so there was never another soul involved in the decision, because it was determined that its physical life was never going to get to that point.

So abortion is not a taking of a soul's life?

Certainly not. A soul does not enter into the mix until there is true viability, and even at the physical point where medical people argue there is "viability" (after a certain number of cellular divisions), the soul chooses when it is going to come in, knowing the pathway that the mother has chosen for herself—that is, whether to go to full term or to terminate.

So the soul would never attach to the baby if the mother decided to have an abortion?

That is correct.

Carmen, you were known as "The Brazilian Bombshell" who wore marvelous costumes and towering headdresses, sometimes made of fruit. What do you recall as the most exciting time in your life?

The most exciting time was performing live before vast numbers of people. I took what was then my personality, my persona, that of being a broadcaster of the energy which was communication through music, and watched that energy enter the people who were listening and feeling what I was doing. I was seeing that spark within them of recognition of the marvelous way the language of music connected all of us together and all of us with the universe. It was what the hippies used to call a love fest, but a love fest on a cosmic level.

We never even mentioned the bananas in your headdress! Thank you, Carmen Miranda, for talking with us.

[Toni laughs: "She's showing me a banana peel, so I guess that's the end."]

Commentary

Toni: Whoa! That was an up-and-down ride. When Carmen was talking about the music, there was a strong enthusiasm that permeated her energy. When we were discussing the physical challenges that she went through, there was a hesitation—"I could have handled that better," or "I'll have to repeat these lessons because I didn't learn them the way I had intended." But there was no recrimination, just a little bit of disappointment that the lessons weren't really experienced the way they could have been. She had such a zest for life, and a true sense of sharing when she talked about her impact on people. It was as if the energy built and built and built and built, and as if all of these souls who had shared her life energy were contributing to the energy of the conversation we were having with her. It was a fun interview.

Peter: They don't talk with human languages back Home, so Carmen Miranda's poor English did not hold her back as she spoke through Toni. She communicated very clearly her rise to fame as a singer, and brought an even-handed approach to the problems she had endured from her conservative parents and her many vocal Latin critics. As with other entertainers I have interviewed, the pressure on this singer was almost overpowering, and she resorted to drugs and alcohol in self-defense, which eventually destroyed her health.

Among her comments was the negative appraisal of shock treatment therapy, which destroys the memory centers and effectively removes the possibility of the soul's continuing its lessons related to self-destructive behavior. So the soul must repeat the lesson.

In common with other souls, including Pope John XXIII (whom I interviewed for volume one in this series), Carmen seemed to have few spiritual problems with her abortions, the number of which I did not think wise to ask! There were human regrets, certainly, but on a soul level, since no other soul is involved when termination has been decided by the mother, she had caused no harm to anyone else, so it was no big deal for her soul to reflect upon.

What I found most helpful in this dialogue was the way in which Carmen described the working of her soul group. Souls are broken off from the Source (the Creator), usually in batches of up to 144 at a time. There are an immense number of souls in the celestial dimensions, and this grouping system appears designed to give coherence to overall management, and support for individual souls. Her husband, David, a member of her soul group, had contracted, prior to incarnating, to be a controlling person in her life, in order to help her develop her sense of self-worth. Their plan did not go well as she self-destructed from work pressures. It was a tough call which, presumably, Carmen's soul will need to try and meet in a subsequent lifetime. The Masters tell us, however, that once a soul has learned a life lesson, it will never be repeated.

"What my human concept of prayer was, is not now

what I conceive of as prayer. What I could not conceive of was that all souls are divine."

Mother Teresa
1910-1997

The First Dialogue

Agnes Gonxha Bojaxhiu, you were born into an Albanian family living in Skopje, Macedonia, but when you took your vows as a Sister of Loretto you were named after Saint Thérèse of Lisieux and now are known worldwide as Mother Teresa. Tell us about the choices and influences which led to your vocation as a nun.

You might well say that our life in the family was one of hardship. Being just able to eke out a living, what we presented to the world was, for all intents and purposes, the happiness inside of us. I was very acutely aware of all those around me who were less fortunate than I, and how they weren't given an opportunity to better themselves but were held down by those who could have given them a helping hand.

I went into the service of the Lord to carry forth his policies, his beliefs, and his teaching of taking care of others. I felt the best way to do that was by being in a position where I had nothing that would hold me in the world, no belongings, no family, so I would simply be able to dedicate all of my energy to helping those less fortunate. I knew this was my pathway when I first joined the convent.

After you joined an Irish missionary order of nuns, you taught catechism and geography for seventeen years at St. Mary's High School in Calcutta. Was that a stepping stone to your future work among the very poor?

Only in that this assignment created an incredible desire to get out and help others whom I was able to observe as I passed through the town. The need virtually welled up inside of me. What I could provide for the students was but a philosophy and a feeling to carry them forward. I did not feel that I was actually able to help those outside of the school. I spent my spare time walking the streets, getting to know the people and aiding them in any way that I could. It was as if I were in the starting blocks with the gate frozen so that I could not get out. This built up within me an energy that told me that I had to get out amongst the people and that I had to spend my time there, but I was always the servant both of the Lord and of the community, so I did what was asked of me.

Your health was poor; you had tuberculosis, didn't you?

I had tuberculosis, but as we talk about it now, it was mainly because I had that turmoil within myself and the energies were being held back instead of flushing out. I could not have fought against the community because I was doing what I had said I would do when I joined the order, but it didn't keep me from holding in this energy because I wanted to go out and do more. That caused the "dis-ease" within my body.

On a train to Darjeeling you received a second call to serve God. You said it came as "an order." What was that like?

[laughs] When spirits from this side wish to contact us in human form, if we are open to it, it is as if they have a megaphone at our ear! I was invited—no, more *commanded*— (although I had freedom of choice and did not have to follow the invitation) to begin true missionary work, which had always been within my spirit. It was during a time of meditation as I was watching that land outside the window of the train. Clearing

thoughts from my mind allowed this voice to come in and say, "Your time is near."

Was that a healing? Did it relieve your tuberculosis?
At the same time as I heard, I also felt the energy go through my body, re-aligning the various chakras (the energy centers) in my body to a point which allowed the body to free itself of blockages. So in that respect it was extremely healing.

Then you went out on your own and started an open-air school for slum children, which led to work among the poor and dying. In 1950 you created your order, The Missionaries of Charity. What was your purpose in creating that order?
While I was on my path of service there were others who would come to me and say, "We wish to help, we wish to be like you." I was still somewhat under the auspices of my original convent, which did not exactly care for what I was doing. I wanted to allow these young ladies to get a sense of belonging that couldn't be had within some loose-knit collection of women. They had to have a title because that's what they needed in order to feel that they were truly dedicated. So it was at that time that, with some assistance from my guides, I formulated a plan for developing my own order.

Were you aware of getting help from your spirit guides?
Most assuredly! They were with me a lot.

How did the Pope feel about your application, coming from a relatively unknown source?
The Church has a very stringent hierarchy, and normally things of this magnitude are only presented to the Vatican under the auspices of a sponsoring cardinal or bishop. Because of the fact that my work would not provide any monetary contributions for the church, it was not looked upon as being favorable for the church. They decided immediately that I wouldn't be able to accomplish what I outlined—the soup kitchens, the schooling, and the harboring of those women and

141

children thrown out of their homes. They believed that I wanted documents from the Holy See proclaiming my group an order so that, were they sent to me, I could siphon money out of the coffers of the church. That was not my desire; it was rather that if they wished to contribute I would accept, but I knew that I could get contributions from people in the area.

So your work became well known. Supporters of your order's relief work now number over a million in more than 40 countries. You became famous and were given many humanitarian awards, including the 1979 Nobel Peace Prize. How do you now view your fame?

Fame, while I did not seek it, was very helpful. As they say, it was the grease that made the wheels go round. A lot of people and organizations saw as an irony that this diminutive female in a country where, at that time, males were everything, could have established such a far-reaching charitable organization with so many people contributing to it. Had I not garnered that fame from so many corners I would not have been able to establish the network and have it grow to the extent that it did. It would have been a little local group that maybe assisted a hundred instead of the world-wide organization providing for millions.

So what was fame?

Fame was a gift and, to some degree, a necessity for me to accomplish what I did.

Is there anything you regret about that aspect of your life?

I found it more an annoyance than anything else. When people came to me for advice I could not deny them, and to be readily recognized wherever I went meant that I could never have any time to myself.

Thinking of having time for oneself, you said, "Before you speak, it is necessary for you to listen, for God speaks in the silence of the heart." Talk to us about prayer.

I have a little difficulty with your question. What my human concept of prayer was, is not now what I conceive of as prayer. What I could not conceive of then was that all souls are divine—we all have the ability to create and manifest. In listening to the heart, the stillness, we are doing two things. We are tapping into our own souls, our own higher selves, our own God-selves, and the wisdom we have stored there from previous experiences. When we are also allowing a break in our own commentary, our ego intellect, we allow for our guides to contribute advice. Prayer is utilizing our own abilities, with guidance from our spirit assistants, to use our freedom of choice to have our earthly experience.

Would you discount prayers made to Mary or to Saint Jude?

[laughs] Communication with those on the other side, such as Mary and Saint Jude, wherein you put forth requests for the way you wish them to assist you, are not useless because they are pinpointing areas that you can then use yourself. It is not that you are asking them to do something for you. Prayer is, for most, asking for assistance, direction, and guidance how to do whatever you feel needs to be accomplished. One who just sits and prays to be delivered is going nowhere. When you contribute to the intention you wish to have accomplished, you are beginning to manifest the change. If it is for your highest and greatest good and you demonstrate your freedom of choice in a particular direction, those from whom you are seeking assistance will contribute to the energy necessary to accomplish your goal.

If you are in extreme agony of soul, what can you do?

You must first accept where you are. Go into the situation and find out why you are in such agony. Most agony comes from a denial of the situation and its cause and fights any attempt to remedy the situation. It is, as for a lot of the people with whom I dealt, getting into a pattern or belief system and just staying in that rut. They would go and spend the entire day begging for food, but they would never at any time offer to assist another with their daily chores in exchange for food.

Tell us about Jesus.

Jesus is a magnificent, loving energy, one who shows the way to allow your passion to take you from the physical back into the spiritual, the non-physical, while still maintaining body form. He was an example to us; he opened the pathways between the dimensions. He was the perfect teacher, as I tried to be. A lot of people see my works as just charitable contributions, but there was much more to it than that. With each handout I gave I also tried to inspire and instruct the recipients to better themselves, or at least improve the feelings that they had about themselves, in order to carry on through life. This is exactly what Jesus did in his ministering to people. He showed them the way to reverse the patterns into which they had put themselves. People called that his miraculous healing, and in a way it is because healing occurs on many levels; it occurs on a physical level, it occurs on a spiritual level—that's how, with energy coming through me, my healing occurred. So the energy that others received from me could affect then on all levels (physical, mental, and emotional), if they opened themselves to the process.

What place does Jesus have at Home?

More often we refer to him as Sananda up here, because that is his cosmic name. Jesus was just one of the incarnations he had. He is the great teacher. He works between lives with advanced souls who are embarking on their last, or one of their last physical lives. As when he was in one of his physical incarnations, his main gift is that of instilling in all those who seek to learn the pathway of ascension how to move through the lessons that they have come to learn, and also to discover, while in physical form, how to reconnect with the spiritual, so they may assimilate everything they came into a physical body to learn, and thereby grow and become enlightened.

You said he had more than one earthly life. Was he a teacher in any of them?

Yes, in all of them.

Do we know his name in any of them?

He had many names. Abraham was one, Gautama Siddhartha, the Buddha, was another.

One last question about Jesus: is it true that he is the "only begotten son of God"?

[laughs] Absolutely not! We are all sons and daughters of the Creator. There is no "God" who is a man with long white robes and white hair.

You said, "There are so many religions and each one has its different ways of following God." Tell us more about the Creator.

The Creator is the energy from which all of us broke off. It is a term that people want to define and understand so that they can aspire to "be there" or rather accept their true nature. If you want to call this force "God," you must understand that God is within all souls because all souls are part of the original energy.

Each religion has visualized the supreme Power (or Source) in one way or another. For all the organized religions it is the One toward whom you aspire to move, but whom you hold as being above anything that you can ever become—instead of seeing it as a completion of what all of our individual souls are together.

All souls have divinity within, a little spark broken off from the original energy Source, the original Supreme Being. But with this divinity comes the responsibility of being that Creator, of being that Divinity. This is why so many people want the God Source / God / the Supreme Being / Mohammed / Jesus to be outside of them—so that they don't have to take responsibility for their own lessons and enlightenment.

This is a time on earth of great strife between Muslims and Christians. Can you tell us about the Prophet Mohammed?

Mohammed was a prophet and a teacher who came upon the earth to instruct people in various types of laws and beliefs, to integrate the various groups that were upon the planet. But that did not happen. People regarded his pronouncements as an elitist set of laws that related only to certain groups of peoples. Mohammed in his teachings wanted people to know that they were all the same, that they were all brethren, but some of his words got turned around. Some have become catch-words in your time, such as *jihad*. This is a holy war—not a war defending one religion against another, but a war within yourself to connect with your soul, and by connecting with your soul to know that you are connecting with the entire universe. If his teaching had continued to be perceived the way he delivered his message, there could not be warfare upon the planet because you would know that you would be killing yourself.

You speak as if you have had direct contact with Mohammed.

Yes, I talk with a lot of people up here who meet in peer groups. There are spontaneous groups of people who have done various tiers of things upon the planet. By tiers I mean, "Have you affected just your family?" "Have you affected 10 people, 100 people?" or "Have you been able to do something big enough to affect a whole generation?"

Those of us who have achieved that generational level compare the various ways in which we were able to do it, and the various things we had to use in order to accomplish it. The purpose of all this is for us to be ready to advise the next souls who are to come down to have that effect, and to help them plan their contracts in life. Mohammed is in one of these groups.

You had great concern for the dying and for the unborn child. Talk to us about euthanasia and abortion as you see these issues now.

I see all issues concerning human bodies as involving contracts, which are not just between a single body and one other individual but between a group of souls who are going to share some aspect of that body's existence.

146

When it comes to abortion, the contracts may not even involve a soul. A soul may not be assigned or may not have chosen that particular conglomerate of cells, knowing that it is not going to go through the entire gestational process. Again, it comes down to lessons that have to be learned by the various parties: mother, father, extended family members, sometimes society in general. It is what needs to be experienced and therefore is neither right nor wrong. You cannot kill a soul—it is impossible to kill a soul. That soul has agreed to the situation—if there is even a soul involved—surrounding that abortion.

When it comes to euthanasia, there also are contracts. There are decisions to be made. If a body is in a consistent vegetative state, there is not a soul trapped within it. The soul is only tenuously connected to that physical shell. The physical shell exists as it does because of the contracts that that soul made with all those around it, whether it be those in the hospital discussing the ethics of what can be done, the medical associations discussing how much their members should become involved in such a situation, the family discussing the financial burden with no possibility of return. All of the contracts are out there being played out, and—quite honestly—the soul is enjoying itself somewhere else.

When a poor person died of hunger, you said, "It has not happened because God did not take care of him or her." Why do people die of hunger in this world? Is it just our fault?

There is no fault to be assigned here. When masses of people transition (die), whether it is from disease, natural disasters, or man-made disasters, it is because *they* have agreed to have an impact on the consciousness of other souls who are in human form at that time. It is not because God has forgotten them, but (as I said) their God-self is inside of them, directing them to be in the position that they are in, and they have chosen to be there.

In 1985 you opened a hospice for AIDS victims in New York. Does this disease exist because of human sin, as some believe?

Absolutely not, absolutely not. There is no such thing as "sin" in the religious connotation that a sin is the breaking of one of God's laws. There are consequences of the contracts we make. Consequences is not quite the right word as it has the overtone that something hasn't gone as planned. These are all people who wished to experience illness of one form or another, though they don't know when they come down to earth what form the illness may take. They experience their spiritual pathway through having that illness.

People are overwhelmed by troubles, death, and disaster in the world. Are Earth and her people reeling into chaos?

The world is very closely approaching a transition, which is coming into place for a number of reasons. It is a normal cycle through which the life on planet Earth moves. It is that, as the planet goes through various shifts, the ability to communicate between the various dimensions becomes easier and easier. [She is referring to the levels, or strata, of human and spiritual vibrational energy.] What is happening at this time is that there is a dichotomy being created on the planet between those who are becoming their spiritual selves (reconnecting with their knowledge and raising themselves *above* the polarities of the Earth's third dimension), and those who are left as a residue who are thoroughly mired in the third dimension and are experiencing the basest emotions and experiences, such as pure hatred, death, murder, destruction. Those with spiritual aspects, who are being winnowed out and separated from the chaff, are much more aware of what is going on because of the ability for inter-dimensional communications at this time. While we have gone through cycles like this on the planet before, this time it is in your face because [laughs] we can bring it to you live and in color!

In the Bible, St. James writes that "faith without works is dead." You said, "Like Jesus, we belong to the world living not for ourselves but for others." What do you say to those people who believe in justification by faith alone?

They do not want any responsibility for what they do, for what others do, or for the consequences of their actions. We must have faith that each one of us, because we have that part of the Creator within us, can do whatever it is that we wish to do. That is the faith that we must have in ourselves. As Jesus said, "Greater things can you do than I." We now have the energy of many like-minded souls in existence at the same time, which creates a mass of energy that can change the effect of one philosophy or another on the planet.

So we don't have to live by faith specifically in Jesus?
    Faith of the kind that Jesus had, not faith in the soul who was Jesus.

Do you plan to return to planet Earth anytime soon?
    Not as of this time. I am very engaged as a member of many advisory consults with souls who are now about to come into body form.

Thank you, Mother Teresa, for speaking with us.
    It has been my pleasure.

The Second Dialogue

Eight months after our initial dialogue with Mother Teresa we learned of the publication, with Vatican approval, of a book about her inner life: *Mother Teresa: Come be my Light.* In letters to a number of her spiritual advisors over half a century, the nun vividly describes how deeply she doubted her faith in God and how she believed that God had abandoned her. Knowledge of this problem area in her life had been only hinted at in our first conversation. It raised further questions, so we were grateful when her soul enthusiastically agreed to another session.

Mother Teresa, you described to me your tuberculosis-weakened physical condition and your troubled state of mind when, on a train to Darjeeling in 1946, you heard a voice calling you to serve the world's very poorest people. You said to me, "I had that

149

turmoil within myself and the energies were being held back instead of flushing out." Up to that time did your turmoil include doubts about the presence and love of God?

Yes. It included an entire scenario of wondering why I was doing what I was doing—if it was something fanciful in my mind or something that the Lord wanted me to do. I did not have a ready connection to the God-outside-of-me who, at that time, I believed was the only Source, and I kept on looking outside of me. My daily life was very structured by the tenets of the religious society I had given my allegiance to, believing at that time that I was only a pawn to be directed by others. I was looking for a direction in my life, and when it didn't feel that I was getting one, I despaired to be alone in what I was doing.

When did all this turmoil start—when you were a teacher in India, or before, when you were a novice?

It was there a little bit when I was a novice. I had expected when I entered the convent to walk from darkness into light. I expected to be embraced, to be always in the presence of God. My definition of God at that time was of a man in a white robe (outside of me), who was a father figure taking care of everyone. I expected to be openly comforted by him, since I was there to dedicate my life to him. As I began working, I thought there would always be somebody there directing me. I did not think that the orders from my mother house were all that I would receive. I believed that part of the vocation I felt so strongly within was that I would have a day-to-day contact from outside of me. In searching for such a thing I was mistaken, because the contact I looked for so earnestly outside of me was, in fact, inside me—so I missed it completely.

After you heard the voice calling you, your health did recover and you set to work, certain of the loving presence of God in Jesus Christ. You've reminded us that you do not now believe that God is a man with long white robes and white hair (and perhaps a beard like mine as well). How, then, could your faulty traditional faith cure you of TB and so support your new ministry?

I don't know that it was actually faulty because it instilled in me the power that I thought was coming from outside of me, but that really I was tapping into from inside of me—this power of manifesting those driving forces that said I had to go out and help people. Once I had this passion (which I thought was outwardly driven but was really more inwardly driven), there was no way for the blockages to remain, because there was a constant churning of energy. What the passion did within me was not allow any of the organisms to remain in my body, because the intense energy was constantly flushing, constantly ridding my body of the things that were causing disorder inside me.

When you say you thought it was "outwardly driven," you mean by God, outside of you?

Yes. I did not see it as the God-force inside of me and all around me, as it truly was. My only impression of God was as I had been taught while growing up—of this person, this energy outside of us directing and caring for us.

By 1957 the darkness of doubt and sense of your abandonment by God had descended upon you. Did this bleak state of mind result in any way from your work with the dying?

I did not make a connection that way, but so many of the dying with whom I dealt were fearful. They were in fear of Judgment Day—that they were going to be judged both for everything they had done and for all the things they had not done. I felt that, as a representative, so to speak, of God, I should at least have his ear, and to me that meant, if not in a physical appearance to me, at least a voice talking, consoling, and guiding me.

Was the darkness partly anger at the fact that you didn't hear that voice?

It was anger, despair, frustration, stemming from a sense of abandonment.

Like St. Thérèse of Lisieux, was it ever the fear of death for you, your own death?

I may have thought of that at times but I don't dwell on those feelings now. It wasn't death as much as it was that, not being able to hear God, I couldn't do what he wanted me to do, so in consequence I was letting him down.

You prayed unceasingly for Jesus to make himself known to you, but in our first discussion you told me, "One who just sits and prays to be delivered is going nowhere," and also, "Most agony comes from a denial of the situation and its cause and fights any attempt to remedy the situation." Tell us what your despair felt like, and what you meant by those words.

My despair felt as if I were but a single person floating alone in an ocean. I knew that there was other life around me in the water, but none of it interacted with me. It was as if I had been placed in (as the church believed), purgatory, a place of waiting, where I could not have contact with those I sought. I thought that, to some degree, I was being punished for something I had done wrong. I began to realize that, however much and fervently I prayed, I was looking for a particular type of contact, which I did not make. I was trying to structure my contact with God.

When I said before that prayer of itself goes nowhere, if you pray for a particular type of contact, and that contact has a missing element, as mine did, it accomplishes nothing. My missing element was that I wanted somebody *outside* of me who was going to tell me exactly what to do, who would take responsibility for what I was doing, because I was just following orders. It was asking, almost, as you would say today, to "let me off the hook" for what I perceived I had to do but had failed to do.

Did you pray for stigmata?

I prayed for any sign that what I was doing was what I was supposed to be doing, but none came.

152

You suffered doubt in this way for about fifty years with only one short break. You wrote that the "terrible pain of loss," was "of God not wanting me, of God not being God, of God not existing." Yet all this time you were teaching the Catholic faith to your nuns, and asking for other people's commitment to God. How do you answer the charge of hypocrisy?

I was but a human at that time. The only thing I knew was that I was living within the church, which had become my family and told me what I should do. I simply repeated that to others, thinking that the church (to which I had given all of my life and my decision making), would not steer me wrong. I so embraced the belief system they wanted me to have that I became a parrot, a recording of what they taught others—and therefore I taught their beliefs. Never once did anybody say, "Go inside of yourself. Find your soul." Had I done that, I would have had everything I sought.

Was the fact that you struggled for so long against doubt, and you kept calling on God, a sign that, at a fundamental level, you still believed in God's presence?

Throughout all of my work, I could feel an energy when I was helping others. This energy I felt came from outside of me and gave me the strength to do things beyond what a normal human could do. My perception was that *this* was God, and I despaired that this energy, God, would not speak to me so I might be sure that whatever I was doing was what was expected of me. I did not realize the expectations came only from my own conscious mind, and that when you follow an expectation, you are doomed to failure because you are looking for something that does not exist.

Did your soul choose spiritual doubt as a life lesson?

Doubt, abandonment, a call to go within—which, in human form, I never answered.

Is the sense of divine abandonment, betrayal, or loss the hardest and most significant lesson the soul has to learn?

If you appreciate what is contained in each one of those characteristics, the common thread running through all is the search for love. That is the hardest of all possible life lessons—the search for unconditional love.

Looking again at Christ on the cross, comparing his sense of abandonment by God with your own—as you did so often in those dark days and nights—should we now abandon the Christian dogma of Christ dying in agony for our sins and the sins of the whole world?

That concept (which you report so beautifully for the organized religions), assumes so many things. It assumes first that there is judgment. Within the realm of what most people call heaven and we call Home, there is no judgment. If there is no judgment, there is no right or wrong. If there is no right or wrong, there is no sin. So, knowing now that there is no sin, knowing now that we choose the lessons that we learn, we cannot be abandoned by anybody for not doing what we thought we were going to do. Our search is always to connect to our soul, learn the lessons, and not to have to do them again.

Many people will ask: if there is no right or wrong, what was the point of helping the dying in Calcutta—which was seen by most people as the right thing, so overwhelmingly right that they wanted to make you a saint?

Part of my life lesson, as we have discussed, was to find myself. My journey was to use my humanness to help others find what they needed, a sense of worth in themselves, a way to sustain themselves. It was not the food that I provided for them; it was not the medicine that I enabled them to receive. It was, if they could go within themselves, a sense of who they were inside. Of course, I tried to give this to them on an unconscious level because it was part of my own soul's journey.

To say, within the physical realm, that doing this was "right" would be understandable, because you are now in a place of judgment, a place of duality, where there has to be "right" and "wrong." So it is still very difficult for you, as it was for me at the time, to say that it doesn't matter, that each of them had chosen the path that they chose, and I was but a means, through contracts that we had made, to help them complete their life's work.

So ethical right and ethical wrong are judgments that are made on Earth, but the ultimate judgment is one of love?
There is not even any ultimate judgment. There is only an evaluation of whether we have completed what we sought to learn, or we have to do it again, knowing we are always in unconditional love in our soul form.

Some people may consider your pain of doubt helpful, because they profess belief in God and even a "personal relationship" with Jesus, yet many are filled with longing, doubt, and self-recrimination. What can you say to them?
I would tell those who are in doubt to go into the doubt and analyze exactly what the feelings are behind it. Is it a doubt that they have faith in themselves to be able to see and to learn what they have to learn? Is it a doubt that stems from a judgment that they have guessed or chosen wrongly, and therefore are going to be punished? If that is true, then they are still in the third-dimensional [Earthly] way of having to balance their lives. What I say to them now is, "Go into your heart. Search for the unconditional love that is there. Latch onto that love, that part that connects you to the whole, and then and only then, from within that love, evaluate where this particular human life you are engaged in is taking you."

You told me that now that you are back at Home, you no longer conceive of prayer as you did, and you no longer see God or Jesus in the way you did. Clearly you cannot describe "tapping into our own God-selves" and still believe in the doctrine of original sin— you've just told us that. Is there anything left of Catholic doctrine that you would retain?

155

The basic principles that are taught—respect for yourself, respect for others; the principle that is claimed to be the basic tenet: Do unto others as you would have them do unto you; in other words, examine your life—those tenets are still very important. To blindly follow another and give all of your responsibility to another to make decisions for you, is misguided. The direction that the church can give to souls that are floundering (to help pick them up, to help them make some of their own decisions), is still very applicable for those in human form, enabling them to begin consciously walking along their soul path. As a means of reaching their destination of feeling their soul while in human form, however, Catholic doctrine gives very little helpful direction.

If, with your present knowledge, you came down again to Earth and resumed your ministry among the poorest of the poor, should someone ask you what you truly believe in and cannot doubt in your heart and mind, what would it be?

That we are all the same, that we all are in human form to learn how magnificent we are in our soul form.

Was your life, which has inspired so many people, intended to inspire them, or was it just for you to learn your lessons?

My purpose was to work with a lot of souls. We made a lot of contracts to help people on all levels: to help the poor realize their self worth and the potential they had within them; to be a means for those with prosperity to share that prosperity, and by doing that to feel good about themselves and what they can accomplish when they look and see what can be done. The whole story of my life and my soul's journey was but a footnote to the series of contracts I had made with others.

Thank you, Mother Teresa, for talking with us. We love you.
    And I you.

Commentary

Toni: There were many shifts in Mother Teresa's feelings during the dialogue. In the first session she felt at times like an epitome of the missionary, the diminutive, meek nun going about her duties, trying to provide for as many people as she was able. At other times I felt her incredible strength, as an old and wise teaching soul who was going to straighten everybody out, letting them know that there was a way to take part in everything that was going on and to learn from it, as she had been able to do. Part of the time it seemed as if she were looking down from on high, giving an inspirational talk to a bunch of novices. It was as if she were tapping into different aspects of her life, and serving on the between-life advisory board for souls.

The second session displayed a quite different energy. She seemed to be thinking, "Now you're asking the serious questions. Now you're letting me help you to see how one person's journey can be perceived by others as a film that doesn't depict the original." She was highly venerated, but it was the last thing she desired. Rather than taking personal responsibility—"As a soul, I'm here, and I'm doing what I came here to learn," she had sought instead to grab onto the coattails of the God whom she was feverishly pursuing to demand, "Am I doing what I'm supposed to be doing?"

Peter: Apart from my questions about her personal development and decades of suffering during her "dark night of the soul," Mother Teresa's loving conversation was outer-directed. The soul's sweet character shone through each phrase. While those who may look for confirmation of Catholic doctrine will be sorely challenged by her bruising denials, she never actually spoke harshly of the Church of which she had been a devoted lifetime servant.

Viewed in their starkness, Teresa's answers show a sea-change in her thinking since returning Home. The God whom *she* chased "down the years and down the days" turned out not to be a person, let alone our judge, but the eternal Source, a myriad of whose detached fragments are the essence of all souls within the God-Force.

This fact of each soul's divinity alters everything for her now. There is no difference in essence between Teresa's soul and that of Jesus—only that, reverently, she describes him as "*the* great teacher." Likewise, prayer takes on a totally new direction. As spiritual guides, St. Jude and Mother Mary may help us clarify what our needs and abilities are, but only the individual soul possesses the creative power to manifest the answers and fashion the human remedies for life's pressing problems.

Then, in keeping with her teaching about the nature of the soul and of Jesus, our faith is no longer to be placed in the person of Jesus as someone who is *other* in his nature than ourselves. Rather, we should share the faith of Jesus concerning the direction of our soul's life—through the experiences we have chosen and contracts we have made—toward our ultimate enlightenment and maturity.

Though much less robust in her reply than Pope John XXIII (in volume one in this series), Mother Teresa was crystal clear about the central issue in the abortion and euthanasia debate. No eternal soul is ever hurt, either because it is totally absent from the cellular structure of the fetus, or because it is merely lightly linked to the unborn child or the slow-to-die patient. You cannot kill an eternal, divine soul anyway. What she did not do, however, was to suggest what we should do in such situations—only that we must get our facts straight.

She gave a sympathetic appraisal of the work of the Prophet Mohammed, whose teaching has been misapplied and should rightly lead to peace and human harmony.

While she dealt clearly with the AIDS issue and problems of global hunger—both being pre-assigned learning experiences and not the result of human sin—she was more veiled concerning the global crisis, saying that we are approaching a transition, which is a normal cycle through which Earth moves. As the planet goes through changes, human ability to communicate spiritually will be enhanced. But there is a split happening on Earth between those human beings who are spiritually inclined and those whose focus is on negativity. She did not suggest what we should do about this polarization, only that the situation was being made abundantly clear by our guides. However, in many respects her answer was given in her teaching about prayer and the divine creative center of the soul. She also gave us a hint in this statement: "We now have the energy of many like-minded souls in existence at the same time, which creates a mass of energy that can change the effect of one philosophy or another on the planet."

Our second session built on the first. Because I had not asked about her spiritual agonies, of which I had been ignorant, she had not mentioned them, but she had not deliberately hidden from us her overwhelming sense of abandonment by God while she was a nun. Her first doubts had come while she was still a novice, and they had multiplied until she was living a sham life, clinging tightly like a drowning sailor onto the raft of Catholic teaching as her direction, her eyes searching for Jesus, "the author and perfecter" of her faith. She feels today that it is her faithfulness to the Catholic church at the time which should shield her from a charge of hypocrisy.

There is no duplicity in Teresa's answers. While, I fear, the record of our conversation may never be taken seriously by those who wish to call the Blessed Mother Teresa a "saint," what she said to me constitutes a crushing rebuttal of those whose faith is based on John 3:16 and Romans 5:8, which may be summed up as "Jesus died for the sins of the world." She also now denies that God is *wholly other* than human beings. Teresa no longer searches for an absent God *without*, but looks for the divinity *within* every soul, her own included. Somehow one feels that if the idea of our soul's being divine is true, it is most readily seen in Mother Teresa.

"It was the essence of the energy conveyed from the depths of my soul that was the only important thing."

Ella Fitzgerald
1918-1996

Ella Jane Fitzgerald, you had a hard childhood. Your father left soon after you were born. Your mother moved from Virginia to Yonkers, NY, with her boyfriend, Joseph. When you were fifteen, she died in a car crash and Joseph had a fatal heart attack. You had wanted to be a dancer but ended up a singer whom people called "The First Lady of Song." Where did you get your musical talent from?

Music was within me from the beginning. My musical talent is part of my being. It is who I am. It is a form of communication that started with the individualization of energy, the breaking off of souls from the Source. There needed to be a way to communicate. This became vibrational music—what you would call music, what we would call vibrations. I worked on defining and standardizing the way that such communication would take place, developing a language distinct from other ways—letting someone know what you were thinking but *not* letting someone know what you were feeling.

Then, as I came down into human form, my lives were not only to continue developing musical vibrations, but also to work on languages so that people would understand other people. It began in the earliest of grunts between humans who didn't have developed vocal cords, all the way through developing a

161

language for a region, such as French, Spanish, or Italian, and then, finally, communicating with people solely through music— back to my origins, so to speak. Music is what I am as a soul.

Were you one of the early souls to break off from the Source?
Yes, I was. We look on it as our having been given a distinct individuality, so that we could then have pursuits beyond that of the Source or Oneness. That's because the Source itself can only experience a finite amount of things, even though it is infinite. So it broke off parts of itself, and I am a part of that Source to enlarge experience. It is very much like the octopus who has eight legs and can contact eight different things at the same time, whereas a human only has two hands—two means of contacting things at one time.

Obviously you're very talented—did you have any other lives when you were well known, in music or in literature?
Primarily they were in music. I wasn't, as you would say, famous, because I was developing different processes as I went along, defining accents and colloquialisms in order to have sub-groups of communication. That's just as in music today, you have sub-groups of communication: jazz, bebop, symphony music, classical. So I sang, I danced, I wrote, I was all about communication in all of my lifetimes. In some lifetimes (going back to the first written memorial of things), I was involved also in putting together the means—developing the papyruses, taking slate and making symbols that could be carved into them that would not chip, to avoid them becoming obliterated and the meaning lost. Everything I have done has been about communication. Most of it has been within the field of musical vibration.

Things got pretty wild when you were a teenager. You were a lookout for a brothel and a runner for an illegal gambling outfit. You were arrested, put into a reform school, escaped, and were homeless for a while. How do the two match up?

What we call "tempering." It was necessary for me to have a myriad of human experiences, since I came down into that life with no memory of what I was or what I was about. Each "difficulty" stimulated memories within my physical cellular being that tapped into the records and allowed me to realize what I was here for, which again was about communication, about touching people, bringing souls together in their physical form—but also about speaking to the soul so that it could recognize who it was.

In 1934 you entered a talent contest as a dancer at one of the first African American Amateur Nights at the Apollo Theater in Harlem. Switching to singing at the last minute you won the first prize. Tell us about that experience.

When I was very little, and in several places where I lived, I was frequently told to shut up when I started singing, so I had it within my human programming that I was sub-par as a musical talent. I definitely saw that my body was not as coordinated as those of so many of the dancers during that competition and, as happens, my guides (a little voice) came in and said, "Sing! Sing and reach them with the feelings that you have inside of you." So that's what I did. I won as much for being able to touch their souls as I did for the not-so-great technique I had!

You turned out to have a wide range of three octaves, a pure tone, great technique, and near-perfect elocution. You won 13 Grammy awards during your career. Who actually taught you to sing so well, or were you totally self-taught?

I had some mentors along the way. There was nobody who was totally instrumental in creating who I was. I studied other people, observed their techniques, had perfect pitch. Not only that, but I could *feel* the techniques. It was as if I could feel the way the vocal cords vibrated in the people whom I listened to.

Were you in touch with your spirit self?

In touch with my spirit self, in touch with my pure essence on the soul level, and my pure essence as it existed in that lifetime as Ella Fitzgerald, and all that existed as it had gone through other lives throughout my past physical experiences.

So you downloaded your past into music you could sing?

Yes. I remembered what I had learned and knew.

Do you ever attend the American Idol competitions now?

[laughs] No.

I was going to ask you what you thought of them.

I find that they are totally ego-based, and while a few potential true talents in the physical world have been discovered, it's mostly a personality and picture contest. It seems to be an acceptable way to make fun of people in front of others and to avoid having anyone think it is not of service to the contestants.

You weren't much of a picture when you started singing. You were described as "gawky and unkempt, a diamond in the rough" at that time. They called you shy and lonely, and later you said, "I don't want to say the wrong thing, which I always do. I think I do better when I sing." Was shyness one of the lessons you had agreed to learn before incarnating?

Shyness was a piece of the lesson. The entire lesson was about being able to feel the reaction of the people to what I said and what was going on around me. The shyness came from not knowing my place within the dynamic of socialization at that time. When I sang, I gave them the feeling of who I was, and they could accept me or not. In a realm where communication and mannerisms dictated whether or not you were accepted, I wasn't as polished. I didn't have a line of experiences to call upon to reinforce who I was, so it was a lesson in accepting the physical limitations placed upon any soul within a physical body.

Despite the appearance of shyness, you had a one-nighter that turned into a week with Chick Webb's swing band, which led in turn to a touring contract with his big band and a chance to record songs. Your first recording, "Love and Kisses," was a hit. Tell us about making your first record.

In the vernacular of the world, it was awesome. It went beyond anything that I, a poor street waif, could imagine. It was, however, just a step that was planned on the way to opening the hearts and the energies of multitudes of souls by the vibrations that I was able to produce with my recordings. I knew at that time that the way to reach the millions was via the "platter," as they called records then, and was able to finally see that coming. As I did it, I knew that there was much more going on than just the simple making of a recording. I had this sense of an immense beginning. I had no idea, in my physical form, what that energy was, but I reveled in it.

Then came "A Tisket, A Tasket." The song was written by Al Feldman and you in 1938, based on the 19th-century nursery rhyme. It became a major hit—17 weeks as Number One. This came only four years after your first venture into singing. The following year, Chick Webb died of a heart attack and you took over as bandleader of what was now called "Ella Fitzgerald and her Famous Orchestra." What on earth was inside of you that drove you to be so successful?

It was the essence of who I was as a soul. I was finally beginning to accomplish what I had done in many, many, many, many lifetimes, and that was stimulating the souls of other people with vibration. The more people I could feel and sense come into synchronization, into resonance with the vibration of the music, the more powerful the energy around all of us became, and the more I was propelled forward.

After recording 150 sides with your band, you quit to start a career with Decca as a soloist. Then Norman Granz became your manager and booked you to appear at his Jazz at the Philharmonic concerts. How did you get on with Norman?

165

Norman was a perfect ally for me. He had the business sense. I was not that concerned with the planning and the logistics and things that had anything to do with anything but music, and it was so nice to be able to rely upon someone to do it for me. It allowed me to concentrate on just doing and being what I was.

Did Norman come from your soul group?

Yes. He was a member of my soul group who had helped me in prior lifetimes, and I had helped him in some, though not in the same way. It was not in physical ways; it was by means of picking him up out of despair, again with the vibrational music.

Next you moved away from swing, to jazz, and to lots and lots of bebop with Dizzy Gillespie's big band, and then to scat singing as your distinctive vocal jazz art form. You used scat in your famous recordings of "Flying Home" and "Oh, Lady be Good!" You worked with Louis Armstrong, a great scat singer. Tell us about that relationship with Satchmo.

Another soul mate of mine. We were perfecting a dialect of vibration that would reach into a particular embedded group of souls. By "embedded," I mean souls that are so deeply into the physical experience that they have no connection whatsoever with their essence as a soul. It was as if we implanted little boring devices with our music, our vibration, that got into the very essence of the person and just made them move, made them come into the vibration, recognize more about themselves, and recognize their connection with those around them. It was a form of opening and connecting. Louis was just the instrument upon which my tones rode.

Before you left Decca, things began to change. You recorded "Ella Sings Gershwin." Norman created Verve, a jazz record company, for you, and you recorded the "Cole Porter Songbook." Was this a turning point in your life as a singer?

At that point I had reached certain groups of people such as with the scat, and I had a legacy there of my recordings that would continue to spread from the nucleus that had been implanted. Then I needed to start the vibration, start the connection, start the soul searching with another group of souls: those that would eschew the bebop and the jazz but would go completely with the feelings in their heart. The first songs touched the heart, but in a different way—touched the heart through the movement of the body. The new songs touched the heart through the soul and the intellect with fantastic wording, so I was moving into another area for expansion.

Verve published a very successful series of eight songbooks of great American compositions. These were later seen as the first attempt by a popular artist to explore this broad musical genre seriously. Did the inspiration for this cross-over series come from you or Norman?

Norman had the human foresight to know when I had just about played out a certain area, and to know that I could then take my energy, take my tools, into another area and expand beyond what I had already done. He was sort of like a gatekeeper; when you bring all of the animals in (I've seen the stockyards) to the pens, you have to open gates to allow the pens to fill up so the cattle don't back up. It was allowing the energy that was no longer pouring out of me, because it had become sated in one genre, to move into another, and allow that to begin to fill.

You married Benny Kornegay, a drug dealer, then divorced him and married a bass player, Ray Brown, whom you met at a Jazz at the Philharmonic concert. Did you marry Thor Einar Larsen, the Norwegian who was later jailed for stealing from his Swedish fiancée, or was that just a story?

That was just a newspaper story. It was a wannabe of his imagination. He wanted to be known. He wanted to use the fact that we had met and had spent time together as an intro to get him in to meet other people, or people who wanted to know "what was Ella like?"

Did you ever feel that your private love life didn't match the romance you sang about?

On the physical level, it never did—it is impossible to match the unconditional love of the soul, which is what I poured out in my music, in the physical setting.

Marilyn Monroe once helped you to sing at the segregated Mocambo nightclub in West Hollywood by promising to come and listen to you every night. Did racial discrimination affect your career much?

Very little. The vibrations almost created a wedge that cleared things out of my way. People would hear my voice and they didn't see race. They saw nothing but the purity of what was there. There were minor instances where I could have contacted more people had I been allowed in somewhere, but it wasn't to be. That was another reason why I changed the genres through my musical career. I went where I was totally accepted because I sang the vernacular in the beginning to start the fire there, to start the communication there, and then I changed direction and went where another genre would be accepted in new locales. There were those who would have been turned off by the color of my skin who just had to hear the vibration of my voice and then became color-blind, because all they felt was the vibration.

You worked very hard, made films, traveled the world, and created an enduring legacy of wonderful singing. Then came decline, first in your voice, but then in the form of diabetes. The disease blinded you, and three years before your death both your legs were amputated. Had you made a decision to suffer like that before you came down to planet Earth?

I had made a decision to learn the lesson of despair, of having everything taken away from me that I held dear, allowing me to go inward and to examine my physical values, something you can only do in physical form—what was really important to me in my experience of life.

The physical part of me realized that I was there to help people and to touch people, and I had done that, and even though I became an invalid and unable to carry on the task, I had set out a foundation that would remain and would touch people, and touches people even to this day when they come across my recordings. Who the physical person might be was unimportant. It was the essence of the energy conveyed from the depths of my soul that was the only important thing. That decrepit, decaying, dying shell was but the physical remains of what is left behind when we move on. It does not define who we are. That was what I had to come to grips with.

What is the point of such deliberate suffering?

When you exist in total unconditional love, as I did for—in your time frame—many, many generations before I first entered into a physical body, you accept that this is the way things always are. You do not know how grand it really is until you have an experience and taste of the negative, the opposite. So each moment spent in despair, in pain, in degradation magnified my feeling and my concept of what I possessed when I returned to my true essence.

After your death, Frank Rich of the New York Times wrote that you made an extraordinary cultural transaction. "Here was a black woman popularizing urban songs, often written by immigrant Jews, to a national audience of predominantly white Christians." How do you now view your career?

[laughs] I just did what I came to do, which was to open souls in their physical bodies to know the potential of communication, which is all about sensing the essence of the other people around you. It allows people to realize others are not simply what their costumes tell your eyes they are, such as their race, their nationality, their ability or disability. It asks you to step back and let your feelings sense who they truly are and then let the communication, let that vibration—in my case, the music—let it all unite the two of you, the biased with the prejudged, enabling the blind to see the essence of who you are.

Thank you, Ella Fitzgerald, for the wonderful conversation. I only regret that the channel is not able to let me convey my thanks to you in music.

Commentary

Toni: There was a great amount of visual communication, pictorial data, that came to me with everything Ella said. It was as if I were simultaneously in two dimensions. She was describing the physical, but she was also giving me examples from the realm that she's in right now. So when she talked about breaking through crowds and the like, I saw a snowplow cutting a swath through deep drifts, and then an icebreaker breaking up huge chunks of ice. That's just one of many examples. When she talked about the essence of the soul coming down, it was like a massive cloud of energy and one little atom breaking off from it but still connected to a Source and responding to vibrations within the mass. It was all quite mind-boggling—there was so much going on all at once.

For me, this may well have been a meeting with one of the oldest souls I've ever encountered while I've been in physical form. The depth she brought to everything was definitely not on the level of simply bringing her into the physical dimension of the room, and not merely of contacting her on the single level of an individual soul who had lived as Ella Fitzgerald. It went far beyond that. It was as if my consciousness had been raised to levels within simultaneous multi-dimensions far exceeding where I had ever gone before. Wow! What an experience.

Peter: The powerful energetic feeling experienced by Toni was matched by Ella's claims. True, she had a tough upbringing and looked at first more like a shy, tousle-haired waif than a future world-class singer. But eventually her soul's long and distinguished background broke through and she took amazingly powerful steps to develop her art. Probably Ella never consciously knew that she was a wise, old, experienced, and powerful soul, but she drew on her latent powers to inform her physical progress.

This hidden well of experience and talent did not save her from burning out as a bebop artist. It did help her to move into jazz and the scat singing for which she is so well remembered. When she burned out again it helped her to move on to Gershwin, Cole Porter, and the albums of American music that had previously been the domain of white singers. Finally, whatever she had accomplished in past lives did not release her soul from its commitment, made before incarnation, to undergo despair, so she was assailed by the diabetes that finally took her life. Even as a mature soul she had that lesson still to learn, and, by her own account, she acquitted herself well.

Each soul I have been privileged to interview has added some more to our knowledge of the way life in the universe is lived. Ella brought her own contribution. It had not occurred to me that souls might be assigned the task of developing human skill in communication, language with all its regional developments and nuances, music in all its forms. Such language, such music, might be seen by us simply in terms of human evolution, but as Ella Fitzgerald (or more correctly, her eternal soul) looked back, it was to remember seeing the potential in words and music to move us human beings out of habitual physical oblivion and preoccupation with the merely physical into a new spiritual awareness both of our own nature and of the essence of all those souls around us on planet Earth.

"My happiness was mainly when I was performing.
My personal life was, as most people would classify it,
a total disaster."

Judy Garland
1922-1969

Judy, it's nice to meet you. In the car going to work this morning, my wife, Sonia, was singing "Over the Rainbow" from memory, and she got the words right, I think.
She did.

You used to sing the words: "Some day I'll wish upon a star and wake up where the clouds are far behind me, where troubles melt like lemon drops..." Is that your experience?
It's more than that! That was based upon my experiences as a human being. There are no problems here, there are no troubles, [laughs] and there are no lemon drops. Here there is just a sense of total well-being, total love, total connection— something that never even touched the hem of my skirt when I was in human form.

Your song "Over the Rainbow" was tremendously popular and was voted Number 1 in the recording industry's Songs of the Century list, and also Number 1 Movie Song of All Time by the American Film Institute, yet your life seems mixed in terms of happiness and sadness. Looking back and being there now, what mood do you feel in?

A sad and depressed mood. My happiness was mainly when I was performing. My personal life was, as most people would classify it, a total disaster. A lot of what I did was an attempt to get stimulation for myself, and of course, because of some of the destructive directions I went in, it was more taking me deeper—away from what a normal person would consider a normal human existence, into chaos.

Was meeting this challenge part of your life purpose?

My life purpose was to experience the struggle, the depths of depression which would come if you were totally run as a puppet by an outside force. I always felt there was a string of puppeteers marching me through life experiences, not allowing me to make any decision, not allowing me to choose any particular direction. The only thing that I could choose to do was to numb myself to the experience.

MGM provided most of the puppeteers in your life. They did a good job of numbing you by introducing and providing drugs that kept you going during your working life.

At first it was done because I was in rebellion and suffering from anxiety. It was done to sedate me to the extent that I could carry on with their plan and not openly tell society that they were jerks, that they were abusing me in mental and emotional ways. They wanted their vision of the "Girl Next Door" to be carried through, and one way to prevent me from opening Pandora's box to society was to keep me in a sedated, fuzzy mood. At first it started out that it was a little something for my nerves, a little tonic, a little pill. Then it became something I was dependent upon because I did not want to deal with the reality when I was out of its influence.

You had a run of films, with Mickey Rooney, but you did struggle against their image. Weren't you really the archetypical girl next door?

That was what was selling movies at the time, so that was the way the studio wanted me to exist. When I wanted more was when they diminished my desire [with drugs] for contact with the outside world.

So when you were filming For Me and my Gal *they wouldn't let you be yourself?*

Not at all. I was never myself. Even in the periods when I rebelled, such as my marriage, it was only a minor foray into what might be considered near-normalcy.

But you were given the glamour treatment in Presenting Lily Mars, *weren't you?*

Oh, absolutely! That was what was needed for the acceptance they sought from the general public. Dottie Ponedel, my make-up artist, gave me a window into the outside world, but then even she was a kind of minion of the studio. She was told to make me glamorous. What I was just referring to was how during our sessions I would ask her what normal life was like, and I began to have visions of what it might be like to be normal. I was getting a bit more enthusiastic about slipping the bonds that the studio bound me with, based upon what she was telling me, but when it got to the point that I was becoming a little bit too disruptive, she was told to calm it down, and she was almost given a script to tell me what was going on, based upon the studio's script. Then it seemed to her that the world had just become a very nasty place.

Did you cast yourself in a victim role at that time?

Oh! I was playing the role of the victim though almost the entirety of my life. It was a victimization, but that was something I had wished to experience in all of its various facets; it was one of my intentions when I came down to earth. The others were to recognize the worth within myself (which I struggled with during my entire physical existence), and to search beyond myself for any connection with what it was to be a soul (something, again, which I did not do very much).

You started your life very successfully. You were 2½ when you joined your sisters Susie and Jimmie to sing "Jingle Bells" in 1924. Then you all went on tour as the Gumm Sisters; I remember that you were born Frances Ethel Gumm.

Yes, I was, and I was happy as Frances Gumm.

Tell me, why did your manager, George Jessell, want to change the group's name?

He always said that Gumm was grim.

So why did you become the Garland Sisters?

Garland portrayed hope—a garland was something you decorated people and scenes with. It brought joy and beauty to the theme. So I became a Garland!

At the age of 13 you sang "You Made Me Love You" for Clark Gable. Did you fall in love with him?

Of course! Didn't everybody?

Was that the beginning of stardom?

Yes, it was my march into stardom, the experience of people taking me into their lives, that girl next door, and dreaming with me. As I dreamed to be with Clark, they dreamed that the average girl could actually be with this beautiful hunk of a person.

In your very next role, you sang as Dorothy that "the dreams that you dare to dream really do come true."

Was that prophetic for me? No, it was not prophetic but was always out there as a light in the distance—which, as I approached it, would retreat from me.

That part of Dorothy was in the full-length movie The Wizard of Oz.

Initially I was excited by the prospect, but then—as the grind of the production wore on—that was the beginning, the turning point where all freedom, all self-expression was taken away from me, and I was being molded exactly as the studio wanted me to be. I lost all sense of personal identity as the powers-that-be assumed all aspects of my life. It was presented to me thusly: "If you do exactly as we tell you, you will be on everybody's lips; you will be on the cover of the magazines; you will be the girl next door that everybody wishes to befriend and have on their social list. It will open the doors for you; it will allow you to expand the bleak existence you have now into a party atmosphere." Of course, that wasn't true.

In fact you did make a notable unfettered comeback at the end of your cinema career. One of your final movies was A Star is Born, *which was your attempt to get back into popularity. You very nearly did it, until Warner Brothers cut the film by thirty minutes and you lost the Oscar.*

Yes. I wanted recognition. I wanted something that was mine, something I couldn't just attribute to the expertise of a puppeteer. I wanted to be able to feel in that particular film that I did have some say as to what took place. But I couldn't get off that cutting-room floor.

Groucho Marx said it was "the greatest robbery since Brinks."

I felt it even more deeply than that. I thought [laughs] that it was the robbery of my humanity, the robbery of my hard-fought expertise.

You were a victim. You were robbed. Do you have intense regret now?

Oh, no! I look back and see that the lessons that were laid out there were exactly what I needed to experience, because in other lives prior to being Judy Garland, I had always been extremely successful. In a previous life, I had been an opera star on the stage in England where I was touted by the monarchy. In another life I was a very successful violinist in Vienna—a man.

177

So you have had lives as a man as well as a woman?
Yes.

Do you feel yourself to be a woman or a man, now you are back Home?
[laughing] I am everything that I have been. Wherever my concentration is I would be what you consider either male or female.

But at the root of things you are neither male nor female.
That's correct. I've had a lot of past lives, a number of which were very successful, and most of them in the arts. There were some which were unsuccessful, where I did not have the physical talent to be accomplished—where I was in the chorus rather than being the star. There were some where [she chuckles] I could not carry a tune, or where music was something I was occupied with just to entertain myself while I did other work—one life that's coming to me is when I was a farm hand and hummed and sang as I worked in the fields to entertain myself. But in none of those lives was my very existence controlled by outside forces, by puppeteers, as happened in my life as Judy Garland.

You raise the issue of "life lessons." Can you explain what that means?
As souls we can view a movie but we cannot be an actor in the movie. We have to assume a physicality [put on a body] in order to do that. Once we are in physical form and actually take part in a movie, we can then experience, and know, and gain the wisdom, of what it takes to play each one of those particular parts, rather than just see someone acting and assume what it feels like to experience what the actors are experiencing.

Why do you have to play these parts?
Because otherwise we would not have the wisdom, the feeling that the experience brings to us. Take sports—you can be an avid sports fan but you do not know the amount of practice,

the degree of exertion that is needed to be a top-notch athlete, unless you do it yourself. Once you have the experience of the performance, then that is something which cannot be taken away from you, because you know what it takes to reach the level of the top athlete, to reach the level of being the best.

You reached that level, singing reputedly the best popular song in the twentieth century. Did you regret the experience?

No, I enjoyed the acting that I was allowed to do unfettered. Once I was on the stage I was allowed to be myself. It was my off-camera experiences that were molded and constrained. So I learned both things through that lifetime. I learned the experience of being a person who could bring joy through my voice to others. I learned the experience of floating on the music and through the music. But then I also learned what it was to have my every moment monitored and controlled.

Did you find it better when you left filmmaking and took to the stage as a singer? Many people called your concert at Carnegie Hall on April 23, 1961, the "greatest single night in show business."

I loved the live performances because they were the real Judy Garland. Those gave me the most satisfaction because they couldn't be cut or re-done. I had to be myself. I had to be "on" at all times, to be in connection with what I was doing and the energy I was conveying. It was as if I floated through those performances because that was the essence of Judy Garland coming out.

In the tie you were in a sorry physical mess. At performances in Australia you slurred your words and were badly hung over. Were you destroying yourself with drugs and alcohol?

It was at the end of the destruction. Even in the earlier times I was able to reach a level of self-medication which allowed me to still feel and be myself. It was why I was successful in those performances. I didn't particularly want to go to Australia and I wasn't happy at that time—my entire personal life was beginning to crumble around me. I went for more and more self-medication, so I was constantly in a stupor. It wasn't that important for me to convey who I was any longer, because I figured I had done it to the world that was important to me.

At one point you attempted suicide, didn't you?
Yes.

Did you want to leave the world early?
I wanted out of the pain. I wanted out of the misery.

Was your death at age 47 of a prescription drug overdose deliberate?
Yes.

Do you have a view of drug use by other entertainers?
There are those who go for self-medication, drugs and booze, to deaden the experience they have. Some fear they are not really who they are becoming, they will fail, they will not always be able to be "on," and not always be able to satisfy the audience. From another viewpoint, it is the first time they have the financial wherewithal to do whatever they want, so they jump with both feet into partying, and then they get in with those who say, "Oh, you haven't lived till you've experienced this, or till you've done that. Then they get in and become addicted to the experience. With me it was depression; I self-medicated.

You started singing and acting very early. Did you have genius given to you?
I don't really know that I made the connection. It was just something that I loved. Music was my life. Music was what allowed me to sing to the world and to be a free bird, jumping from bush to bush, singing and entertaining.

But you were exceptionally talented.

Part of that was what I had brought forward from other lives. When you have had a tendency to be a singer in past lives, it is much easier for you to adopt that mode in a new human physicality.

All of your five husbands have now left planet Earth. Do you see them all from time to time?
Occasionally, yes.

How do you relate to them, now you are all back Home?
As we relate to anyone with whom we had experiences in physicality. Since none was what would be considered my "Twin Flame" (that part of me which makes me whole), there is no light and show-time when I see them. It's just "Hi, how're ya doing? Remember the good times we had, and the laughs? Remember how we got into those pickles—did we think we'd ever get out of it?" It's just re-living old times, and "Thank you for letting me have the experiences I had (whether I considered them good or bad). You did a good job there." There is no real discussion of my experiences and feelings compared with their inner feelings. Such feelings are individual to each soul. I don't say, "Man, I felt horrible when we had that experience together." That's a personal thing. What I share with them is the laughter of the external appearances of what we did together, not the internal turmoil.

What was your main aim in that life?
When I was in my physical form in my "Over the Rainbow" life, everything I tried to do was in order to be loved, accepted, received, nurtured, and protected. So I tried to set myself up in situations that would facilitate that sense of self which involved the feeling of being accepted.

So now, "way above the chimney tops" is where we'll find you. Do you have any final thoughts?
I think it could be construed, by anyone who studied it, that I had very little happiness in my life. Even the beginnings of

my courtships and my marriages were performances. I was always looking for something just beyond. My predominant feeling while in physical form was of numbness. I felt very little. I always looked for those feelings. My plunges into marriage were always to find a safe harbor, to find somebody who could give me a sense of security and safety that I didn't see in my life. And throughout my life all I ever wanted was to have a house with three children and a couple of pets—with my husband going off to work and me staying home, baking cookies.

Thank you for coming and talking with us, Judy Garland.

Commentary

Toni: There was such a wistfulness to Judy when she was talking about her life. It was a nostalgia, as she tried to remember things as better than they were, a sense that she hoped her life might be some sort of model that people could see and then decide *not* to emulate—not to be sucked into things just because other people thought you should experience them. When she went back to Judy's life she seemed to be caught up in a tornado over which she had no control. Her life had its highs and its lows, but she never had a true identity because she was a piece of the storm—her life had been overwhelming. The only time she felt internal peace was when she was performing— when she was someone other than Judy Garland. She was almost too numbed to feel the pain, and so when she was playing someone else she wasn't playing that pathetic, tortured soul Judy Garland. She felt able to have free self-expression only as she played other people.

Peter: The acting profession often shows a suffering side to its life that is at odds with the cheerful face it puts on for the public. Judy was manipulated more by the studio managers and less by the media than she might be today. The bosses were indifferent to the cost borne by the young artist from her grinding work-load. They dealt with her anxiety by unleashing the Rottweiler of prescription drugs, designed to keep her on the job. She could have been a small-time singer, but she was entitled to her ambition and her search for happiness, both on and off the stage. Looking back she said, "Everything I tried to do was in order to be loved, accepted, received, nurtured, and protected." She nearly made it several times, but she had started out on the mountain top of popularity as a child performer, with her acclaimed *The Wizard of Oz*. So after that it was downhill all the way despite her attempts to prove it otherwise. By the time her singing career began to take off she was already too far down the path of self-destruction to climb back up again. What was troubling, listening to her, was the feeling that her soul is still overwhelmed by sadness.

Becoming a human being does not mean that we must suffer until life is not worth living. The Masters are very clear that we do not have to be crushed by our experiences. Our task is to learn the lessons that we have set for ourselves, and to carry on intact spiritually. No lesson is too much for the soul to tackle. We don't always learn easily and well. Earth is the toughest environment out there. But each one of us has chosen this fast track to knowledge and wisdom, and we get what we've asked for, because over the rainbow, skies really are blue.

"One thing I miss up here, is being able to fill
an auditorium with a depth of vibration so intense that
the very introduction of a human form into that massive array of
vibration absorbs and intensifies
the emotional feelings of those present."

Maria Callas

1923-1977

*Maria Anna Sofia Cecilia Kalogeropoulou, you were born in
Queens, New York, and despite your Greek family name, the world
knows you as Maria Callas. Your father, George, was not interested
in the arts, and he and your mother, Litsa, were not well suited,
but they say you had a good relationship with him. Is that right?*

I was the apple of Papa's eye. I could do just about
anything and be able to charm him. I didn't have any
expectations for him, as Mama did, so when he wanted to
smooth the anger that was below the surface, we would go off
somewhere and just talk.

*In 1937, when you were a teenager, your parents separated and
your mother took you and your older sister, Jackie, to Athens.
Jackie was her favorite. You said, "My sister was slim and beautiful
and friendly, and my mother always preferred her. I was the ugly
duckling, fat and clumsy and unpopular." Did you put on weight
because of her hostility?*

It was one of my defense mechanisms. Food for a while,
particularly after the breakup, was the way that I felt

appreciated, as happens with a lot of people with weight problems. They know that the one thing they have control over, that they can't be talked out of when they need it, is eating, and it's consoling and comforting. Mama was all about appearances. She aspired to be recognized everywhere she went, and she felt the only way to do that was to be extremely pleasing to the eye of the male folk.

Did you actually choose to be very short-sighted and nearly blind before you incarnated?
It was one of the restrictions that I wanted to experiment with, to have to go inside and feel more. Rather than being able to picture everything clearly through the eyes, I had to take and visualize it, and become a part of it within myself in order to appreciate what was confronting me.

Did it help your singing career?
It did in that I couldn't see some of the distractions. [laughs] It allowed me to focus on the pure quality of the tone rather than eyeing a handsome young gentleman in the front row. [winks]

Your controlling mother recognized your talent as a singer and forced you to sing publicly from an early age, which you hated, but she also sent you to train at the Greek National Conservatoire. There, Maria Trivella became your tutor, quickly recognizing the quality in your untrained voice. What did she mean to you?
My dear teacher was an inspiration to me—not only an inspiration, but for the first time since Papa left, I felt appreciated. I felt that there was a recognition of the uniqueness of who I was and what I could do. Although in the beginning I had no concept of where I could go with my voice, she always had that faith in me and let me know that it was a slow and tedious process to polish the jewel.

Did you have an awareness of having been a singer in any past lives?

Then I had no awareness. Now I know I had been, but nothing of the quality that I had in this life as Maria Callas.

Maria Trivella used a French approach to singing and trained you to become a dramatic soprano. Looking back now, do you feel that in raising and lightening the timbre of your voice she adopted the best approach for you?

She had me adopt an approach that best suited the quality of what I could produce vocally. Through her techniques, she also allowed me to truly feel what I was singing, to feel the power of the words and the chords and conveyance of them to others. It was the way of learning to take one note and develop it into a symphony.

You worked very hard for her, didn't you?

I did, because she was very fair with me; she was loving with me, and she did not treat me unfairly as I had been treated at home. She pushed me to do things, but at the same time never expected more than she thought I could do.

On April 11, 1938, you had your student debut, singing in a duet from Tosca *at the Parnassos music hall. That must have been an exciting moment for you. How did you feel?*

At first, scared. Here I was, still pretty much the ugly duckling, being presented as this fantastic creature that was supposed to move whole hordes of people emotionally. I was overwhelmed in the beginning with the power that I could convey through my voice, but then I let the music take me, and it was a prelude to what I knew I wanted to do the rest of my life.

The next year, at the Athens Conservatoire, the soprano Elvira de Hidalgo became your teacher. You worked very hard for her and she thought you were a phenomenal student. What did she teach you?

She taught me depth. She taught me that it was all right to repeat what others had done, to be mediocre. But to be, as she said, "fantastico"—to be magnificent—you had to take what was

187

in your heart and mold the songs, the music, to your own energy. With the combination of your energy and your uniqueness, you presented to people something they could find nowhere else, and you grew with each experiment you did of altering the timeworn patterns and putting in a depth of newness and excitement.

During World War II your family was very poor. Your husband later said that your mother did not work but sent you out to earn money by prostitution with German and Italian soldiers. Is that true?

Yes. It was a time, again, where I allowed Mother to control me, because she again made me feel that I was the ugly duckling, that I could not provide anything other than in mundane tasks that were required of the very lowly. It was a time when, because of the turmoil around me, I felt that something as pure as my singing was totally overcome, totally suppressed by the moment, by the anxiety, by the poverty, by the cruelty that was going on, and that it was something of little meaning to me at that time. What was important was to be able to survive, and a way to survive was to offer another aspect of myself—my body—instead of my voice.

Didn't you hate the men? They were soldiers who were oppressing you.

I disassociated myself from what was going on and saw it only as a means of survival.

Did you hate your mother?

At that time, yes, I did, but I was still not confident enough in myself to deny her what she demanded.

Did your relationship with her help you interpret some of the roles you played later in your operatic career?

The emotions that we exchanged allowed me to have the personal experience to put those particular energies into the roles I played—most definitely.

188

Your teacher Elvira de Hidalgo helped you to find small roles at the Greek National Opera. Were you aware of the jealousy your fellow sopranos felt about your powerful voice?

I was oblivious to what went on around me, because I had learned to dissociate myself from things outside of me, coming from the wartime experiences, and I just communed with my energy, with my soul.

Do you feel, looking back, that the fact that you were severely overweight, and that you'd had this experience with your mother and with the soldiers, actually helped you to go inside and become a great singer?

It definitely helped me to go inside. I don't know that it could not have been accomplished in some other way—had I, for instance, been crippled and had to go inside. I knew when I came down that this life was to be one of communicating through music, through my voice, directly to the essence and the souls of other humans, and a necessary step for me to be able to do that was to go inside, to tap into the energy that is the essence, in order to project outward with that magnificent force. The way I chose to do it in this lifetime was through the disabilities, infirmities, difficulties that you have mentioned.

In 1942 you sang the lead role of Puccini's Tosca *and then of Marta in* Tiefland *by D'Albert. A critic wrote that you had "God-given talents." Soon you were being called "La Divina." Where did your talent come from?*

They had it partially right when they said "God-given talents." As I now have the wisdom of knowing, each soul is part of the Creator, the God-Force (God, as most would have you believe). Without tapping into that power that is within you and within all people, you cannot reach, you cannot touch, you do not have the ability to shake the very foundation of the people who hear you. By connecting with my soul, I tapped into the God-Force that was inside of me and used that to broadcast outward. So the critic was right, but not in the way he meant it.

The voice you used to broadcast had a very big range, from F-sharp below middle C to E-natural above high C. Some people have claimed you reached high F in concert. Are they correct?

Yes, they are.

I'm going to chance it: F-sharp?

[smiling shyly] Just about.

You were a dramatic soprano whose voice had the distinctive sound of bel canto, which, you admitted yourself, was not as exquisitely beautiful as the voice of the lyric soprano Renata Tebaldi, who had trained in the twentieth-century Italian style. How seriously did you take the heated debate in the newspapers and between your rival supporters?

[laughs] When I first read the reviews, I thought that there was something lacking in the way I had trained, in the way I presented myself to the art. But then I realized it was because of the fact that I put my uniqueness into my singing that I could, in a way, be compared with but not be graded against anyone else, because my voice had a uniqueness that was my very own. It was a matter for the listener's ear what differences were perceived between our styles. It was merely a variation in the vibration of their soul and their body that they received from what I sang. The most pure tone, if it does not come from the heart, is but a noise, yet the most insignificant sound, if it comes from the heart, can move the heart and soul of another.

Back Home now, as you consider the strengths of your singing and acting, what stands out for you: The sheer vocal power you had? Your agility and masterful technique? The distinctive coloring and timbre of your voice?

One thing that I miss up here, is being able to fill an auditorium with a depth of vibration so intense that the very introduction of a human form into that massive array of vibration absorbs and intensifies the emotional feelings of those present. Here we have vibration, but it does not come near to the human body's feeling, sense, and depth in which you can be immersed by means of the human vocal cords. We are all vibrational energy and you need the resistance of flesh to get the tingling created by the sounds of excellence.

I thought you had heavenly choirs!

We have heavenly choirs, but the receptors are energy—the other souls in their energetic form—and they just sense the vibration. They can't feel the power of a note blasted into a human chest.

In 1945 you left Greece for Italy and thence America. Is it true that when you auditioned for the Metropolitan Opera you were offered Madame Butterfly *and* Fidelio, *both to be sung in English, but you declined because you felt too fat then for* Butterfly *and wanted to sing in the original languages?*

I did feel that my size would make a certain percentage of the audience concerned that I did not fit their impression, particularly of the lovely Madame Butterfly. I also felt that the original languages had tonal quality to them that conveyed a vibration that English, which I found to be rather clipped, could not do, so I preferred to sing in the original languages.

Your American debut was, in fact, in Chicago in 1954, and you provided the fledgling Lyric Opera with a stunning performance of Norma. *Do you remember the event?*

I do. I found the Windy City, as you call it, to be a very charming and receptive place. The patrons who came were there to receive; they were open to the experience of riding on the music, being engrossed in the music, being embraced by the music. To them, what they saw meant nothing. It was all what they felt.

You went on to have a brilliant international career. During it you worked with the Italian conductor Tullio Serafin. You said he was a major influence on your work. Tell us about him.

Tullio felt that it was not enough to take a sheet of music and keep to the black and white of the music. He felt that, as any piece of literature, it was to be interpreted. The phraseology put the drama and the feeling into it. He was the one who taught me that there could be a marriage between the voice and the instruments, so that they truly became one—that they could convey a sense of being a womb within which people could be gently comforted, and then stimulated, and then inflamed, and then brought back to peace. He taught me the true drama of music.

Then came your decision to slim, and you lost 80 pounds. Many said the physical change altered your voice. What was your experience of the weight loss? Did it in fact put an end to your career, or were there other causes you know now?

Around that period of time I was hearing a lot of criticism of my personal appearance. I was in one of those periods that humans go through of second-guessing a lot of what we have done—was it the right thing. So I tried weight loss, and all of the various ways to do it that were current then—supplements, starvation, all the cleanses, and some very dramatic things, which had an effect upon my vitality. It just sapped me of my strength.

The result of the weight loss was an immediate impact upon my singing, because it shrank the volume of my lungs so that I was no longer able to fill up like a bellows and inexhaustibly put out the energy. I became a miniature projector of myself. Also, some of the slimming techniques I used had an effect upon the organs of my body—my liver and kidneys—so that my bodily functions did not work as well. I was also getting very tired, so I gave in to the energy of other people running my life and making decisions for me, as I had early on with my mother. This was the beginning of the end.

In 1949, when you were 26, you married Giovanni Battista Meneghini. The marriage lasted ten years, when you began an affair with Aristotle Onassis. Is it true you and Onassis had a little boy who died as a baby?

Yes.

Did you go on seeing Onassis after he married Jackie Kennedy?

We were friends at that point. I respected the intimacy that he shared with Jackie. They were like two kingpins meeting and collaborating, whereas I was the outsider, not from their class.

Franco Zeffirelli has suggested that your death was not an accidental overdose of methaqualone, a sleeping pill, but that you were murdered by someone who wanted to control your fortune. Will you tell us what actually happened?

It was an accidental overdose. All of the drama that people would like to play in the life of a celebrity did not exist. I was very free with taking care of those around me, so there was no jealousy, there was no underground movement to get rid of me. I became careless, and in those moments, thinking I had not taken a dose, and then again thinking I had not taken a dose ...

But in fact most souls plan their death, don't they?

We plan along the line of the lessons we come to learn and the things we seek to accomplish. When we have reached each one of the pinnacles along the way, we are then ready to come back Home, to evaluate, and to decide whether to do something else. I had completed what I came to do; I had gone full cycle within my lifetime.

So was the overdose, spiritually speaking, deliberate?

In strictest terms, yes. In terms of being aware of it within my physical body, no.

Looking back on your career, which was your favorite opera house?

I think what I enjoyed the most of all the places that I have sung was when I did the outdoor amphitheatre. There I felt that I could rise right out of my body into a realm where many before me had gone, and it was there where one time I felt myself present in a time many, many centuries before the chronological time.

Was that amphitheatre in Greece?

In Greece, yes, the main amphitheatre. We had a fundraiser there, and it was magnificent. It gave me a sense of singing to the heavens instead of singing to the walls and having it come in. In the opera houses, as the energy projected out, it reached a point when it folded in on itself. This created an intensification for those who were there that was able to affect their body and their soul more completely. Those were the venues that I liked when I was reaching people. But this was a time for me, when I just projected out into the universe and knew that it went on and on and on.

What was your favorite role?

That depended upon the particular period in my life, whether I needed to get out my anger, if I needed to be coy, if I needed to be sad. The role that I played at the time frequently reflected the stage of my life that I was at, and because I wanted a full experience of all of the human emotions, each role provided me that. I didn't particularly have a favorite, because I enjoyed the variety.

Do you plan to reincarnate any time soon?

I am thinking about it, but I haven't decided exactly what lessons I would like to experience, so you'll have to stay tuned for that one.

Thank you, Maria Callas, for talking with us.

Commentary

Toni: This was an emotional interview. When Maria Callas was talking about her physical problems, the period of prostitution, difficulties with her mother, sadness of her father leaving, it was as if she were reaching deep into a well of sadness and had a very physical feeling at that time. Then, when she spoke of her singing and of discovering the way to reach people and to express herself, it was as if nothing physical mattered. It was just like stepping totally into the energetic realm. When she talked about the performance in the Greek amphitheatre, her energy swelled to monumental proportions, and there wasn't the least feeling of physicality with it at all—it was totally etheric. She gave a varied sense of her energies just as she performed various roles in life.

Peter: An engaging story from a consummate artist. Maria used her youthful difficulties—poor eyesight, obesity, a controlling mother, lustful soldiers—all to good effect. She created a depth in her artistry which, together with her fabulous voice, was developed by her sheer hard work under fine tutors and made her into a true *prima donna*.

Her mother's criticism of her weight came back to haunt her when the music critics called her to account for her size. She was only 30 when, in 1953, during a performance of Cherubini's opera "Medea," she decided her stage roles deserved a leaner leading lady. Her slimming was successful but it took the edge off her voice, and her career lost pace and went slowly downhill.

Maria became known for her friendship with Aristotle Onassis, but then, after Jackie Kennedy had married him, she rather went into a slump toward the end. She cleared up rumors for us concerning the birth of a child by Onassis, which she confirmed, but she refuted the darker suggestion that, at the end, she had been murdered for her money.

There was little new in this dialogue by way of spiritual information. Talking of her "God-given talents," she confirmed the common claim that all souls are part of the God-Force, and claimed that it was by tapping into her soul's divine condition that she possessed "the ability to shake the very foundation of the people" with her incredibly beautiful singing.

"I began to realize that my whole life had been a play or movie and the way we present ourselves on screen is how we want others to see us, not necessarily who we are."

Marilyn Monroe
1926 – 1962

Norma Jeane, your birth certificate lists you with the name of your mother's second husband, Martin Mortenson, who left her before you were born. Then you were baptized Baker, your mother's last name, but historians say that your mother had an affair with Charles Gifford, a salesman for the studios where they worked. Who was your father?

Gifford. Gifford was my father and that was part of the reason why Mortenson left.

But you once claimed that you had Norwegian ancestry.

I said that when I was given a lot of problems for going blond. I had to make up this story that I was identifying with my heritage. Also, the Norwegians whom I had met were very strong people and I wanted to be perceived as strong.

You didn't mind telling a few lies in your lifetime.

I don't know that they were necessarily lies—I think they were publicity-getters.

You had a very tough start in life. Your mother was taken into a mental hospital when you were young. You suffered abuse in a succession of orphanages and foster homes. Did you really choose to have such a life before you were born?

Of course—not that I remembered any of it once I got down there. I thought (and my early life taught me) that you could present an image to people, even if it wasn't the truth of what you were and how you felt, that would change the way they thought about you. After coming to this realization, my plan was to present an image that everyone would want to embrace. At that time "everybody" was mostly the males in society, because they were the ones with the money.

In orphanages, abuse was pretty commonplace, wasn't it?

It was constant. My feeling about that situation now is that the people running the orphanages are there because they themselves were abused, and they want to wreak havoc on as many poor little kids (who can't fight back) as they possibly can. But it did toughen me up physically, and it taught me to be very manipulative, because those kids who manipulated were less abused.

Would you, from your present position at Home, have an answer to the orphanage problem?

There aren't as many orphanages now as there used to be because people are more willing to open up their homes to those who don't have families. But souls who put themselves into situations like that do it for the learning experience, so if they wish to experience an institutional setting they can do it in an orphanage, in a military school, in a prison, or something of that sort.

Much later, in 1961, you were admitted to the Payne Whitney Psychiatric Clinic and placed in the ward for the most seriously disturbed. How much was your life affected by problems of mental illness?

My perception of reality was always colored by my early experiences. To some, the depression that my life put me into was considered mental illness, and the clinic was just one more institutional experience for me before I was ready to move on to something else. At the time I was hospitalized, the façade I had put up was beginning to crumble, and I was forced to look at myself in a new way. I was not being accepted as I was wanting to be, because people saw through to the core of me and discovered a very insecure, very weak person.

When you were sixteen years old your foster parents had to give you up, and you married Jimmy Dougherty. Were you in love with him, or was the marriage a way out of returning to the orphanage?

I considered it my salvation at the time, because I was being accepted by someone who didn't *have* to accept me. My feeling of the foster homes I'd been in was that people were doing it for whatever money they could get, or for the recognition from their church or their society, and that I was merely a thing being passed from place to place as a token of how great those people were. I felt a true love for Jimmy in the beginning, that he accepted me as I was. This was so new to me that I just grabbed on to it and became like a little puppy to him.

Did the marriage break down because you changed or did he change?

Both of us changed. I began to realize, once I was out in the world getting exposure to other people, that my entire vision of life was based upon lies. It was based on institutions and systems that had nothing to do with normal society. Then I wanted to stretch my wings and experience as many things as I could. But Jimmy became very possessive of me and wanted to hold me down—in the same way that I felt my foster situations had held me down.

Taking pictures of munitions factory women for Yank *magazine, David Conover saw you as "a photographer's dream" and helped you begin very successful modeling for the Blue Book Agency. Did you see modeling as your career at that time, or did you already have acting ambitions?*

I hadn't really thought about acting. My idea at that time was just to experience as much as possible in whatever way I could. At the time I found it very ego-building for someone to come and say that I was the best or the most beautiful. It was something that had never before been said to me in sincerity—a little bit from Jimmy, perhaps, but not with the sincerity of the people at the Blue Book Agency. I felt almost an awe about them, as if they were placing me on a platform. For the first time in my life I felt I really was Somebody.

Did you have an affair with David Conover?

We had some little dalliances. I began to learn how powerful my body could be for me, how it was a tool.

Divorced from Jimmy, and working for Twentieth Century Fox, you changed your name and became a blond. Your grandmother Della's maiden name was Monroe, and a talent scout, Ben Lyon, suggested you take the first name of the musical theater star Marilyn Miller. Did your new name have any special emotional significance to you?

Oh, I should say so! It was the washing away of the past, the washing away of the identity of Norma Jeane, that dysfunctional child who was pushed from place to place. It was the birth of Marilyn Monroe, the birth of this woman who could turn heads, who was catered to, who was put on a pedestal. It was as if my personality was recognized for the first time.

Nude photos of you, taken by Tom Kelley when you were young and poor, were bought by Hugh Hefner for the first edition of Playboy Magazine. These photos and your movie successes in All About Eve, Don't Bother to Knock, *and* Niagara, *established you as a sex goddess in the public mind. How do you look back on your powerful use of sexuality now?*

For me it was a tool to gain life experiences. It was what was needed in order for me to move forward. I did not have any particular talents outside of my body that I could rely upon, so I chose the one thing that came naturally to me. The little coyness that I put in grew out of the many experiences I had had of not saying things but looking nice.

One of the people enchanted by you was Joe DiMaggio, the baseball star who was your second husband. He idolized you but was jealous of your star role. What was life like with Joe?

In the beginning it was very nice. I got into what you might call a mainstream family life with him. He had a very well-balanced idea of the male-female roles, and of what family life should be like. The fact that he idolized me kept me there for a while, of course, but then he did become very restrictive. He would go onto the set, when he wasn't on the road, and would sit there and watch what type of interaction I would have with everybody. It was impossible for me to step out of my persona as a sex goddess just because my husband was around. So there was a clash between what his idea of what I should be and my knowing what I had to be.

So he became jealous?

Definitely jealous.

After your divorce he seems to have remained true to his love of you.

It was impossible to cut that piece out of him that I had become. In a very short period of time I had become his ideal woman, and he knew the fear and tenderness within me from our private times together. He told me that he always kept me in his thoughts and in his memory, and that when he saw me doing those other things that he did not necessarily approve of, he knew it was a reaction to my upbringing. He became almost a caretaker.

After your death he sent red roses every week to the mausoleum where your body was stored. When you have transitioned back Home are you aware of something like that?

We are aware of it if our transition is smooth—in other words, when we go in a very short period of time from consciousness in human form to full consciousness in spirit form. I didn't go real fast; I had some hang-ups to deal with as I transitioned. I first went back into thinking that I was in some of my early life situations and that I was still trying to flee from them, so there was a passage of time before I entered total spiritual consciousness. However, because linear time (as you have it) does not exist here, once I did regain full consciousness I was able to go back and observe the homage that he had paid me in the intervening period.

And you meet him at Home now?

Yes, that's right. We joke and laugh over some of the things we put each other through, and the lessons we were able to learn from them. His lessons were a lot about possession and love in that lifetime, and I played a small part in letting him learn those lessons.

1953 was a hectic year, with Niagara *followed by the hugely successful* Gentlemen Prefer Blondes *and* How to Marry a Millionaire. *Then in 1956 your own company produced* Bus Stop *and* The Prince and the Showgirl, *where you plainly showed your ability as an actor. In 1959 you received a Golden Globe for Best Actress in* Some Like It Hot. *Looking back on these films, which gave you the most personal satisfaction?*

I think the one I liked the best was *Gentlemen Prefer Blondes* because it was a turning point for me. Working with the crew and the other artistes on the film, I began to realize that my whole life had been a play or movie, and the way we present ourselves on screen is how we want others to see us, not necessarily who we are. It was as if a light came on, that I could be whatever I wanted to be, not only to myself but to other people.

Laurence Olivier complained about your lateness and attitude during the making of The Prince and the Showgirl. *How did you feel about him?*

Dear Laurence didn't have the whole repertoire of humor. He was very business-like and very intense at that time in his life. I was just then coming into my own, finding that I could be care-free, and catered to, so I took full advantage of it. A little bit of the problem was that I loved to irk him, I loved to see him blow up. [laughs] It was because he was not totally caught up by my charms, like everybody else was. That made me a little upset and I wanted to let him see my importance to others.

He wasn't a man who wanted to go to bed with you?
     That's right.

You surprised the world by marrying the playwright Arthur Miller. In fact, you had a large library and spoke about your interest in classical music, art, drama, and poetry. Were you expressing an intellectual side of your nature when you married him, or was it, as you said, that he made you feel "giddy"?
     It was both. I was able to be accepted by Arthur as not just a body. He thawed my search for knowledge that had begun in the closet, so to speak, because it did not fit well with my reputation as a dumb blond sex toy. He accepted me for who I was, not for this ditzy cinematic robot that everybody else wanted. I was able to be free with him. I was able to discuss philosophical and intellectual issues, something that most people did not believe I could do. It was a quiet sanctuary time for me with him.

During your marriage you had an unhappy ectopic pregnancy followed by another miscarriage. It is also said that during your lifetime you had a dozen abortions. Can you tell us about these aspects of your life as you see it now?
     Well it wasn't a dozen. There were many, but it was not a dozen. I was experiencing in my lifetime as Marilyn Monroe a myriad of emotions—beginning with the sense of worthlessness that I felt as a child, which came out as the callousness with which I treated other lives, and when it came to fetuses (particularly early on in my career). I never wanted to subject another little being to what I had gone through, but easy birth control was not readily available in society at that time, making things very difficult and resulting in several unwanted

pregnancies. I saw it as wrecking my career were I to have a child. So whenever the situation arose that the result of my encounters was a pregnancy, I could not and would not let the child come into the world—that is until I was with Arthur. With him I felt more of a whole person than with anyone else. He had accepted the whole package, which included my mind. I would have loved to have been able to present him with a child. A child of ours would have been extraordinary, but because of my previous terminations, my body was not physically able to carry a fetus to term.

Have you ever lived as a man in a past life?

Of course! The one whose energy affected me most as Marilyn was when I was a traveling minstrel back in the fifteenth century, complete with puffed sleeves and tights. At that time I fitted into whatever was needed. [laughs] I had a kind of sinister side to me in that I was a spy, because I could easily get into royal chambers. It was kind of a lark. Going back (in your time) many, many years, I was a bushman in Africa. I had beautiful black, bushy hair. I laugh about it now as I remember those things. Kinky too, it literally flopped the way my blond hair did.

Any notable women's lives?

I was a French noblewoman. That life was one where I spent all my time with the classics and with music. I was an excellent pianist. It was a time for inner contemplation as the nobility, outside of spending time refining their talents, did not do much of anything. So you spent your time in introspection.

And some of that carried across into your life as Marilyn?

Without a doubt—everything builds.

Arthur Miller created Roslyn Taber in The Misfits *especially for you, which brought out your air of naïveté and vulnerability. How did you view the part then and now?*

I wasn't sure what I thought about it then because it seemed that he was poking fun at me, which I did not realize at the beginning. Then when it was pointed out to me, I was deeply hurt. I now know that he was simply taking advantage of the human condition, using it to explain to all who watched that this was a regular human characteristic. We laugh about it now.

Was it a reason for your marital breakup?

That play was the major reason because I didn't allow anybody to make fun of me at that point in my life. It tipped me back into my predisposition of doubting people's sincerity and motives.

Tell us about your romantic relationships with Jack and Bobby Kennedy.

They were very highly sexed people, in the physical sense. They were men who had been raised in power, knew how to wield power, and expected everyone to cater to them. At that time I was totally enamored of the whole mystique of political maneuvering. To me, being able to be a part of the scene, even in an ancillary role, was one of the most exciting things that a person could ever do. So I was a very willing participant in the dalliances that took place.

Was your early death an accidental prescription drug overdose, a suicide, or were you murdered?

It depends upon your perspective. I was in a depression at the time and was self-medicating. The medications were provided to me by people who knew that I had a tendency to take too much, so I can't exactly tell you their motives, whether they were trying to get rid of me, but I was becoming a liability to some people.

So, does the fact that you took two unusual drug combinations suggest they might have been provided deliberately by somebody else?

The medications were delivered to me. I was unaware of what I was taking at the time. I only wanted to drown out my feelings.

With your present knowledge, what is the answer to the question: Were you murdered?
Yes.
Do you know by whom?
Strange as this might seem, it is prudent that I not say.

You helped Ella Fitzgerald to play at the segregated Mocambo nightclub in West Hollywood by promising to go and listen to her every night. Did race relations mean much to you?
No. All I saw was discrimination and injustice, the same as I had been the victim of throughout my early years. I saw Ella as a beautiful, beautiful person with a voice which was from heaven, conveying the messages of the living soul. This was something I would not tolerate being pushed into the corner. Race was not the factor; discrimination was the factor.

Are you going to return to planet Earth any time soon?
I don't have any current plans now. I haven't decided what I would like to do the next time around.

Do you have freedom to make that decision, or are you pushed into it?
Oh, no, no—total freedom. We have a council of advisors who are always sitting down with us, and we are saying, you know, I've experienced this and this. I haven't done that and that. Do I want to try that? Well, I don't know. We go back and forth until we come up with a plan. Then, once we have a plan, we start finding the best ways to implement it. But it's all about things we wish to learn and experience.

Thank you, Marilyn Monroe, for talking with us.
A big kiss to my fans out there.

Commentary

Toni: What energy! It shifted during the interview from shy and somewhat demure to showing pride in accomplishments, and even into complex character traits we do not normally associate with Marilyn. I saw the Dumb Blond she portrayed so well. But she was very proud of her private side, her apparent ability to become an intellectual—as she was with Arthur Miller—although that was not recognized by other people. There was a sense of mirth in her dealings with men. She had no hidden agendas in her relationships. It was just being who she wanted to be and experiencing what she wanted to experience. It was quite a delightful interview.

Peter: The soul of Marilyn Monroe painted a clear picture of the psychological imprint of her many adverse childhood experiences, and how they affected her conscious choices as an adult. This manipulative screen idol, who used her blond hair, her fluttering eyelashes, and her body to control powerful men and enhance her success, was also always, inside, the damaged little girl in many abusive institutions. But the effect of her continuing use of manipulation was disastrous in a cyclical way.

Fame did not bring her peace, and her sexual successes brought her multiple abortions and destroyed her chance to have a family with the one man who had consistently valued her real talent. But then that husband, Arthur Miller, misjudged the depth of her vulnerability when writing *The Misfits*. The pain the play caused her was too great to bear, and it snapped the marriage bond. How interesting it would have been had this odd couple, Arthur and Marilyn, actually stayed together.

The list this soul gave us of its past lives seemed to have genuine connections, but did not lead very far. The abortion issue (which needs to be read together with comments by other women in this book) was simply very sad to learn about. It was not a great surprise that she took too many prescription drugs, commonplace among those at the top in the entertainment industry. What was truly awful to hear was when—after some pressure had been applied by me—Marilyn confirmed what many had already guessed, that she was indeed murdered. Her unwillingness to identify the person or group who arranged and carried out the overdose does not signify an inability to do so. Everything is known in the spirit world. In the non-judgmental atmosphere of unconditional love that exists at Home, however, such a thing as identifying a murderer may not always be considered appropriate.

"The lessons that I learned at that time were of total degradation, of the impact that one human being can have upon another to strip away every sense of being human."

Anne Frank

1929-1945

Annelies Marie Frank, you were called by the seemingly Christian name of "Anne" by your family and friends. Was that because your liberal parents were Reform Jews and you lived in a religiously diverse neighborhood in Amsterdam?

There were a lot of reasons. I preferred Anne—it was simple and plain but had a ring to it. Also, at that time we did not want to draw attention to ourselves by using a Hebrew name, or an old family name.

Would you call your parents secular Jews? Your mother was quite religious, wasn't she?

There was a lot more religion practiced behind closed doors than openly for the world to see. This was not a time when we wore our religion on our sleeve for the entire world to know what we were. The ideals behind the religion were maintained and practiced; the strict procedures, mandated by some Orthodox Jews, were not. We still had Seder and times of celebration, but though we were conservative we were not strict in our practice.

Your father was scholarly and had a big library. Until the Nazis forced you to go to the Jewish Lyceum you attended a Montessori school. Tell us about the development of your ability and interest in being a writer.

209

From the beginning, Father let us know that the written word was tremendously powerful. He would read to us from some of the books he had in the library where we would be transported to different lands and exciting adventures. Very early on I saw that within the word was a whole world. It was not just the act of putting things down in writing—you could convey your entire imagination and your world onto paper. So, at a very early age, long before the period of our confinement, I began to experiment in transporting my life to paper.

Someone said that you used to shield your writing from view.

I was very forthcoming about all of my personal thoughts and desires in my writing. Because some of it was bridging on fantasy or flights of fancy, I did not want people to think I was not a dutiful daughter, or a religious person, or something like that, so I did not want to share my innermost self and my feelings with other people. I kept my journals personal for the most part.

The day came when you had a place to put it all down. Your father gave you an autograph book for your thirteenth birthday on June 12th, 1942. Did you intend to write a diary at the time?

Absolutely! And Father was sure that that was what I would do with it, as well.

Why did you address the diary to Kitty Egyedi?

She probably understood me better than anyone else. We would have long talks when I would pour out my innermost thoughts to her.

Was she your own age?

She was a couple of years older than I, but she was a very good listener, and she was not judgmental of anything that I thought, or imagined, or fantasized.

Three books containing your diary were recovered, but the period from December 1942 to December 1943 was missing. Did you keep a diary during that period?

Yes. During that period there were actually two additional books. They were very small in size, and one went missing when we moved. The second was discovered by a mouse where I had hidden it and torn apart to make a nursery nest. I let mother and family keep the shreds since they were no longer legible when I found them.

You re-wrote parts of the diary that we have; was there anything of special interest that was lost?

Not in that particular period. I was experiencing a period of fantasy expression and created my own little domain where everyone was the same.

Your family moved from Frankfurt to Aachen, then to Amsterdam to escape Nazi persecution. Then when things got bad, you hid from the Gestapo by moving into the Achterhuis, a secret annex at the back of your father's offices. Were you living in fear all that time?

Not in the beginning. At first I thought that people were overreacting to what was going on. But then I witnessed through the window the development of cruelties wrought on the people, which became very pervasive.

You had to wear the yellow star of David.

Yes, that was around the time when everybody was made to identify themselves and we were told we had no rights.

Please describe the people with whom your parents, your older sister, Margot, and you shared the Achterhuis.

Everyone was very gracious and sympathetic in the beginning. They were against the invasion and the occupation that was taking place. But throughout the period we were there they developed a frantic sense that my family was the cause of all of their problems! We were constantly in fear that somebody was going to say something to the authorities.

Fritz Pfeffer, a dentist and friend of the family, joined you. Was he useful as a dentist?

He was useful throughout the whole community as a dentist. He was called out in emergency situations—people with flaming infections...

He left your hiding place?

Only in the most structured of circumstances. There was an underground message system that went back and forth with people passing messages during the day and signals from window to window. We had quite a good method of communication which we don't believe the Gestapo ever picked up.

Did you personally ever leave the Achterhuis for a while?

No.

That must have felt very confining.

At first it was extremely irritating because I longed to take walks. To be totally confined caused me to go more and more into myself and take long strolls within my own imaginary world inside, where I could venture wherever I wanted to, and do whatever I wanted to do without repercussions.

Did you miss your cat, Moortje, whom you had to leave behind?

Tremendously. That was one of my deepest regrets in having to move because I no longer had it as a constant companion.

You don't mention your sister, Margot, much in your diary, but we do hear a bit more about Peter van Pels. How did you young people get on together?

Margot and I did not have the same ideas about a lot of things. We were sisters and there was a love for my sister there, but she was constantly in rebellion, forever arguing about what we should do and where we should go, and was basically unhappy. She seemed to jeopardize us sometimes when she would go out on little forays, looking for things and making contacts with people outside.

She was the quiet one, wasn't she?
That was the way she was portrayed, but as they say, "quiet waters run deep." She had a streak within her of rebellion. I was less rebellious. Instead of rebelling about outside things, I would retreat inside and get my satisfaction there.

How did you get on with Peter van Pels?
Peter was interesting to talk to and be with. He had some worldly experience of things that I had only read about. It was nice to have a live person—almost like listening to a recording of his adventures at times. How much of it was actual experience and how much was from his imagination I don't know, but it was delightful nonetheless.

Were you romantically interested in Peter at all?
Of course. [laughs] There wasn't much else to be interested in.

Were any of the people with whom you lived, and those who smuggled supplies to you, from your soul group at Home?
No.

Will you tell us about soul groups?
Soul groups are energies, which you call souls, who split off from the Source about the same time. When we prepare to go into human form we make our most serious contracts with soul mates to learn the most in-depth lessons. They have shared so many lives with us that we can depend upon them, and they know us well enough, and we know them well enough that we are confident they will do a good job of helping us learn our lessons. Some lessons are considered "good" lessons, such as being a loving spouse (if we are going to examine the lesson of

being in physical love and having a family). Others are considered "bad" lessons, such as when you want to experience degradation and depravation, with your soul mate possibly being a slave master over you.

The experience that I went through as Anne Frank was mainly one of being forced within myself and, during that time, of leaving a record for human posterity of my emotions and feelings about the various stresses and activities I experienced. This lifetime did not require soul mates to be present with me to fulfill my lessons because that would have detracted from the purpose of its being essentially an individual experience.

Do you know what happened to your soul group?

I cannot say there were no soul mates around at that time because, in fact, some of those who persecuted us were soul mates. I have had many lives together with the same soul mates prior to my life as Anne Frank. In any one lifetime not all of your soul group is incarnate.

How big is your most intimate group of soul mates?

Well, the entire group, which is loosely related, can be up to 144. The group that I have most often incarnated with—not all at the same time—is about two dozen people.

Then you were all discovered by the German Security Police on August 4, 1944. Someone tipped them off. Do you now know if the informant was Tonny Ahlers, or Willem van Maaren, or Lena van Bladeren-Hartog, and how do you now feel about that person?

Who the informer was really is immaterial because that was the next step along my lesson path. It was Lena who did it. She was trying to curry favor with someone because she had been caught out after curfew. I have no (what you would call) "hatred" or anything like that, because she was just a person who provided for the next step in my human experience. There is no judgment here at Home, just understanding of what occurred.

From your place now at Home, how do you feel about those

who have claimed that your personal diary was a fake and that the Jewish Holocaust never even happened?

[laughs] In human terms I feel sorry for them because they are denying something that took place from which they could learn. The diary itself, although it was part of my mission while in human form on Earth, was more for the lesson I got from writing it than it was for those to whom I left it. To deny something that is real shows the depth that such people are at in their spiritual development. People who do not believe in the existence of souls, or of the energy around us, will not see a tree even when they bump into one.

You wrote that it was hard to understand why the Jews were singled out for persecution so often. Do you know now that you are back Home?

Well, every group of people on planet Earth has to have a feeling that they are better than someone else, if they are in the early stages of their development. Those who are spiritually awake know that everybody is alike, identical at the core. The population on the planet during the time of my existence there, and for periods of time before that, had chosen to persecute the Jews for various reasons related to their personal characteristics, such as concentrating on becoming astute businessmen, and purveyors of fine arts and gems—so there was a jealousy factor. A number of people did not understand Jewish religious beliefs, which were at variance with the beliefs of Christianity; therefore, because we were not Christians, there was something to be hated about us. Every time one group does not understand another group, suspicion can grow into hatred. In my time period that is what happened with the Jews, and it is still happening now all over the planet with anyone who is different, which results in genocide or in persecution of different sects because beliefs are not the same.

You were all taken to the Gestapo's headquarters and then sent to the Punishment Barracks for hard labor before being herded onto the last train from Westerbork to the Auschwitz concentration camp. Tell us what that was like—were you brutalized?

We were all brutalized. It was as if every ounce of hatred that could be engendered by anyone on the planet at that time was funneled through our handlers, to be meted out upon us to assuage their angers and their fears. We were not looked upon as human at all; we were looked upon as animals, and sometimes even less than animals, as we were herded from place to place.

Were you physically attacked?

Not in a sexually physical way. I was hit with rifle butts and riding crops and a number of such objects. There were not so many sexual attacks occurring among the young women because we weren't considered even human by those herding us around, so it was beneath them to have any contact with us.

You were separated from your father, who survived. You escaped being sent directly to the gas chambers because you were just fifteen. But you were tattooed with an identification number, your head was shaved, and you were forced to do slave labor. The women were herded together in the freezing winter. Typhus broke out, and first Margot, then you died. What have I left out that was important to you during that experience?

The lessons that I learned at that time were of total degradation, of the impact that one human being can have upon another to strip away every sense of being human. During that period it was as if we existed only for the energy we could expend for the pleasures and the desires of those who had taken control of us. We lost all sense of identity at that time, all sense of personality, and we strove only to survive in whatever way was possible. What we became was—I cannot say "human"—we became biological animals who groped for every bit of nourishment that we could, from whatever source and in whatever way. That was the primary thing occupying us during every waking moment. It was a desire for survival.

In your diary you have written about your belief in God, and how you felt about human nature. How did your beliefs fare in your last weeks in the concentration camp?

I began to see that I had not had all of the material necessary to venture the opinions that I had penned on paper previously. My education was very definitely expanded while being in the concentration camps, so that I saw that the part of the world to which I had been exposed was minimalistic. The extent to which a person could go in treating another was way beyond the propriety that I thought had a firm hold on controlling behavior.

My belief in God was definitely tested during this period because I didn't like being tossed from place to place at the whim of others. I didn't feel that God should or would allow such a thing to occur. But, at that time, my belief in God was of a force outside of myself that had ultimate control. I now know that it was what I had contracted to experience, and that what I considered to be God at that time is the energy which is within the soul in each one of us. With my present knowledge I would have to deny myself in order to say that God does not exist.

Now that you are back Home, what would you say to anyone here who cannot understand why the Creator allows such brutality by some and such suffering by others?

I would say each one of us decides what it is in the physical realm that we wish to experience. We set up the parameters, whether it be that we wish (as I did) to go through degradation, physical pain, and deprivation, or else that we wish to be one of those who are experiencing total control over others and a total lack of what may be considered human compassion. We choose which roles we play, and it isn't a single God but the energy within us that makes the decision of what the lessons are going to be.

So was the whole Holocaust set up in advance?

The Holocaust was agreed to by all of the souls who participated on both sides of the gas chamber door.

Was the God-Force in agreement with this?

The God-Force is contained within all of us. Religious teaching that God is a singular old man with white hair and a beard in a long white flowing robe who directs from on high those who are on the right and those who are on the left, those who are privileged, those who are in the gutter, is in error. It is the energy within us, which is part of that Force, that makes those decisions. It is our freedom to choose to determine our individual experiences, and since we are each the God-Force, yes, we are in agreement.

Have you had any contact at Home with souls who were once in the Nazi Gestapo, or prison guards, and have you met the soul of Adolf Hitler?

I haven't taken the time to meet the soul who was Hitler, but I have met a number of the guards who were my physical contemporaries. We have discussed the various parts that we played and the lessons that we learned, so that I might get some knowledge of their experiences, and they could also gain knowledge of my experiences.

What is the nature of the lesson they went through?

They wanted to be in complete control of others, to have no sense of compassion whatsoever, to have a steel intent to break other humans to their will.

This was a role they took on?

This was a role that they wished to experience, a set of lessons.

Now that you are back Home together, do you accept that it was just a role, that it wasn't their inner nature?

Perfectly correct. In a lot of cases we thank each other for being the counterpart which enabled us to learn the lessons that we did.

What is your present occupation?

My present occupation is as an historian, you might say. I collect and document various experiences that have been had in human form. If anyone is doing research whether or not they may wish to go down to planet Earth and experience a certain characteristic, they come to me and ask me for whatever information I have of what that particular role might entail.

As an historian, do you work in a particular location?

Oh, no—I'm everywhere. The soul has the ability, being an energy form, to be in more than one place at once.

You don't need a library to do your work in?

I don't need a library; I have it contained within the energy force that is me. I can tap in energetically to what you would call the "akashic records," and I can tap into the universal experience and categorize and take millions of soul experiences and condense them into all of the experiences of that particular human characteristic for the curious person.

Sounds as if you are too busy to come down again.

Well, I haven't planned coming down yet because it's so much fun helping other people to decide what experiences, what lessons they wish to have.

Have you met with Peter van Pels since your return?

Just briefly. We laughed about some misconceptions we had about each other and the experiences we went through.

Thinking about the way your life and your diary have been handled by historians, is there anything they've got particularly wrong which you would like to correct?

Wrong is in the eye of the perceiver. What people get out of the writing depends upon each individual person. I was young, naive, not too worldly. Some see it as having been written by a very selfish person. Some see me as a very cold person, just observing things. Others see me as very compassionate and

219

involved in the writing. It all depends on the reader and whether they identify with the energy that is contained within the book. So some people have totally wrong impressions of what I went through, because they are judgmental and they cannot see the growth and dawning awareness, the fluctuations in my emotions reflected in the writings, the moodiness that occurred sometimes because of the desolation that I found myself in. To say that somebody has it wrong is only to say that when you read a book you may not allow yourself to feel and remember exactly what is within it. That is not what the book is for; it is so that you may find a piece of yourself within it, and experience within those feelings the type of lesson that I went through.

Thank you, Anne Frank, for talking with us.

Commentary

Toni: This was an interesting experience because Anne's energy went back and forth, at first making me sense her as an innocent, naive person, then feeling her coming over like a school teacher. It was an unusual energetic roller-coaster, as if she were flipping between her current position and her former human self.

I have never heard anybody talk about the celestial akashic records before in the way she did, that she could be a compiler and interpreter of all the varied experiences souls have had. My contact with the records has always been on an individual basis, where each soul goes back and reflects upon the series of their own previous experiences, or taps into somebody else's experience, but solely to see what such an experience was like. Anne was talking about comparing and contrasting lots of experiences to see what a model of them all might be like. Fascinating!

Peter: Some of the mystery and the pain of Anne's life is revealed here in this serious and helpful interview. Apart from letting us into some of the secrets historians have longed to know—who would have guessed that a mouse destroyed one of the missing diaries—Anne also spoke about two important spiritual issues: the nature of the soul group, and the nature of adverse experiences as soul lessons. She did so with a clarity that justifies her working with the Akashic database at Home to help other souls choose future lessons for themselves.

It was helpful to have further detailed confirmation of soul groups, which have been well documented by between-life regression specialists. The large basic group numbers up to 144 souls who have been detached from the Source. This larger group forms a talent pool from which individual souls may draw helpers, though usually a smaller selection is made from the 12 to 24 souls who are known most intimately

In most lifetimes personal contracts are made between incarnating soul group members for mutual assistance in learning lessons. It is interesting to hear that the members of Anne's human family did not number among her soul group. She did, however, say, "Some of those who persecuted us were soul mates." She calls the concentration camp guards "my physical contemporaries," though they appear not to have been members of her soul group. But despite the physical degradation and anguish she suffered at their human hands, she makes it clear that, back Home, she shares laughter and not recriminations with her former persecutors.

The larger issue of souls' deliberately choosing to experience negativity (both as perpetrators of "evil" and as their victims) is most helpfully addressed in the interview. Readers of my interview of Adolph Hitler (in book one of the series) were faced with his soul's incredible assertion that a prior agreement was made by millions of souls to take part in the Holocaust—not only as his supporters, but also as the many victims of Nazi oppression. Here, as one of those victims, Anne gives her confirmation that this was true for her, asserting, "The Holocaust was agreed to by all of the souls who participated on both sides of the gas chamber door."

Strange as it may seem to the human mind, Anne, the child-victim who has returned Home, is now concerned with exploring the various parts which she and other souls, on both sides in the Holocaust, once played, and the lessons they learned, so that each side may gain insights from the experiences of the other side. Listening to what she has to say (if we are at all willing to learn from this harsh aspect of living as a human being), we might be enabled to see that our own lives, like Anne Frank's, are lived for the purpose of learning the lessons life has to teach our soul and, as a result (hopefully), growing in spiritual wisdom.

"I accepted that which I wrote about, and in accepting it,
I became it. That took me then into what would be called clinical
depression to such an extent that I felt so trapped that I no
longer wished to continue."

Sylvia Plath
1932 –1963

Sylvia Plath, your father was a professor of German and a specialist on bees. Did you get your passion for writing and for art from him or from your mother, Aurelia, who was a high school teacher, or elsewhere?

I got my love of being able to record what was important to me from both of them. Neither one of them had my particular interests. Also neither one of them spent that much time with me, nor with each other. They were very much involved in their own pursuits, and it was almost as if we had a compartmentalized house, with each person staying in their own drawer or cupboard.

Your mother had been your father's student and was 21 years his junior, wasn't she?

Yes, and it was almost as if he had grown tired of her and she had grown up and no longer needed a father.

Was their relationship one of the sources of the feminist viewpoint you developed later on?

Absolutely. I saw within my mother what, first, a sense of hero worship could do to a person, and how, when you became infatuated with someone, you gave up your power to them. Then, when the disillusionment set in and you tried to recapture your own essence, there was difficulty.

223

Women who love too much?

That's exactly what it was. When your infatuation so encompasses the definition you make of yourself—but it is not reciprocated—you are left with a disconnect from the picture you brought into being.

Was your mother's problem solved by your father's death?

It gave her a sense of being cut off from that which she desired but which she could not truly possess.

Did you inherit a depressive tendency from your father's family? Did you choose before incarnating to experience clinical depression?

That was one of the lessons I wished to experience in human form. I wanted to know what it was to have a sense of foreboding overriding my entire existence and have a cloud over me that I had to find my way in.

[Toni: She's showing me a fog so thick you have to feel with your hands to find out where you're going   and who else is in the fog with you.]

What would the benefit of such a choice be for you?

To enjoy the sunshine, to enjoy a sense of freedom, and a sense of being able to see and connect with everything that was out there. Unless you experience the opposite of something, you can't truly appreciate what the ultimate experience can be.

That opposite (depression) was overwhelming for you.

It proved overwhelming. I did not anticipate it was going to be as devastating on me as it turned out to be, but then I set the parameters so that I got what I wanted.

Your high school and college education were supported by the scholarships you won. You graduated from Smith College with top honors and, later, taught there for a while. Did you have the idea of an academic future for yourself then, or did your heart embrace poetry more?

I knew from the experience of seeing my parents that academia gave a sense of continuity to one's life, and also that there were certain advantages—summer breaks and various times when you had total freedom to do what you wanted. When I first finished school, I had no real opportunities to do anything other than to remain in academia, so I let it be my prison, but my security.

Prison?

I feared the unknown. That was because my depressions were starting to come. Staying where I was familiar defined the limits of my world, so that I didn't have to have a fear of coming up against something that I didn't know or didn't understand. I knew the limits that existed within that institution (Smith College), where I could go, what I could do, and what was expected of me.

You wrote "Ennui" at Smith, It was a poem of bitterness and disappointment. Did you feel let down by life at that time, or was your emptiness a reflection of depression?

First and foremost it was an expression of where I was mentally going at that time. As I have said, I felt that Smith was my prison, and that was a sense of being contained and not being able to reach outside of myself to have new experiences. Depression is like that. You lose a sense of anything but what is there with you. You can't envision going beyond where you are at that time, and you sense that if you try to go beyond where you are, you will be so overwhelmed that you will be destroyed in the experience.

As you were writing that poem, were you influenced by F. Scott Fitzgerald's The Great Gatsby?

More than anything else. I could feel exactly where his writings went. I could sense the frustration. I could sense the limits that were there, and it very much mirrored what I was feeling.

225

Then in 1953, during your junior year at Smith, came work at Mademoiselle *magazine and experiences in New York, which feature in your novel* The Bell Jar. *They brought about a major episode of depression and your first suicide attempt. Tell us about that time.*

The Bell Jar was almost a diary of what I was going through at the time—set, of course, from somebody else's perspective, but it mirrored the energies and the depressions and the frustrations that I was feeling. Even though the very words weren't there, if you take and put yourself into the energy of the book, you will be able to feel the state that I was in then. In putting it down on paper, like anything that you proclaim, you claim it, so that at that time I accepted that which I wrote about, and in accepting it, I became it. That took me then into what would be called clinical depression to an extent that I felt so trapped that I no longer wished to continue.

Were you influenced by Salinger's The Catcher in the Rye*?*
Not really.

That's a mistake that commentators have made.
There were some similarities, but if you compare the two, the energies are totally different.

Some of the energies were of a feminist response. Can you tell us about that?
When people feel trapped, every experience within their universe takes on monumental proportions. We were going through a time where women who wanted to do things were prevented from doing them simply because of their gender. Very insignificant little things, such as going into a store or a restaurant and seeing a gentleman who had come in after you served first, created in me an energy of being totally slapped and totally relegated to the gutter. It made me want to respond, to say, "Women, let yourselves be seen!" Of course, because of my depression, I did not have the strength to come full bore into the

fight, so I did it subtly within my writings, because I saw it as one of the biggest things affecting the feminine gender at that time.

In particular, wasn't it the erotic choices available to men that were not available to women?
That was but one part of it. That was what would sell. That was what would be embraced by men. That was a way of taking and shaking them by their private parts as a means of getting their attention and letting them know that there was some seriousness.

But there was also a positive element in the book.
There was a positive element in that it was a clarion call for all people to examine where they were and to know that they did not have to remain there, that there were ways of examining their situation, dealing with the elements of it, and creating anew.

Shock treatment was a part of your human experience. Tell us about it.
It is something that I would rather not have done. It is a dramatic way of dealing with a situation. I liken it to taking a 20-lb. sledgehammer to kill a fly. It has such an impact that it deals not only with the problem that you are experiencing (which is an electrical and chemical malfunction within your body), but impacts the very essence of everything that is you. The electricity may come in and be directed toward the brain, but it impacts your motor skills, it impacts all centers within your brain, and it is as if you give yourself a stroke and then have to go through rehabilitation.

Looking back now, do you think you suffered permanent damage from this shock treatment?
I know I did.

And you had it more than once?

Yes. At that time I was in such a state that I was crying out for anything that would alleviate the pain that I was in—pain on a mental and emotional level rather than the physical.

You won a Fulbright scholarship to study at Cambridge. Angry at double standards in male behavior, you demanded sexual freedom as a woman and believed in matching intellectual with erotic pursuits. You met the poet Ted Hughes there, and married him. Was your life at Cambridge a time of awakening for you?

I like to see it as one of the times of peaceful seas.

Peaceful?

Peaceful seas, calm oceans. The majority of my life was stormy and wave-tossed. Cambridge was my most calm time, when I wasn't totally assailed constantly by the depressions, by the fears, by the anxieties. It was a time when I was able to sit back and see the sun, although in England that was a bit difficult all the time! But I was able to get out of the fog.

Back in Boston, as a married woman, did you submerge yourself in helping Ted develop his poetic voice, but at the expense of your own?

One of my experiences from my childhood was the intensity of my mother's desire to do whatever she could to get the attention of my father, to sacrifice aspects of herself for his pursuits. I fell into that pattern with Ted. I had grown to need him. I had grown to almost worship him, as my mother had my father, and I was experiencing her life all over again.

In fact, commentators have said that you were very demanding of his attention when in groups of friends.

I was extremely jealous. As I had seen, when you are totally infatuated with someone, you want their time. When you are alone, you throw yourself into the situation. When you are in public, you are constantly setting up a defense perimeter that protects (as you feel) your territory. One way to make sure that he was not wooed by others was constantly to be between him and anyone else who was there. So to the perception of others, I was constantly demanding his attention. It was to divert him from the allure of anything.

You failed in your attempt, I think.

I was so overly protective that it drove him away.

While you were in Boston, you attended Robert Lowell's poetry-writing class, where you met Anne Sexton. Tell us about your friendship and the development of confessional poetry.

Anne had a totally new perspective from anything that I had previously experienced. She came from a different background. She came from a background where trust allowed people to accept themselves and exactly what their situation was, and not to be intimidated by it. I was never able to adopt all of her various qualities as I would have liked, but it gave me the opportunity to see the other side of the fence, and in that to be able to do some comparisons, to be able to feel and to long for some of the freedoms that she had. Some of those freedoms were denied me because of my mental problems.

Your first book of poems, The Colossus, *was somewhat confessional, as was your religious allegory "Lady Lazarus." Recalling your work from the perspective of Home, with knowledge of the adulation and criticism it has received, how do you now view your poetry, essays, and children's stories?*

In my work I was attempting to allow others to feel what I was feeling—the good parts, I hoped, of what I was feeling. I now see that I had planned this as my Earth's work, so that I could act as a catalyst for those who read my work. My audience was varied, and my poetry was like a field of wildflowers, not of one variety but of every possible and imaginable species and variety, so that in my work, if there were only one poem that resonated with a person, that someone could identify with and therefore get a heightened experience of life or a needed change in direction, that was my ultimate goal. In my incarnate life, however, I did not have that view of it. I was writing for myself. I was pouring out the aspects of where I was at, where I would have liked to have been, and a happy medium.

You had half a dozen years or so living with Ted Hughes and bore two children. Then things fell apart. He had affairs, and you separated. Was there violence in that relationship?

Physically there was frustration on both sides, because neither one of us matched the expectations of the other, and out of frustration we acted out. It much more affected me on an emotional basis, because it was again stripping away all my ideas of what life could be, what a relationship could be, and saying they weren't true—they no longer existed. It was like removing wallpaper that you had spent eons and eons of time perfecting exactly the way you wanted it, and then having someone come in and tear it down and throw it in the fire.

Your father, whose big medical mistake led to his death when you were only eight, appears as the driving force in the poem "Daddy." There is reference to Ted Hughes as well. You will have heard the criticism about your references to the Jews. Would you like to tell us about the poem and your reaction to the critics?

I would like at this time to say "critics be damned!" but in my place here, there are no such things. [laughs]

While I wrote a majority of my poems for people, this poem was for and of me. This poem was talking of my frustration, talking of some good times that existed, talking of the lessons that I went through as I progressed through my life, of the frustrations I had in various situations. It spoke of how my soul felt, mirrored through my physical body. It was of experiences. It was of a perspective of just one person, one persona, and the perceptions that I had then. It was not meant to be instructive, condemnatory, judgmental. It was an expression of my heart and soul crying out about what I perceived at that time as my triumphs and injustices.

You held grief at the Nazi debacle very close to your chest, didn't you, because that poem was written a long time after Hitler had gone.

It was of the concepts of people being taken and led by others and suffering the consequences, because of giving their soul, their existence, to another in faith, in trust, and then seeing that there was nothing of themselves in that picture.

Much has been made of Ted's editing of Ariel and Other Poems, *removing 12 of your chosen poems and substituting 15 others. He has also been criticized for destroying the final volume of your Journal. How do you view these issues now from the literary and the personal point of view?*

From the literary point of view, it was jealousy on his part, trying to make something that would have been spectacular, less so, so that the shining of the star was dimmed. From a spiritual lesson aspect, it was another example of my allowing myself to be diverted, directed, controlled by others, not knowing enough of who I was and what I could accomplish to speak up for myself.

You speak as if this had happened during your lifetime, but it took place after your death.

The actuality of "time" is a very difficult thing for you to understand. We have no linear time here, and the energies of what we learn while we incarnate can be examined and revisited from Home after we return. To him I was still alive, so I am talking of it from the perspective of whatever time in my life that it occurred. The energy was the same—he knew he could control me in life so he thought nothing of doing it in death.

The destruction of the last book in your Journal—was that because there were unflattering things in it?

Yes. It was when I finally recognized how I had allowed myself to be manipulated, how I had allowed myself to give up my energy to him. And also it recorded some of—what would be construed in normal society as— the negative things about him, some of the lies and manipulations.

Have you met with Ted's soul at Home since his death?
Oh, yes. We have joked about the dramas that we put each other through for the purpose of learning different energetic lessons.

How do you now view his poetry?
His poetry was of a different kind. His poetry was more for entertainment and a little stimulation. It was more of an intellectual genre, whereas mine was emotional.

You didn't feed off each other very much.
Not at all.

You had attempted suicide before, and you ended your life at the age of 30 by gassing yourself in an oven. People have said Ted murdered you: Is that true or false?
Did he physically turn on the gas? No. Did my emotional turmoil over his not meeting my expectations play a part? A very big part. Did my interaction with the world and not thinking, because of my mental condition, that I could stand one more moment play a part? Yes.

Was it a long-planned suicide?
Suicide? Practically from my childhood suicide ideation was my constant companion.

Did you, at the time, expect to have life after your death?
No. I simply thought, because I was not spiritual at all in that incarnation, that I would be out of my suffering.

What actually happened to you when you died?
[laughs] We partied as soon as I went to the Other Side. It was a matter of my having accomplished a lot, lesson-wise, during my short physical encounter, but also leaving a legacy of

energy that would help many. I realized that I did not complete the lessons that I had signed up for—primarily that I would learn about myself, and be able to triumph over the depression, and triumph over the control of others—so I will have to come down and experience them again. But at the same time, there were no recriminations from anybody; it was just sort of a "Whoops! Pulled the plug a little bit too soon."

You weren't censured for ending your life so early?

Oh, absolutely not, because a soul has freedom of choice, and the freedom of choice is at all places throughout our existence. It's when we start the lessons, how we do the lessons, if we want to re-do the lessons, when we go on to something else. There's no censure, because we're the ones who decide what we're going to do, and all we are doing, say with a suicide, is rewriting our own script and choosing to approach it from a different direction.

What is the purpose of taking all these lessons?

The purpose is to have the wisdom of them. In the realm of the soul there is nothing but unconditional love. There is no sense of emotional fulfillment, such as the satisfaction of helping another person, or the emotions that you get in loving another human, which is a romantic love, as opposed to the universal love we have. There is no experiencing the pain of a depression that you can't seem to get out of. All of those give us a sense of the magnificence of the unconditional love.

There's no judgment?

Absolutely no judgment. There's simply evaluation: Did we learn enough, did we experience enough to truly appreciate and to understand and have the wisdom of that particular aspect of existence, or should we do it again?

Are you coming down to suffer depression again, Sylvia?

I'm going to come down to conquer depression in the human form.

And will the Earth be available for you to come to?

There will be a planet. There will be a plane, a third-dimensional stage to experience on.

Thank you, Sylvia Plath, for talking with us.

It has been my pleasure.

Commentary

Toni: There was much depth in Sylvia's soul. At the beginning I had a sense of a very Earth-bound soul as she flashed back to herself in that body. During the interview it was as if we were going back and forth between Earth and Home. When we talked about problems I felt her perception of the depth of her despair, the depth of the experience that she had gone through. Then she became the spiritual evaluator weighing the experience and the wisdom that the physical problems provided. She was taking me back and forth, reliving some of the experiences and stepping back and taking a look at what she had gained from the lesson. It was very interesting, almost like a seesaw—going back and forth: physical, spiritual, physical, spiritual, physical, spiritual. I sensed she may have been in the process of deciding how to complete the lessons next time.

Peter: With the exception of a paragraph where our notation needed a little clarification by her, this dialogue spoke of Sylvia's carefully nuanced use of language, as one would expect from a writer of her caliber.

She was very forthcoming, very eloquent, especially when talking about her husband, Ted Hughes. I expected her comments to be more hurt (she got close), more angry, and quite a lot more feminist in tone, but the calming atmosphere at Home may have smoothed her feelings out somewhat.

The dreadful use of shock treatment clearly did her no good, though at the time she desperately craved a solution to her massive depression. I was the one who felt angry as she explained what it felt like to receive that barbaric therapy.

What intrigued me most in our dialogue was when she gave us a helpful glimpse of social life at Home. "We partied as soon as I went to the Other Side," she said, and I was struck by the normalcy of it all. Sylvia Plath and friends—there just had to be a party! (I wonder what they could substitute for booze?) But the revelry was followed anon by self-evaluation, which felt almost like a sigh of disappointment that her suicide had snuffed out too soon not only her talented life, but also her freely chosen lesson, which, in consequence, must be experienced again. She left no room for us to doubt that it would be her decision to suffer depression again, because otherwise her soul would not grow in wisdom as fully.

Sylvia did not qualify her statement that souls have freedom of choice, a freedom at all points throughout their existence, on Earth and at Home. There is no judgment nor censure, not even requirements concerning what must be experienced on Earth, because each soul decides what it is going to do when it incarnates, and if it fails in any attempt it will choose a different way to learn the same lesson. And the soul of Sylvia Plath will do so as well when next it incarnates, whenever and wherever that may be.

"Words are magical.
Words paint pictures in the minds of people, and if you put your
own coloration into the words, you have captured
the imagination and the heart of your listener."

Barbara Jordan
1936-1996

Barbara Charline Jordan, you were the very first African-American woman from a southern state (Texas in your case) to serve in the US House of Representatives. Were your parents among the people whose influence got you there?

My parents were extremely supportive. From the time we were very young, they always put the energy out that we could do whatever we put our minds to. They facilitated placing me into situations so that I could learn my strengths, learn to deal with people, learn to manipulate the thoughts of others so they just had to have me as their spokesperson—I don't like the word "manipulate," but it is correct.

Tell us about your special relationship with John Ed Patten, your maternal grandfather.

If ever there were someone who could provide you energetically with the strength of the Rock of Gibraltar, that person was my grandfather. He believed in having faith in himself, and in imparting to others faith in themselves. He would be one of your biggest motivational speakers were he alive today, because he could take someone who had scraped a knee and was crying hysterically and transform that event into a lesson on how to better yourself, how to learn from it and carry that message on to others.

You learned to do this while you were helping him with the scrap metal business?

Well, you might call it scrap metal. He used to say it was taking the things other people didn't want and enabling us to have the things we wanted.

Truly motivational.

He could put a twist on anything and everything.

Was that a good background for a politician?

[laughs] Oh, you'd better believe it!

You won a national Baptist church oratory contest and awards at high school for your skill as an orator. In 1952 you won the Texas State Ushers Oratorical Contest; then the national oration contest. You become a first-class debater at university. What inspired you to develop that skill?

To me it was going into a world where you could have—I don't like the word "control," but you could have direction over how people perceived what was going on. Words are magical. Words paint pictures in the minds of people, and if you put your own coloration into the words, you have captured the imagination and the heart of your listener. In debating, in particular, I would take obscure topics, things that people either couldn't possibly be interested in, or things that they would be diametrically opposed to, and I would find the right words to shape an image that the listeners just had to have and had to be a part of, which was training for my future life, of course.

You didn't become a preacher like your father, grandfather, and great-grandfather. You said, "It is reason, not passion, which must guide our deliberations, guide our debate, and guide our decision." Were you a religious person?

I had a strong connection to my sense of the Creator, the Source. I was very comfortable with my relationship with the Source. I did not feel that I had to go out and convince people. I thought that was a personal passion of my relatives, that they needed to reinforce their beliefs within themselves by getting others to share them. I found that it was more of a personal challenge to shape a whole group dynamic in order to better people's physical lot. I left the afterlife and spiritual issues to the preachers while I dealt with the physical issues.

How do you view the virtual insistence in America's current political scene of being willing to say the word God and being seen going to church?

I think it's an absolutely ridiculous problem that small minds have put up to take away a person's freedom of choice, to deprive them of having their own concepts, their own feelings about their connection to the Source, and who they are. We cannot mandate what a person says. In fact, by reason of the Bill of Rights, we do have freedom of speech, but the politicians now do not apply that freedom to a handful of words such as "God" and "church." There is fear within political circles that someone will find a power, a sense of safety, a redemption within themselves, that will take them away from the control that can be exerted over them by others.

How do you then see the proclamation by a president, for example, that he is guided by God?

[laughs] People can convince themselves of anything of which they want to be convinced. Various leaders throughout the planet have empowered themselves with their ideas of the source of information. In point of fact, all souls have a connection to the God-Source, so all souls are empowered by the God-Source, not just one who will stand on a soapbox and proclaim it.

Were you specially gifted, or was your success in graduating magna cum laude *in political science at Texas Southern University, and then excelling at the Boston University School of Law, a matter of sheer determination and hard work?*

Study came very easily to me because I could identify with the words. I could feel the words. If I read something, I was within the mind of the writer, and I knew what they were saying. I didn't have to sit down and memorize what they were saying. I had the experience of it, so it was very easy for me to accept or reject the principles that they were putting forth. But at least I had the experience of knowing what had been said by the author, so when it came to the way in which professors decide if you've learned things—examinations—I was right there and I could, as they say, regurgitate for the person asking the questions exactly what they wanted to know. But I had a deeper feeling for what the author was putting into the material. And even in a lecture, when a professor would say something, I heard his words but I felt his energy behind them. I felt whether he was saying the words because they were part of his syllabus, or he was saying them because they were part of his soul, his energy.

Was this intuition a gift that you had prearranged before you came down?
         It's something that I had honed over many lifetimes. I was around in the time of Cicero and in the time of the great philosophers, where we debated the words. I was among the Egyptians when they began to record thoughts. I was part of the time of Gutenberg and the printing press and the way of using words to get them out to the masses, not just the super-intellectual means used by the educated. I played around in several lifetimes with phraseology to be able to get people to feel the thoughts that were being carried upon the words and going through them. Many lifetimes were spent on physical communication.

Would any of those lifetimes be regarded as significant by historians today?
         Potentially. It depends upon your choice of horses.
By which you mean historians? Were you someone whose name I might recognize?
         You might recognize Plato.

Thank you, Plato! In 1959 you (as Barbara Jordan) were admitted to the Massachusetts and Texas bars and commenced practice in Houston. But almost immediately you became involved in the Kennedy-Johnson presidential campaign. What drew you into politics?

The potential of what can be done within the arena of politics; the fact that, particularly during that period of time, the emerging politicians (Kennedy in particular) were not of the same mold that we had seen. These were people holding beliefs different from those of the common politicians. These people brought a freshness, a new awareness to the political scene, and with it the possibility of getting out of the male Anglo-Saxon Protestant groove into Catholicism, and women, and including those of other beliefs and religions.

After two attempts to gain public office, you were elected in 1966 and served two terms in the Texas Senate, the first black woman ever to serve there. Later you said, "We are attempting to fulfill our national purpose, to create and sustain a society in which all of us are equal." Do you now see significant progress having been made toward that goal during the past 50 years?

[laughs] Significant progress on some fronts, only to be slowed down on others. What has shifted more than anything else is the importance on the political scene of the war chest—the money. In my time, if a person had an ideology, an openness, they could create a group of volunteers around them who would help get the word out, and it wasn't necessary that they have the elaborate media blitzes that are needed nowadays in order for a person to become recognized. It was what you might call a grass-roots approach. It was very, very effective because you had personal contact with as many people as possible. Now "personal" contacts are made through the media, through television commercials, and billboards, where the money that is generated within the elections puts the face out there, and it's the face that is accepted, not the message.

There's also the Internet, isn't there?

241

The Internet is playing into the whole political scene in two ways: It's giving the exposure to people, but it's also giving people the ability to study some of the issues. There are actually interchanges that can take place where people can examine what's being said, the feasibility of it, the practicality of it, the authenticity of it.

That raises a question that many people wonder about. How much detail of our life on planet Earth are you able to see from your place now at Home in the Spirit World?
As much as we want. We can tap into anything. We can tap into everything.

Thoughts? Conversations?
We can tap into those if we choose, but normally because of propriety we don't. We allow the souls to have some sense of privacy within their thoughts. But even if we do tap into thoughts, we don't interact, so it's in most cases sort of like tuning into a dumb sitcom.

Most sitcoms are dumb!
Well, I don't want to take anything away from those for whom it's their sole means of entertainment—but they do need to get a life!

Are there any other inhabited planets that you monitor?
Yes, there are a number of other planets. They have different types of existences from that on planet Earth. Planet Earth is the only one that is in the total duality stage at this time.

You mean that Earth has positive and negative energy?
Where there's positive and negative and there's an opposite for everything that exists. There are some planets that are just inhabited for people to experience one particular thing, which might be the development of the mind, or the development of a physical prowess, the experience of warfare, or developing different means of communication. There are no

other planets that have the emotional lessons that the planet Earth has, because to have the emotional lessons, you must have the duality, the presence of diametrically opposed action.

Then you became heavily involved with the Democratic Party and, in 1972, you were elected as a Democrat to the United States House of Representatives, the first black woman representative from a southern state to serve there. Did you encounter much racism and sexism in the Congress?

[laughs] Absolutely! But it wasn't really any more than I had anticipated. I had been well trained, by the various experiences I had had during my education and when I was first an attorney, as to the prejudice that can be heaped upon one, so it was more or less just an aside that I swept away. I did not let it bury my message or bury me emotionally so that I was unable to function. I just acknowledged that it was there, said that's the experience that those people need to have, and I went my own way.

On a camping trip, a year or two before going to Washington, DC, you met your partner, Nancy Earl. You both kept your lesbian relationship a secret for 20 years. Was your joint silence to protect you from political discrimination?

At that time there was only one thing worse than being a black southerner, and that was being homosexual. My word, my message, my mission would have been totally ignored and unimportant, because the only thing people would have seen was an aberration in nature, which was how homosexuality was thought of at that time. I would have been condemned by mainstream society, by all the religious organizations, and by the political parties, as something that detracted from their mission.

Remembering his Symposium, *was Plato also homosexual?*

Plato played the field. Plato experienced what there was to experience in all its forms.

You said, "There is no way that I can equate discrimination on the basis of sexual preference with discrimination on the basis of skin color." Did you mean that being a lesbian involved making a sexual preference rather than being homosexually hard-wired from birth?

That wasn't what I meant by the statement. The statement was that there were things that could be excused of a person because society believed they had no choice. Society did believe, in some realms, that homosexuality was a choice, so to that degree, yes, that was what I meant. To a larger degree, I meant that all blacks were lumped together as just being the progeny of slaves and of people who were lesser. Homosexuals at that time (and to this day by some religions) were considered to be evil, abnormal, a threat energetically to anyone who came in contact with them, almost as if we had a virus that was contagious. A leper is a perfect example.

But is the homosexual hard-wired—in other words, it isn't a personal preference but something that you have to do?

How you perceive it depends upon the lesson that you came down to experience. If a person's lesson is to experience homosexuality, with all of the condemnations of society and dealing with all the lessons of being hated and considered outcasts from society, being considered crazy, evil, then, yes, it is "hard-wired" and a part of you from the very beginning of that lifetime.

It may, however, also appear to be a choice that one makes because one energetically connects with a member of the same sex but cannot energetically connect with someone of the opposite sex, so it becomes a choice as to how to spend the majority of one's life. People may deny their feelings and enter a heterosexual marriage, or they may lead dual lives. Your wording of "hard-wiring" implies only that it was a part of the plan decided before incarnation with no way to deny the tendency. I differentiate in that souls may choose to hide from their feelings even if they had planned to have that as a lesson.

Lyndon Johnson helped you secure a place on the House Judiciary Committee. Tell us about your relationship with President Johnson.

Lyndon was a fantastic person. He was a down-home boy who thought we needed more Texans in places of power. He was a person who didn't see color, didn't see religious connections, didn't see sexual connections. If he thought you had your head screwed on right, and you were from Texas, he would do anything to help promote you in your career.

Lucky you were from Texas! In your famous Judiciary Committee speech in 1974, supporting the impeachment of President Nixon, you said, "My faith in the Constitution is whole; it is complete; it is total. And I am not going to sit here and be an idle spectator to the diminution, the subversion, the destruction, of the Constitution." How do you feel about the health of the US Constitution today?

[*Toni: I'm being given a picture of a document in scroll form with band-aids on it.*]

Parts of the Constitution are in the intensive care unit. That is because some people in power think that the reasons behind the founding fathers' wording of the Constitution should be interpreted with new meaning. They want something that fits into their desired use of the words. They resist going back to the original document, to the energy existing at that time, wherein the people were being endowed with individual powers that had not previously been allowed them because of the tyranny of the oppressive rulers they had been under.

The country is leaning toward a power struggle within the government—not just from the presidency, but in the various levels of government where each section has its own power struggle going on, its own thrust to dictate and mandate to others. The interpretation of the Constitution is being done by the light of the reader of the Constitution. If their light is red, there is anger and the taking away of freedoms. If it is white, there is a benevolence in the interpretation. If it is blue, there is an adherence to their speech at the time. There is an ever-living, ever-changing energy around the Constitution. They could just leave it alone and let it speak for itself and not try to rewrite it with their interpretations, but they're never going to do that.

Your speech in 1976 to the Democratic National Convention is considered to have marked a high point in modern political oratory. Was it exciting to give such a speech?

To me, any time that my feelings could be felt by others was a highlight, and I felt that I was reaching the people. I felt that they didn't see me; they didn't care about my past, my future, my present. They hung on the words that I delivered.

Talking in the U.S. Commission on Immigration Reform, which you chaired, you said, "It is both a right and a responsibility of a democratic society to manage immigration so that it serves the national interest." Developed nations worldwide are struggling with this issue. What is your view of the way forward to a just solution?

The way forward is that we must respect the rights of all human beings. That said, we must also understand that there are conflicting rights that exist in a situation such as immigration. We have the rights of those whose country it is, who work to support the government, to provide the schools, to provide the health care, against the rights of people who come into the country illegally and want to become leaches upon that system without giving it their energy. We must honor them as individuals, but we must be firm in saying that those who provide the government have the right to say how that government functions and how their monies are being used. It's not taking away from the honoring of the person who has come in, as a human being; it is just making them comply with what society calls fairness.

In 1973 you had a heart attack and were found to be suffering from multiple sclerosis. You kept on working but ended up in a wheelchair and retired from public service. Do you know now why that happened to you?

246

By 1973 I had completed all of the lessons I came down here for. I had created new pathways; I had created new energies; I had put out a standard for others. It was time for me to live out the last of my life just enjoying life as Barbara.

Could you have healed yourself of MS?
All of us have the ability to heal ourselves, but on an unconscious level, I knew that had I been restored to health, I would have gone right back into the fray.

What do you see as your greatest achievement?
My greatest achievement was showing that if the soul puts out the energy, it may experience whatever it wishes to experience. If your energy is employed in communicating with others, and you do that by exchanging ideas rather than dictating to them, then, after having enlightened multitudes of people, you can have them make their own choices based upon their conscious beliefs without just following you like lemmings. You have then provided the light for them to remember their wisdom.

Thank you, Barbara Jordan, for talking with us.
It has been my pleasure.

Commentary
Toni: Very powerful energy! Barbara was very particular and thoughtful about the words being used. There were times when a lexicon of words flashed in front of me, as if there were a selection available of exactly the proper and most powerful word to use. It was interesting to see this going on in the background, almost like a computer screen.

The depth of her feeling for humanity and drive for communication involved her total energy—everything in her being was geared toward and energized by a sense of sharing, whether it be in communication or experience. A very powerful lady, but somewhat understated. There was so much dynamism, yet no sense of trying to overpower. The image I see is of the neighborhood "Officer Friendly" trying to keep everyone out of trouble and headed down their respective pathways.

Peter: This was a remarkable interview. Her confidence, expressed with elegant and thoughtful choice of words, was only part of the equation. There was a special energy about this soul that even I felt strongly. As we finished and had switched off the tape recorder, I asked about other lives the soul lived previously. It mentioned that in the Elizabethan era it had lived the life of Sir Francis Bacon. That plus Plato—wow! All this might seem a little hard to grasp, but in that moment it was totally believable. As Shakespeare might have put it, "One soul in its time plays many parts."

Barbara brought down immense talent, which, sadly, was only half-recognized by others. The Democratic Party delegates did have a moment to recognize it the day she blew their convention away with her oratory. Congress applauded her wise leadership in the impeachment debate. But Barbara Jordan allowed her talents to be understated. Perhaps she did not need to excel as a human being, though well equipped to do so. She had to learn the specific lessons that she had chosen before incarnating, and then she was free to go Home again. Still, having this valuable glimpse of her depth of character, we may choose to wonder now why she was not given more recognition. Racial discrimination was largely to blame. Lucky for us that L.B.J. was somewhat color-blind and he did give that nice Texas gal's political career a helpful boost.

I hammered Barbara on the homosexuality issue, as it is a thorny one. There is still a lot of misunderstanding as to whether homosexuals have a choice in the matter of their sexual orientation. Barbara acknowledged a measure of personal freedom—the freedom to be true to one's pre-destined homosexuality and Come Out, or to choose to hide it from society (and even from oneself). She and her lesbian partner chose the middle ground. They had to be secret about their relationship in order to avoid the shame society would undoubtedly have poured upon them both, a torrent of abuse which they foresaw would wreck her career and endanger the happiness of their togetherness. The secret endured, so their choice proved successful in the event. But that choice apart, her sexual orientation was hard-wired within her human physicality.

"My life purpose was to go through adversity, strengthen my resolve, strengthen my courage for going against what seemed to be impenetrable walls, and then to use that as a basis for instilling the same virtues in thousands, even millions of people around me."

Wilma Rudolph
1940-1994

Wilma Glodean Rudolph, you were born prematurely, weighing only 4½ pounds. Historians don't agree on the number of children in the family. Were you really number 20 out of 22 kids?

Give or take some. It depends upon how you count. There were some stillborns and various other calamities, but for the record, yes, I was number 20 of 22.

Your mother was worn out, I should think, after that!

All she did was get pregnant, have babies, and change diapers.

Your folks were hardworking poor and lived as African-Americans in the segregated town of Clarksville, Tennessee. Being a very sickly child and crippled by polio, you were educated at home until you were seven. You must have been very sure of yourself when you chose to come down into such a situation.

I came down with the idea that I was going to show what could be done. I was going to be in a situation where I had to overcome physical, mental, emotional, and societal belief systems that other people tried to impress upon me, and I would find the strength within me not only to pull myself up—as they say—by the bootstraps, but also to be a guiding light for siblings, friends, relatives, and the nation.

251

"The nation" part of it was related to segregation, I take it?

Segregation was the starting point, but also to prove that a woman, as well as a black, could be recognized on a world scale for achievements when she put her heart and soul into accomplishing something.

You once said, "My doctors told me I would never walk again. My mother told me I would. I believed my mother." Was she the major influence on you as you struggled to survive?

My mother was an absolutely fantastic person—gentle, kind, encouraging, but like the Rock of Gibraltar. If she said that you were going to do something, you found a way to do it, no matter what it took, because you had total confidence in the pronouncements that she came out with. She was able to organize all of my brothers and sisters and to instill in them a sense of who they were, what they could do. She was my heroine during my entire life.

We have been told that incarnating souls leave part of their energy at Home, and bring part of it down with them. Is that true? If so, how much energy did you bring down?

To say that there is a division between "up there" and "down here" may be a little confusing for people. The truth is that our entire essence as a soul is not contained within the physical body. We do not bring down with us all of the experiences that we have gone through in other lifetimes. We do not bring down all of the wisdom that has become a part of our being as we review between lives what has happened in prior lives. That is the part of us that remains outside of our human self. We can connect with it if we go searching for it in this lifetime, but it's not as if we are a dozen eggs and we are only one egg out of the box. We have a connection to all of those other parts of ourselves, but it is an unconscious one in our physical mind.

But you can bring more strength into the human situation if you wish to, or less if you think you don't need to, can't you? That's right. We decide as we come down what the lessons are going to be, what we want to have the experience of developing, so that we get the wisdom of what it takes to, say, overcome a disease that is thought incurable by human standards. We learn how we can rewrite the belief that if we have polio we will not walk, how we can tap into the energy to reprogram our physicality, as well as how to re-pattern the mental restrictions that may be placed upon us by society. We set up the necessary events that will allow us to then develop our wisdom for completing a particular task. Sometimes it is the first time that we have attempted such a task and we don't need as much energy, and sometimes we have not completed the task in other lifetimes, and when we repeat a task it becomes more difficult and we need more energy.

If souls bring down more of their energy, are they more able to tackle difficult problems?

If they have the wisdom that comes from experiencing a lot of different lives in which they have overcome things, they have the potential of tapping into the store of energy, that wisdom they have already gained. When they come down to Earth they may bring all of that wisdom with them, or they may bring just part of it so that they have to work harder on the lesson that they're undertaking. If their lesson plan includes, as mine did, reflecting energy out to other people, then they will bring down, as I did, a stronger connection to the energy. I had to have a force that could be recognized, so I could do things that other people thought impossible. It's interesting, because not long ago you interviewed Helen Keller, and the two of us sometimes discuss how our pathways were rather similar in what we chose to develop within us and how we spread the energy out to society.

Regarding the wisdom that you brought down more strongly into this life because you needed it more, did you develop that wisdom from a series of past lives, or was it the wisdom of the universe as a whole?

253

Everything is a combination of both, because just as you can pick up a book and read what somebody else has experienced, you can tap into the energy of the universe as a whole. The application of that energy can be trial and error, or if you have had similar experiences in past lives, they can magnify the energy that comes down. So it's a combination of taking universal wisdom together with personal experience and being able to apply it. I had a number of lifetimes where I had overcome what might be considered extremes in human existence. That gave me the strength to know how to go within myself and rekindle the pilot light there and fuel it into a blast furnace of energy.

Segregation barred you from the local hospital, so every week for two years your mother took you 50 miles to Nashville where the black medical college of Fisk University had a clinic where you were fitted with a leg brace. Was this a sign of hope for you?

As a child I didn't really think about it. I just knew that my mother had said that I was going to walk, and I had a feeling inside of me that I could do whatever she wanted me to do, and that she would find the way to facilitate allowing me to go through the various stages I had to go through to accomplish her goal.

Did your brothers and sisters, as well, help you to recover, take off the leg brace, and grow strong?

Well, they did—sometimes with intelligence but also with typical sibling behavior such as hiding my brace, and kidding me along, and teasing me, and inciting me to do things that all of the medical people said I shouldn't do. It was all by an agreement that we had beforehand, of course, that there would be many instances of instigating and igniting and helping me that would lead me to get the physical exercise that would strengthen the muscles in a way the medical world didn't believe possible because it had never been done before.

You give me the feeling that you were the child in the family that everyone looked at and talked about.

Well, I was the only one who was different. All of the others were very active, scrappy kids, and I was the cute one whom they didn't want to leave behind. Mom was very protective of me, so an easy way for them to get on the good side of Mom was to take care of me.

I think your sister Yolanda was important to you. You named your first child after her, didn't you?

Yolanda was like a second mother to me. When I thought Mom was pushing me too hard, she was the one who was there to console me, and keep me going, and give me hope. She and I had been together in many prior lifetimes, so we had the closeness of what most people call soul mates, and she helped me with the lessons.

When you were in junior high you actually joined the school basketball team, but you weren't picked to play for three seasons. Was that a frustrating time?

Frustrating, yes, because as a human child I had a strong desire to be able to participate in something. But it was also very instructive because I watched the way the other girls' bodies moved. Then I would mimic in private the way that their legs moved. It was as if it was my own private medical physical therapy ward.

Eventually you became a basketball star at high school. You set state records for scoring and led your team to the state championship. Was this when you first had confirmation of your desire to become an athlete?

I had a desire to become an athlete from the first moment I felt the movement of my body on the court during our practices. That was when I felt the interaction between my human body and its potential to join with and become a part of the energy that is around us, the energy of the universe. That's what an athlete is—somebody who communicates with and rides upon the energy that surrounds us. Most people ignore tapping into the energy that is around them. I knew, I could feel, that there was a way to take the physical body I was in and stimulate the muscles, and coordinate the hand and the eye when shooting baskets. It was like having a goal in the distance that came ever closer to you. You just let it pull you in as you were going toward it.

You said, "I ran and ran and ran every day, and I acquired this sense of determination, this sense of spirit that I would never, never give up, no matter what else happened." Was this really how the Law of Attraction worked in your life?

[laughs] It is the Law of Attraction, and people who find their passion use all of the attributes of the Law of Attraction. In your time on Earth right now, everybody is referring to it as the "Law of Attraction," but it is the passion, it is the goal that draws the soul through a particular lifetime, through a particular experience, and if you put all your energy into it, you can accomplish whatever you set out to achieve.

Then at age 16 you became a track star, winning a bronze medal in the 4x4 relay at your first Olympic Games in 1956. How did you come to be picked for the US Olympic team?

I was fast. They couldn't deny the fact that I could accomplish what needed to be done on the team. There was a lot of talk by doctors, because we had to go through physicals in order to make the team. They had a partial history of my health record, and they feared that my muscles might shut down under extreme stress, so at first I was considered not worthy of being on the team. But then when I kept beating everybody out, people said, "She has to go!" The coaches were on my side. So they took a chance on me and I was able to produce. But they only bet on me where I was a quarter of the event—a relay.

The Tigerbelles women's track team's coach, Ed Temple, spotted you during the state basketball contest and invited you to a

Tennessee State University sports camp. You won a scholarship to study there. Tell us about that time.

That was the time when I knew that everything Mother had predicted was possible, a time when I knew that I was in control of the physical processes of my body. I also knew that my intellect was going to be sated. I envisioned myself as a sponge that was able to suck in as much as was presented to me. Not that many of my brothers and sisters were able to go on to college, because they weren't unique in the special way I was in sports, although Mother made sure that those children who were capable did find some way to go to college. It was as if there was a recognition that all the work I had gone through to get myself out of bed, and get myself out of those braces, was now patterning the rest of my life.

Eventually you got a Bachelor's degree in education. How do you feel about the issue that colleges should expect sports stars to also prove themselves in scholarship?

I believe it's the pathway that each of them is on. If their pathway is through the college system, simply to be able to avail themselves of sports experience and have no desire for intellectual pursuits, they should be allowed to follow their pathway. As a teacher, however, I believe that schools and universities are for teaching, and that there should be other ways for people to get their athletic education—but in reality that's not what happens. So it's for each individual soul to decide whether to juggle athletics and intellectual pursuits or just go with the athletics. The real problem is for those people who are at a university for the education and not the athletics, who are slighted because so much money is going to the athletic department. I think this is an injustice. But again, it is the pathway that has been predetermined.

What's your feeling about the imbalance between men's and women's sports?

That's a problem that the human race is not going to solve in the near future. While the primary leadership on the planet is masculine, that is going to maintain or increase the injustice. People don't want to watch women's athletics on television. They watch men (the macho angle) because the average Joe, a blue-collar worker, who gets all of his entertainment sitting in front of the boob tube watching baseball or football, wants to be able to identify with another macho man.

In the Summer Olympics at Rome in 1960 you won the 100- and 200-meter dash and were in the winning team for the 400-meter relay. That made you the first American woman to win three gold medals in the Olympics. How well did you handle fame as "The World's Fastest Woman"?

In the beginning I didn't handle it quite as well as I could have, because in my human experience here I was going against all the odds—I was a woman, I was black, I was poor, I had been an invalid—and the accolades showered upon me went to my head a little. At one time I became rather insufferable in my pride, but then my family came into play and reminded me of how we grew up and of the values that were instilled in us. So then I came down to Earth and used my experience to help others understand that they, too, could do what I had done.

You received many awards, including the Olympic Hall of Fame. What do the awards mean to you now?

Absolutely nothing. The only thing they mean to me is that there is a historical record at which souls facing challenges can look and see that another soul, Wilma Rudolph, overcame what they are facing, and that if they put their effort into it to the same degree that I did, they can accomplish the same things.

Was it your idea to insist that Clarksville provide a desegregated homecoming welcome for you when you returned from the Olympics?

Interestingly enough, it was the whites who really wanted to congratulate me, because there weren't as many of the blacks who had followed my continued pathway up the athletic chain. I wanted the blacks there to see that they could be accepted by the whites if they were steadfast in their beliefs and in their pathways, and that they could share in the joy of a single individual's accomplishing something.

In 1963 you married your high school sweetheart, Robert Eldridge. You had four children together but later divorced. What went wrong?

Primarily what went wrong was that I continued to grow and to expand in my understanding of what I had accomplished and how I could be a role model and a stimulus for others to accomplish the same thing. Robert was a bit jealous of the exposure and the limelight that I engendered wherever I went. He could not understand why it was as important for me to tell the world my story as it was to tell our children my story.

You became a coach at Burt High School in Clarksville, then took coaching jobs in Maine, and at DePauw University in Indiana. You represented the US as a goodwill ambassador in Africa. Dr. Billy Graham sent you to Japan as one of the Baptist Christian Athletes. Did success make you restless?

I don't know that it was success; it was the success schedule that made me restless. My own family was as important to me then as my family had been when I was growing up. As I began to be away more and more, I felt myself being torn away from them, not being able to interact at each stage of their development. The children grew and I wanted to be a part of their maturing as individuals, but I found that that was increasingly difficult to be able to do as the demands of society and ideology overtook my personal desires. My own life became somewhat drowned in the scheduling.

You became a motivational speaker to young people in schools and universities and took part in a national athletic program for underprivileged young people. Your foundation provided them with free sports coaching and academic support. Did people make use of your fame or were you the driving force behind all you did?

The driving force primarily came from within me, the knowledge that I could ride upon my accomplishments and my fame to spread a wave across the country that would nourish and uplift those who thought they were forgotten. They wouldn't have been able to develop a sense of self but for what was provided by my programs, my athletics, my insistence at the time that they have good grades in order to stay within the programs. Even though I recognized what the universities were doing, to me each student's education was important. They might not succeed in athletics, or the time they spent in athletics might be only fleeting, but education would provide them with a strong basis for going forward in their life.

You said, "When I was going through my transition of being famous, I tried to ask God why was I here—what was my purpose? Surely, it wasn't just to win three gold medals. There had to be more to this life than that." Before you incarnated did you define a life purpose?

My life purpose was to go through adversity, strengthen my resolve, strengthen my courage for going against what seemed to be impenetrable walls, and then to use that as a basis for instilling the same virtues in thousands, even millions of people around me. So my life purpose was to be a beacon of hope and a light of direction. Of course once I was in human form I didn't remember any of that and fell into my religious belief that God had the answers since He made all the plans.

Was that purpose chosen by you, or did it come from the elders who advised you?

We all have a council of twelve that helps us decide what we want to do when we incarnate. But even in spirit form we have freedom of choice, so while we get advice and suggestions from our council, it is solely up to us to decide exactly what we want to do. In this particular case, a lot of the ideas came from me because I was building up to that sort of lifetime. I had many dry runs, or previews, in different lifetimes of being a leader, being a guide, being able to overcome obstacles, and this life as Wilma Rudolph was designed to put all the pieces together into one gigantic, dynamic example of the power and strength of the soul within a body.

You died of brain cancer quite young, aged 54. Was that illness a further pre-planned experience, or was it just that you had finished your work here and it was a way out?

It was time to transition. I had everything set up exactly as I had wanted it to be. By then I had become superfluous to the movement I had started. Had I remained, it would have been an air brake in some of the programs. People would not have taken the initiative; they would have relied upon me instead of following their own momentum. I withdrew at that time so that they had to take the initiative of the forward movement.

What was the most exciting moment in your life?

The first race I ran without having to have braces, when I felt the freedom of being with the wind—and no, I didn't win it, but I ran it.

Thank you, Wilma Rudolph, for talking with us.

It has been my pleasure. I hope that those on planet Earth will still take those principles that I helped shine a light on and use them to fill their pathways.

Commentary

Toni: Wilma had a dynamic energy, but with a modesty, almost shyness. It was like, "Yeah, I'm this big dynamo, but anybody can be; don't make a whole lot out of it. It was just my purpose to be there and to be the signpost for others." There was almost a contradiction between the way she spoke and the way she had lived her life. As she described what she had done and what she could do, and talked about her programs, she displayed a drive, as in running a race—she had to get it done, full speed ahead! I had visual images playing through my mind, of all the various steps she had to go through, racing by at an incredible speed.

261

Then she was gentle, even timid, as she shyly discussed the principles of why she did what she did. "And, oh yeah, no big deal!"

Peter: It was interesting to hear Wilma compare herself with Helen Keller. The strength of their purpose in life was equally dynamic—what has been unequal is the acclaim people have afforded them. Helen is more widely known. The difference may be our racism. Wilma acknowledged her obstacles to be that she was black and a woman.

We talked about the amount of soul energy she employed to accomplish her incredible journey. Briefly, souls at Home are a cloud-like amorphous mass of energy, some of which is used by them to incarnate; the rest is left behind. The amount of their individual energy, and the amount of general energy from past-life experiences, that souls bring down with them varies greatly. Having chosen their lessons, souls decide how much energy to allocate to that life on Earth. Difficult lives require more energy, regular lives need less. Wilma needed a lot and judged correctly. Had she not done so, she might never have healed herself of polio and become a gold medal Olympian.

That raises an issue we did not discuss. If other people are inspired to copy Wilma's powerful life, will they be able to achieve their goals? Will their energy be sufficient? A soul may have made a small energy allocation (there's no going back for more once incarnation has taken place). Wilma herself provided us with some of the answer, teaching young people to believe in themselves, and making practical provision to help youngsters get ahead. Above all, we must develop an intention to succeed, because, as she said, "it is the passion, it is the goal that draws the soul through a particular lifetime, through a particular experience, and if you put all your energy into it, you can accomplish whatever you set out to achieve." We look gratefully to Wilma Rudolph's life for inspiration— just as she planned.

"There wasn't anything that shone about my qualities;
my beauty was what got me in and kept me there."

Sharon Tate

1943-1969

Sharon Marie Tate, you were an "Army brat." Your father was in the US Army so you moved around the country, and then you were sent to live in Italy.

Being a military dependent creates the extremes of emotion. You go to a new place and really have to be outgoing in order to fit in, or you're swept under the carpet. At the same time, when making friends you know that there's a short duration to the friendship, at least on a one-to-one basis, so it makes you sense that nothing is permanent. I had friends all over the world—people I had met at school and in my different activities. I was brought up to be able to make do with anything that came about. Father and Mother were quite indulgent with us so that we would be able to find our own identities.

But you were a bit shy, weren't you?

Yes, I was, when compared to most of the kids. I was also a bit small when I was a child, and it was easy for people to pick on me.

Is it fair to say you were aloof?

I think it is unfair to say that. I did have certain fears of being taken advantage of, since I had been teased so much as a child.

You were a pretty girl and a beautiful young woman. When you were a toddler you won the "Miss Tiny Tot of Dallas Pageant," but

263

I don't think your mother was ambitious for you in show business. Did the event have any impact on you?

It was exciting but also boring. It felt very unusual to be there and to have adults talking all about you but never to you, so it was a time when I retreated into myself and just let those people pose me if they so chose.

In 1959 you won a contest for "Miss Richland," a Washington State town, and wanted to enter the state competition, but you all moved to Verona in Italy. You attended the American school there. Tell us about your feelings at that time.

It seemed as if every time I got into an activity where I was really succeeding with something, we would uproot and be off again. What was good was that my looks didn't give me a problem in Italy. I had thought that with all of the beauties over there, I would just be shoved into a corner, but I was pretty enough to attract the boys to me. Of course, I could speak English, and most of the American boys at school didn't bother to learn Italian, so it was easier for me to have people to talk to and go out with.

A pretty picture of you in a bathing costume had appeared in the Star & Stripes *armed forces magazine.*

Yes. I did have slightly proud parents, and I think it was at my mother's urging that father submitted the photo. It could only be submitted by service personnel, so mother couldn't do it herself, but her force was definitely behind it.

What was your ambition at that time?

Mainly just to be happy and to be able to settle down in some way, so that I wasn't being constantly uprooted and there wasn't a constant change in everything going on. I did like the attention paid me with the pageants. I was becoming quite enamored of some of the actresses at that time and the way that they seemed to dictate what they did and where they went. That was something that definitely appealed to me, because as a military dependent I was sort of military "luggage."

So you and your friends landed parts as extras in the film Adventures of a Young Man. *One of the stars, Richard Beymer, noticed you and introduced you to his agent, Harold Gefsky. You had a brief affair with Richard, didn't you?*
Yes.

Did most of the men who helped your career expect sex? That was the payment in the industry at that time. If you wanted to go anywhere, if you wanted to have your name passed along and have yourself considered for different parts, you had to be willing to please them.

In 1961 you appeared in a TV special with Pat Boone, which was shot in Venice, followed by a film test that led nowhere. So you went back to the States, and your mother had a nervous breakdown worrying about you. Am I right?
Mother had never really been considered to be anything special, so she began to live vicariously through me. At the start she was the mover, the shaker, the pusher to get me into things. She wanted her daughter's name up in lights. I wanted some of the same things, but not to the same degree, so while I was a little reticent to jump into bed with everybody to get the parts, she was back there encouraging and pushing—whatever it took for me to become a star.

Finally, when you were 19, you moved to Los Angeles where Harold Gefsky got work for you in TV and magazine advertisements. You got bit parts in The Beverly Hillbillies *and* Mr. Ed. *Did you feel hopeful about your acting career?*
At that time I was just having fun, being accepted for who I was. I wasn't the new girl on the block, as I'd always been growing up. I was a local at the time. I saw that this was an exciting business in which I could really go somewhere, and I was in seventh heaven, as they say.
Then you were engaged to an aristocratic French actor, Philippe Forquet. A row broke out about his being violent and putting you

in hospital, but some said it was all a nasty negative publicity campaign from which he suffered unjustly for many years. What was the truth about your relationship?

The truth about the relationship was that in the beginning it was a whirlwind of romance and excitement. Then I realized that there were so many differences between us that I really could not envision spending the rest of my life with Philippe. So there was a time when I was trying to gently break it off, and in exasperation, he struck out at me. It wasn't big, but it was sufficient for the publicist to use the beautiful, battered heroine approach.

Whose publicist was that?

Mine. My team saw that this was a way for my name to become more of a household name out of sympathy for the poor, battered, abused woman, because that was one of the things of deep concern in the country at that time.

Should Philippe have been dragged through the mud?

Not to the extent that he was, but yes, he did cause me some injuries.

Is he forgiven?

Oh, absolutely. I know that a lot of things that I said were quite biting, because when I first proposed that we sever any connections, he was very heartbroken and indignant, so in order to get through to him, I became quite terse with my comments, and it was in response to some of them that he acted out. I'm not justifying the hitting of a woman, but I did instigate the response.

Your career gathered momentum. Your engagement to Jay Sebring didn't stand in the way of work. You appeared with David Niven and Deborah Kerr as a witch in Eye of the Devil, *for which a critic described you as "chillingly beautiful but expressionless," but David and Deborah said you had latent talent. What did you think of them?*

They were beautiful, beautiful people. They were so experienced, so giving. It was a pleasure to work with them. Whenever they would see me doing something that would be conceived as a poor presentation of myself, they would coach me in how to play the role. In that particular film, for some reason, I could never get totally into the part, and I gave a sort of wooden appearance to it. I just could not identify that much with my character.

You weren't a witch?
[laughs] Not at all.

Too beautiful?
I didn't think beauty had anything to do with evil. Evil is what is inside, not the package it is presented in. I knew a number of beautiful people who were playing totally evil beings in this incarnation, and their beauty helped to ease their acceptance by others.

Then at a London nightclub you met the film director Roman Polanski. He agreed to let you star in The Fearless Vampire Killers *in place of Jill St. John. She had red hair and he made you wear a red wig. He made you work really hard on the set. Polanski was a perfectionist, wasn't he?*
Roman was insufferable when it came to matching his vision of the way things should be done. He would be ruthless in staging what was in his mind's eye. But the finished product he created was magnificent.

If he was that difficult to work with, what attracted you?
His intensity. I had never come across anyone who was so passionate, and he was as passionate in bed as he was about his craft. Everything he did was to the ultimate.

You became busy in movies: Eye of the Devil, Don't Make Waves, Valley of the Dolls, The Wrecking Crew. *Looking back on your brief career in films and fashion, how do you view your own abilities and performance?*

I would evaluate myself as average, compared to others in the business. There wasn't anything that shone about my qualities; my beauty was what got me in and kept me there. I was able to follow directions and therefore seamlessly play into the scenario, but I didn't bring a particular vim or vigor or attraction to the part that some other actresses did.

Would it be true that, like the part you played of Jennifer North, you were "admired only for your body?"

That would be an adequate way to sum it up.

But there's another aspect of this: Was your life purpose on track at that point?

My life purpose was to experience different things in order to come out of the shell that I had possessed early on, to stand up for myself, and to be able to make decisions—discernment, we call it up here—as to what was the best way for me to have the most experience within the time. It was all setting me up for the climax.

Your marriage in 1967 to Roman enhanced your status as a star. In August 1969 you were 26 and famous, and your baby boy was nearly due to be born. You rented a house in Benedict Canyon in Beverly Hills and there hung out with your many friends in the movie business, as Roman preferred, "like hippies." Did you have any premonition of what would happen to you there on the ninth of August?

Consciously I had no idea. We were just totally enjoying life. I was preparing to be a mother, adamant that my baby would not have the same disjointed early life that I had, and that, while he would travel, there would be as much attention paid to him as was humanly possible. I had a great group of friends who supported me in that idea.

Did your soul realize what was going to happen to you?

Back here, I recalled the contracts I had made.

Then followers of Charles Manson came to the house and murdered you with your unborn child, together with the driver of your car and three friends. My first question is: was this an act of free will by the followers of Manson or was it in some way planned before you incarnated?

Oh, this was definitely planned. I was going to go through a violent death, which would bring attention to a way of life and to a whole pattern of brainwashing that was going on—not only in the Manson sect but throughout a lot of other quasi-religious and hippie groups at that time. The exact person or people who were going to be the perpetrators? It was sort of a loosely gathered contract. My soul knew it was going to be from the group of which Manson was a part. The exact people who did it—that was the freedom of choice within the group.

So the reason you died at that time was to show up the iniquities of these religious groups?

Religious groups, fanatical groups, gangs, all of the accumulations of people where power was totally given to one or two people to dictate what everyone did. It was more than just the religious groups because it related also to gangs that would take retribution for things done to them, or would make some type of statement within the territory of another gang. It was all about people's wresting power from the establishment or from normal society and then saying that they were right over everything else, that they did not have to comply with societal norms.

You and your friends were the sacrificial lambs?

To the outward appearance we were sacrificial lambs. To our souls we were volunteers.

Do you find this same problem still here in the United States?

Absolutely—throughout the entire world during your time. People who are fanatical about their cause, thinking

269

human life has no value, need to be highlighted and dealt with. Anyone who believes that all the world must do, think, and believe as they do must be made to see that each person has his or her own truth. All souls are the same; no one is better or righter than any other.

But these are souls who are doing it. Have they deliberately taken on an evil role?

For us here at Home there is no evil. We have no duality on a soul level. But incarnate, we are in that physical form known as the "Third Dimension," which is Earth's polarized vibration. There, in order to demonstrate what is good you must also know what is evil. There is evil within the third dimension. This is the way that we may get the attention of the other souls who are incarnate at the same time.

Souls who take on this negative role do so deliberately?

They do it quite deliberately, and the reason is in order to experience it themselves and to give other souls the experience of knowing what it's like. One example is the demolition of the World Trade Center. Those perpetrators within the airplanes had agreed to be evil incarnate in the eyes of the world, again under the guise of some fanatical idea of what was right. All the souls who transitioned (died) at that time had agreed to be on the stage, to communicate emotionally with everyone else on the planet, in order to change perspective, and to help them see that the world was tipping in the direction of anarchy.

You were stabbed 16 times. How much suffering did your soul go through before it left your body?

The perception I had was more of shock and disbelief than actually of any pain in the first several thrusts. After that my soul separated [from my body].

Did you have difficulty returning Home?

No, not at all. As soon as I was out of the body and saw everything that was going on, I began to have my memories return of the fact that I had agreed to be part of this experience on the planet.

Before this interview, the Masters told us that no soul had been assigned to your unborn baby. Are you aware of this?
Yes.

Jennifer North, whom you played in Valley of the Dolls, *had an abortion. Did you ever have an abortion?*
Yes.
Are souls assigned to fetuses that are aborted?
Sometimes. The determining factor is whether the mother, the host of the baby, is to exercise her freedom of choice. Part of her life lesson is to make a decision whether to bring the child into the world, and then, whether to raise the child herself or put the child up for adoption. Since that is freedom of choice, and if it has not already been determined, in order for that fetus to have a soul if the mother chooses to bear it, a soul has to be assigned.

So if the mother chose at the last minute to have the child, and walked out of the abortion clinic, would a soul then be assigned to the child if it had not already?
A soul would be assigned at the first joining of the sperm and the egg if the fetus is going to have the possibility of going full term.

And the Universe knows whether it will have that possibility because it sees into the future?
The universe is aware of the mother's desired life lesson. Unless the mother has chosen from the very beginning to have an abortion, so that she has to deal for the rest of her incarnation with all the guilt and the energy surrounding her thinking that she has killed another individual, a soul will have been assigned.
In the case of your abortion, was the soul assigned?
No.

271

Are souls directly involved in an abortion procedure? Do they suffer?

No, they never suffer, because the soul is just loosely connected with the fetus until it comes out. The only time that a soul may experience something is in the case of a baby going through difficulty at the time of delivery, such as a breech birth with the cord around its neck, or something like that. Then a soul may experience something. But that's a lesson that's been set up ahead of time, to go through the struggle, whether it has the strength to hold on and to make it through the difficulty, and whether it wants to come out as an injured human from some birth problem, to deal with that throughout the rest of its incarnation.

Going back to Charles Manson and your killers, do you have an opinion about the death penalty for murder?

[laughs] No. When people transition (die), it's something that they pretty much know ahead of time. So that if people commit murder, and the State does away with the death penalty, and they had wanted to transition then, they will either die of medical reasons or somebody will hasten their departure.

The death penalty is sometimes seen as either retribution or a means by which other people will be dissuaded from evil actions. Is there any substance in either of those ideas?

Historically there is no truth that it has any deterrent effect. It is only important for the experiences that can be had in society. For instance, if I want to experience judging the actions of another person to the ultimate, by imposing the death penalty, I would arrange to be on a jury making those decisions. Then, as that person was on death row, I would agonize over whether that was right decision. As the sentence was carried out, I would experience emotions concerning it. The same if I were a relative of the deceased—it would be to examine the emotions I had at each stage. Does the termination of the life that caused my loss lessen my loss? Those are the things that our souls set us up to experience.

After you died, your mother, Doris Tate, championed the cause of victims' rights. How do you view her campaign?

Mom was really hurting. She had some guilt herself about whether introducing me to the limelight led to my being a potential target. It was therapy for her, dealing with other people who had been victims or were families of victims.

You were in love with your husband, Roman. How has your separation by physical death affected your feelings for him?

It's rather difficult for you to understand the various stages of love upon the Earth. The attraction of one human for another human, which we call romance, is on a very physical level. It engenders all of the emotional and physical reactions that occur within a human being. As a soul we unconditionally love every other soul, and that goes for those who helped terminate my existence on the human plane, as well as those who are here and those whom I left behind. It is across the board an acknowledgment that we are all the same. Do you not love your hand, your arm? It is as difficult for you to say that you do not love your hand or your arm as it is for us to say we do not love another soul.

So your love is unconditional?

Love is totally, absolutely, positively unconditional.

Thank you, Sharon Tate, for talking with us.

It has been my pleasure. I hope that I have cleared up some questions in people's minds.

Commentary

Toni: The feeling I got from Sharon's soul was that it was much older and more mature than my physical picture of the actress would lead me to believe. It was as if, in place of my impression of her as a flighty little thing, she were a very mellow, balanced, thoughtful soul who set herself up—put herself out there as a target—and said, "You need to have this experience. I'm here. World, take note."

Peter: One of the hardest pieces of information coming from the Other Side relates to evildoers and to personal sacrifice. We are told that, before coming down to Earth, souls actually contract with other souls to do things to them that the world considers evil, and that their future victims willingly agree to suffer at their hand. This idea puzzles and infuriates many when told of the arrangement.

In a milder way before her death, evil happened to Sharon many times as suffering in her relationships. She claimed that her mother had supported her making use of her body to climb in her profession. Then it happened as powerful men took advantage of her sexuality. Sexual exploitation is a major lesson to which we are exposed in one lifetime or another, and to which we souls expose other people as our victims from time to time. The point is that our souls come here to experience both sides of negativity in order to value ultimate, unconditional love, which is the nature of the eternal Source of all being.

The lessons we learn do not end in mere exploitation. The murderer is playing a role agreed with the victim. Sharon's soul says that those who brought down the World Trade Center and all those who died there were in the same relationship of perpetrator and victim.

The requirement is for souls to learn lessons, whether to suffer at the hands of megalomaniacs like Charles Manson, or to oppose dictators like Idi Amin, or on the other hand to grieve— as Sharon's mother did for her daughter and as millions did when the Twin Towers fell down. This is the reason why all of us have "chosen" (that word is selected with care) to live in Earth's dimension, polarized as it is between the positive and the negative. It is a learning experience for which our souls are all here. Our lesson may be to give love, cherish hope, share worth—or it may be to vent hatred, dash other people's hopes, rob, and rape. We choose positive and negative experiences in order to grow and to mature as souls.   To misquote

Shakespeare: "All the world's a classroom and all the souls of men and women merely students."

This cosmic spiritual arrangement is all far too serious to be seen as mere theater. Were it not for the freedom of choice that is ours at every stage of the journey from Home to Earth and back again, we would appear like puppets on strings. But, as Sharon Tate made plain, that freedom exercised by her soul was that she and her companions might become Manson's innocent victims in order to draw the attention of human society to a growing social evil. She does not regret making the choice now, does not hold anything but love toward her murderers. Would that it were so easy for those of us she left behind!

"I was singing outdoors. It was, to me,
an exchange of energy like a celestial chorus,
and I heard some of the angels join in.
It was an absolutely beautiful experience"

Selena Quintanilla-Pérez
1971-1995

Selena Quintanilla-Pérez, you were the youngest of three children. You grew up in Texas speaking English at home. Your Mexican-American parents ran Pappagallo, a restaurant in Lake Jackson which failed, and you all moved to Corpus Christi, taking your musical instruments with you. Do you remember that bus ride?

There was so much going on right then. There was sorrow, but there was elation that something new was coming. They tried to keep an upbeat air about everything so that we children didn't get sad. We were leaving so many friends behind that we naturally felt sad, but they were telling us how great things were going to be.

Were your parents quite ambitious?

They knew that they were going to succeed as soon as they got the right formula together. There was no doubt in their minds whatsoever.

The right formula involved music.

It ended up involving music, but it was something that to them was so non-defined. With the restaurant there was definition—food, people, work, money—but with music it was "how do you sell them a song?" So it was something that took a while to work into their acceptance.

Your parents were Jehovah's Witnesses. What did the religion of your childhood mean to you?

That there was a strong faith in a Power outside of us that would take care of us, that would nurture us if we lived within the principles, and if we gave witness to the power of the Lord.

Did you remain a Jehovah's Witness all your life?

No, I did not. It was something that for the longest time seemed to be right, but then as I began to move within the music, I remembered something bigger than a doctrine within which you had to follow rules and regulations. I remembered a freedom. I remembered a connection and that all of us were of the Power.

How do you view Jehovah's Witnesses now?

It is a very helpful religious practice for people who need to be directed. It is a religion for those who need to have answers for everything provided to them, where you get rid of a certain sense of faith and trust. There is underlying faith and trust in God, but at the same time, the religion tells you everything that you have to believe, and everything that you have to think. You don't need to have faith and trust in something that you can't touch or feel. It's very palpable to them because it's the way they exist.

It's something of a sales organization, isn't it?

It's perceived that way by a lot of people because of the missionary work that is part of the program itself—selling Watchtower, selling the belief systems within the religion and the "salvation" that comes with that belief. It is something that the people so strongly believe in, and it's like with anything: If you speak of something, it becomes your truth, so in putting the people out on the streets speaking their religion, they unquestioningly accept the truth of everything that they are told to say.

When you were about three, your brother and sister were given musical instruments. You did not get one but delighted your musician father by singing "Blue Moon" to him. Do you remember the occasion?

[laughs] Yes, I do. You might say I knocked his socks off. I had always had a fascination with music. When I heard it on the radio, I would instantly be able to sing along. I had what you

would call perfect pitch, and if I heard something I could repeat it. So he was a little taken aback because he was into a regimentation of getting lessons for my siblings, and then, out of the blue, I showed him I had more musical talent than either of them. It was quite funny.

Did you draw from a past life or two?

Or three or four. Just about every life I have lived has been something musical.

Anything in particular that was special?

In Spain I sang arias at the outdoor amphitheaters, and that was a way to express myself and connect with the universe. I did a little bit of outdoor work in my incarnation as Selena, but nothing like I had done in Spain. That was where I felt the vibration of Earth intermingling with the vibration that was coming out of me. It's rather difficult to have that feeling when you're in a studio with headsets on and microphones and everything else. It takes away from the pure experience of joining the vibration.

Later, in 1994, your hit single "Amor Prohibido" told your grandparents' love story. Were you close to your grandparents?

Yes. In our family everybody was close. We moved as a unit. Even when we were separated by distance, any important decision was made jointly with the guidance of the whole family.

In that same recording your brother, "A.B." (Abraham Quintanilla III), was on bass, and your sister, Suzette, was on drums. Were you musically particularly close to them, as well? A.B. was a song writer, wasn't he?

A.B. was beautifully adept at taking an emotion and putting into music. He was fantastic in that regard. Suzette just liked to make noise, but there was a very comforting closeness between us.

And you created music together that sold well.

We all created from our souls. We tapped into the music that was there. It was almost as if you would get us together and the room would vibrate with the energy that came from inside of us.

Then at only nine years of age, the future "Queen of Tejano Music" became the lead singer of a band named by your father "Selena y Los Dinos" (Selena and The Boys). Was that quite a rough time for you all as you tried to make your music a commercial success?

We kind of went from engagement to engagement. Other members of the family helped us out from time to time because they believed in what we were doing, but it was very difficult for us because there wasn't a steady income. Father didn't scrimp on anything we needed when it came to costumes and instruments and recording time. He believed in what was developing. All of the resources of the family went into the future, not into the present.

You cut your first album when you were twelve. As English was your mother tongue, you had been singing in Spanish phonetically. At what age did you become really fluent in the language?

I think it was always within me. In Texas during that time, speaking Spanish would classify you as a lower-class citizen, as an immigrant, rather than as a U.S. citizen, part of America. That was why our parents spoke English at home, so that it became our first language. I actually had to get some tutoring from other members of the family who had kept with Spanish—cousins, etc.—in order to develop a fluency in the language. Singing it phonetically I couldn't get my heart into it until I understood the words and felt the words. That was when the energy of love could be put into it. It was a gradual process. It wasn't that I could say I got into it at the age of seven or twelve; it came gradually, but by fifteen, I hardly spoke English unless I had to, because the romance of the Spanish had a music all its own, and I wanted to live and revolve in that energy.

You were a good school student, but your parents pulled you out of school when you were about 13, and you completed your education by a correspondence course. Education remained important to you, didn't it?

I had an insatiable curiosity about words, about facts, about what influences a person, and what is important to a person. I studied that to get an idea for the type of music that would appeal to different groups of people. Most people think that singing is just a matter of having a melody that appears pleasing to the ears, but it's much more than that. It's touching the heartstrings of the person. Sometimes that has to be done through the mind, where they hear something that takes them back to another time period, or connects within their memories to a family setting, to some joyous event within their lives. So words and connections, thought processes, became very important to me.

In 1987, when you were only 16, you won the Tejano Music Award for "Female Entertainer of the Year." Tejano music is a mix of Mexican and East European musical styles. You are credited as being one of a handful of musicians who refined and popularized it worldwide. Will you tell us about your music?

My music was a combination of the interest that I put into it, studying what was needed by people, studying where there was a niche that didn't seem to be filled. At first it was a plan by Father, and where I found the best opportunity to shine. Then it was a bringing together of all the energies in which I had been raised—a lot of whites within the United States are European, and of course we were in a Latino area, so it was appealing to both groups and it went across racial and ethnic lines and caught and captured the hearts and imaginations of people.

I see it now as bringing back within me songs which I had sung throughout Europe in various incarnations. I have sung on every continent of this planet, and there are certain music types that work well together and certain ones that don't. Tejano works because it takes the romance, the vigor, the excitement of the Latino world and marries it with the ambition that is found in the European world.

You won the Tejano award seven times in a row. What did that mean to you?

Outside of the fact that I was good at what I was doing? [laughs] It was very humbling to know that I was accomplishing what I had set out to do, to be able to provide for people an entertainment, an inner heart feeling that would take them out of their day-to-day work and let them dream along as I sang, because that's what my songs were about. My songs were about hope, about taking yourself out of troubles and going to the sunny side of the street, to a place where you felt comfortable and integrated and accepted.

In 1988, two albums, Preciosa *and* Dulce Amor, *were released, and the next year you signed contracts with Capitol/EMI and Coca Cola. You were 18, and already becoming rich and famous. What was that like for you?*

It didn't mean a whole lot to me, but it was great for the family. I think I was the least affected within the family by the amount of money that was coming in. I was more affected by the reception that I received from people, by the love that I could feel coming from them, the hope that I instilled in them. This, of course, was all facilitated by having the money to be in the right place at the right time and to have the best of everything, and to be able to present a package to people that they could identify with. There was so much stress taken off the family by the money that it was a happy, carefree time for all of us.

To add to the happiness, Christopher Pérez, a talented guitarist, joined your band, but your father fired him when he discovered the two of you were romantically attached. Is it true Chris was allowed back, "shotgun style," on the condition that he married you?

I guess that would be people's interpretation. You have to remember that within the Latino family, the sense of propriety is exhibited by the patriarch of the family. My father was very, very protective of me, but (I guess) there was always a grudging acceptance of Christopher because he made me happy, and that was the thing that was most important to my father. He wanted us to get married so that I wouldn't get hurt if we broke up.

Was it a happy marriage?

It was a very happy marriage. Christopher made me laugh. I was able to be myself, I could lie around with messed up hair and torn jeans and not be criticized. He never judged any of my decisions, although he did make me think them through.

You took time to support D.A.R.E., the drug awareness organization, and supported HIV/AIDS patients. You did show a bare midriff, but you were sexually modest. How do you feel about entertainers who are blatantly sexual and highly self-absorbed?

When a person doesn't have true talent, they have to use other means of luring in their audience. I never found I needed anything other than my voice to captivate. I also didn't think that exciting a sexual response had anything to do with my type of music. Those who go for the exhibitionism basically are themselves lacking in an acceptance of who they are, and they need to do whatever they can to be accepted, to be recognized. To me that wasn't important, because I knew I always had my family, and I was totally and unconditionally accepted by them, regardless of what happened.

In addition to your growing popularity as a singer, you opened two—and then, four—highly successful fashion boutiques with clothes you designed yourself and manufactured. Was this fashion venture a dream come true for you or just an astute business decision?

When I would go to the concerts and I would see girls mimicking my dress, mimicking my costumes, when in some cases they scarcely had the money to come to the performance, I saw it as a means of helping them by providing a line of clothing that they could identify with me, but do it with a fairly reasonable price tag, not the expense of the costumes that I had produced for the performances. It also was a way to employ more people. Running through my life was a desire to help as many people as possible. That was why I was also involved in the D.A.R.E. and HIV programs, to help people help themselves.

Successful records poured out of you and you toured all over. You won a Grammy with Selena Live! *You were in a soap opera with Erik Estrada. Your album* Amor Prohibido *sold half a million copies, knocking* Mi Tierra *by Gloria Estéfan to number two on the Latin charts. Did you get to know Gloria?*

Yes, there was kind of a closeness among the big name singers. We would be together for award ceremonies and things like that. There was kind of a friendly rivalry going back and forth. We had styles that were very distinctive, so it wasn't a matter of "I'm better than you are"—just "I'm different from you," and "what do the people want or need now?" It was very comfortable at that time with the major Latino entertainers. It wasn't dog-eat-dog as with some of the other nationalities.

February 1995 saw you sing before 61,000 in the Houston Astrodome. Was that the highlight of your career?

They had the dome open—I was singing outdoors. It was, to me, an exchange of energy like a celestial chorus, and I heard some of the angels join in. It was an absolutely beautiful experience, and I think everybody who was there had to be moved by the energy within that arena.

Then you decided to do more crossover singing in English, starting with an album in the summer of 1995. But it was not to be. You believed that Yolanda Saldívar, the manager of your boutique chain, was stealing from the business. When you confronted her, she shot you. Before dying of your wounds you identified her as your killer, and subsequently, she was given a life sentence for your murder. Tell us what happened.

Well, it's pretty much just as you have stated. I had a number of reports from other employees that the profits of the business weren't as good as they had been because monies were going awry. I hinted to her on several occasions that possibly we should have better profits, and should look into some of the things that were going on. Then it was almost as if she became more blatant, because more money seemed to go missing. So I went in with the idea of confronting her.

She had done a lot of good things for me, and if she had a good reason for doing it, such as needing the money for a family matter that I didn't know about, I was willing to work something out with her. I didn't go in there with the intention of outright firing her because we had too long a history together, but she became belligerent. She became very upset, at first, saying that I was questioning her integrity, but I had the facts and figures with me. Then she said that I had so much money, what was this little bit of money to me?—that I should share the wealth. I told her that I wanted to share the wealth with the world, not just with her, at which she became very nasty. It was at that point I told her that I would have to let her go, and she said, "Well, if you're going to let me go, are you going to go to the police?" I said I hadn't decided that yet, and she said that she would make sure I didn't, and that was when she shot me.

Did you suffer much?

There was a sensation of pain. There wasn't an extreme amount, and of course, it's like women say with childbirth—they don't feel the pain afterward. I definitely don't feel it now. I have no residual effects from it. The soul knows when to step out of the body.

How do you feel now about Yolanda?

She had a path, just as I had a path. We had agreed that my life would end with her, and that she would have the experience of incarceration and restriction of freedom, as she is still having.

When you say you "had agreed," was that before coming down to Earth?

Before coming down into physical form. As a matter of fact, she and I have had a number of lives together. We're soul mates. As with practicing something that is very noteworthy within a human life, so you make an agreement with somebody whom you can trust or with whom you've made other agreements, who you know will be able to carry it through.

It seems a bit strange to us, though, that somebody who was so willing to give to other people in the world—to create dresses for poor girls, to give employment, to look after people with AIDS, to help with drug awareness programs, to support her family, all the things you were doing—would suddenly have this shut off by prior agreement. It makes no sense to us. What sense does it make to you?

Well, of course, I understand that I did choose to leave at the time I did because I had accomplished everything I set out to accomplish.

But couldn't you have accomplished more?

I could have accomplished more, but you have to remember that a contract on the planet is not just about one person. There were also contracts with my various family members to go on after I left, to deal with a sense of sorrow and abandonment, to rethink all of the things that we had meant to each other and done together, to come out of the shadow that was me and to become themselves—individuals who had been lost in the shadow of what I had become.

What gifts did your family and fans give you that you treasure?

Sharing with me the joy of unconditional love through the music, through the acceptance that the vibration is universal, that we are all the same at the soul level, as we are all the same in enjoying the rhythm and the sound and the vibration of music.

What about tributes to you? Are souls interested in such things as funeral eulogies, commemorative films, and fans' websites?

Not at all. It's interesting because these are all things that other souls have to work through to deal with their grief, to deal with an identity of who they think they are. It means nothing to us as we pass on, because we go back into the energetic unconditional love of Home, where we have been many times and where we appear as many different people to those who have shared lives with us. I am not just Selena. I am many, many incarnations upon the planet.

Thank you for talking with us, Selena.
     I wish I had a voice to serenade you, but alas, I don't.

Commentary

Toni: Selena had a very, sweet, loving, concerned energy. There were no hard edges with her whatsoever, no flag-carrying, stand-on-the-soapbox remarks, no regrets or excuses for her life experiences. Everything just flowed. Everything was melody, comfort, and love. A delightful soul. The entire interview had a rhythm of its own that carried it along flawlessly.

Peter: Selena duplicated the exhilaration reported by Maria Callas singing in an open air amphitheatre in Greece. Marion Anderson also had a similar outdoor experience singing from the steps of the Lincoln Memorial. Selena said her Houston Astrodome concert brought about angelic participation, though I was unsure whether she meant that she was aware of angels singing along with her at the time. (Not a regular weekly feature at the Astrodome, I imagine.)
     Her extended family played a significant role in Selena's career—not just her close relatives, but the wider Latino family, which drew out from her heart a passion for Tejano music. Whether or not she was consciously aware of her many former lives as a singer, her soul drew from that rich experience and helped her become the Queen of Tejano Music for many years.
     She said that her death was planned in advance. It might be shocking to some that her murderer, a member of her soul group, was party to such a contract—shocking to learn that, despite Selena's youth, she had completed her assignment for

that life and her death would *benefit* in many ways those left behind. Nevertheless, this is how the spirit world organizes our lessons with our agreement.

Selena's self-giving nature, a hallmark of her human life, was rich and genuine. She reached out to people in need to help in drug awareness and AIDS awareness programs. She provided jobs in her fashion stores that were catering to less-affluent girls' dreams. Chiefly she sang to the souls of all who cared for her and her music, who loved her for who she had become, and who may have hoped that they too might become a star one day.

Living Souls

The human soul is eternal. There is little disagreement among the world's major religions about that idea. When I was a boy it seemed to me that a soul was something you were given by God when you died. Maybe you got one if you were good, and if you were bad—well, then there was "outer darkness" complete with "wailing and gnashing of teeth" waiting for you. It never really occurred to me that you did not "have a soul," or "get a soul," but that you <u>are</u> a soul, that the Thing somewhere inside you, who (or which) is doing the driving, is your soul. Maybe when you are forgetful, it's having a nap and letting your brain do the driving instead!

Religious people don't talk that much about the soul; it is sort of uncertain territory for most folk—or it used to be, but perhaps not any longer. A good deal has changed in the certainty we have about the human soul. People have studied thousands of near-death experiences. Scientists have written detailed case notes about little children who vividly remember being someone else before they were born. There have already been many millions of past-life regression experiences in hypnosis, and a whole field of life-between-lives regression with hypnosis is becoming established worldwide.

All these tell the same basic story of the life of the eternal soul. It is a story that supports and amplifies the collection of dialogues in this book and in the rest of this series. Toni Ann Winninger's amazing channeling of our 21 leading ladies deals with the same issues as do thousands of researchers and therapists, to say nothing about other well-known psychics and channelers.

What is remarkable about these brief dialogues with leading women of the twentieth century is that they give us glimpses of what it is like actually to be a soul, alive and flourishing before, during, and after physical life. Our discussions have served to clear up many unsolved mysteries, like the disappearance of Amelia Earhart and the sudden death of Marilyn Monroe. More importantly, these encounters raise new questions about the life purpose each soul is working through on Earth, about soul groups and soul contracts, and the whole question of why, when we volunteer to come down here, we suffer so many problems of disease and death.

For the sake of those readers who may not have read the first book in this series, *Talking with Leaders of the Past* (and as a refresher for those who have), we now summarize the Masters' core teaching. For more details please read volume one—it's not really a good idea for us to write the same book twice!

Summary of the Masters' Teaching

We should never think about God as the "supreme gentleman in a white beard and cloak who has ultimate power over everything upon the Earth," whose wrath and judgment are used to control people and punish evildoers. The Masters prefer to say "Creator," or "Source," or even "God-Force," which they clearly interpret as meaning the collective divinity of all the spirits in the whole universe, including our own individual soul.

All souls are separate energetic portions of the Source which have been "broken off" in order to extend the outreach and deepen the experience of the Source itself. Souls exist in the universal God-Force community, sharing all its knowledge totally, yet possessing individuality and personal wisdom gained from their past experiences.

All souls eventually return from planet Earth to Home, which is an energetic realm of unconditional love. Although there is self-evaluation of our lives, there is no judgment made of us there. All is unconditional love and service.

We have to give up the old ideas of Heaven and Hell: Heaven because our eternal Home, though filled with unconditional love, is not a place of celestial reward for our being and doing good; Hell (which exists only as a state of mind within the energetic dimension of planet Earth) principally because the divine force is non-judgmental. Every soul who incarnates on Earth will eventually return Home. There are no exceptions.

We all incarnate on planet Earth with a copy of the database of our soul's life in our DNA, though most of us are entirely forgetful of our origin and life purpose. Together with guides and counselors at Home, we have already identified those types of experience we need to have, during our time on Earth, for personal growth toward our soul's maturity. We select our parents, and our soul may make binding contracts with other souls who will provide us with challenges of various kinds during our lifetime.

Of whatever nature our physical experiences may be, they are always for a positive purpose within the life of our soul. The lessons will not necessarily be humanly judged to be pleasant or even experiences of goodness. They may involve our role-playing in a manner that human ethics consider profoundly negative or evil. We may have chosen to be subjected to physical or psychological pain and suffering which few human minds would ever regard as benign. Moreover, if we fail to deal successfully with the specific challenges that we have chosen in order to gain spiritual mastery, we will need to face something similar in a subsequent life. The experience of negativity is part of the plan to awaken our conscience, increase compassion, and gain an understanding of the opposite of negativity—the magnificence of unconditional love.

Our soul never dies because it remains always pure energy destined to realize its true identity in harmony with the Source. This fact affects many areas of human life and physical death. For example, abortion is seen by those at Home as a non-issue: The aborted fetus's soul (if, indeed, a soul has even been assigned to the fetus) is not involved in the destruction of fetal tissue and returns Home in advance of the procedure. You simply cannot kill the soul. Likewise, tough life-support and euthanasia issues are challenges which everybody involved with the patient must face, yet the permanently vegetative patient's soul itself will have already substantially detached from the shell of the body and is only nominally connected until, finally, the body expires. With sudden death, as with lingering dying, the soul is unharmed but *transitions* back to the place from whence it came. So our role in the cosmos as incarnated human beings provides the means by which our spiritual selves may learn many lessons. Our egos and our body shells are designed simply as vehicles for this spiritual work, which we will continue to use until it is time for our souls to return Home.

The Authors

Toni Ann Winninger, JD, CH, is well established as a psychic channeler in practice with individuals, and groups large and small. A Reiki master, she specializes in spirit release and teaches metaphysical subjects and Light Language. Previously she worked for 27 years as a prosecutor in the Chicago area. Toni is the President of Celestial Voices, Inc. which promotes the Masters' messages. She channeled for the books listed here:

Peter Watson Jenkins, MA (Cantab.), MH, is a master hypnotist working in past-life regression and spirit release. In the 1960s he studied theology at Cambridge University, England, and served for 21 years in parish ministry. He is the C.E.O. of Celestial Voices, Inc., a spiritual publisher based in the USA. and compiled the books listed here:

> *Talking with Leaders of the Past*
> *Talking with Twentieth-Century Women*
> *Talking with Twentieth-Century Men*
> *How I Died (and what I did next)*
> *Spirit World Wisdom*
> *The Masters' Reincarnation Handbook: Journey of the Soul*
> *Healing with the Universe, Meditation, and Prayer*
> *Exploring Reincarnation (May 2011)*

Our websites

MastersoftheSpiritWorld.com

CelestialVoicesInc.com

Facebook: Reincarnation Guide